ESSENTIALS
of Corporate and
Capital Formation

Jeff

Enjoy the Book!
Pleasure to work with you
and I expect you will
recognize some of
the examples in the book.

David H. Fater

ESSENTIALS SERIES

The Essentials Series was created for busy business advisory and corporate professionals. The books in this series were designed so that these busy professionals can quickly acquire knowledge and skills in core business areas.

Each book provides need-to-have fundamentals for those professionals who must:

- Get up to speed quickly, because they have been promoted to a new position or have broadened their responsibility scope
- Manage a new functional area
- Brush up on new developments in their area of responsibility
- Add more value to their company or clients

Other books in this series include:

For more information on any of the above titles, please visit www.wiley.com.

ESSENTIALS
of Corporate and Capital Formation

David H. Fater

WILEY

John Wiley & Sons, Inc.

For general information on our other products and services or for technical support, please contact our Customer Care Department within the United States at (800) 762-2974, outside the United States at (317) 572-3993 or fax (317) 572-4002.

Wiley also publishes its books in a variety of electronic formats. Some content that appears in print may not be available in electronic books. For more information about Wiley products, visit our Web site at www.wiley.com.

Library of Congress Cataloging-in-Publication Data

Fater, David H.
Essentials of corporate and capital formation/David H. Fater.
       p. cm. − (Essentials series)
   Includes index.
   ISBN 978-0-470-49656-5 (pbk.)
   1. Saving and investment. 2. Capital investments. 3. Capital market. 4. Industrial management. I. Title.
   HG4028.C4F38 2010
   658.15'224–dc22

                                                                        2009035913

Printed in the United States of America

10 9 8 7 6 5 4 3 2 1

To my devoted wife, Alexis; my sons Brian, David Jr., and Murray; and my grandchildren, Caitlin Marie, William Edward, Aaron David, and Evan Patrick. Without their support and love this would not have been possible.

Contents

Contents

Contents

Contents

Preface

Entrepreneurship has existed since the caveman. When individuals first began to barter, commerce was initiated. As society evolved, the business of conducting business became more complex, and structure and capital resources also became more complex.

Entrepreneurship is often defined as the practice of starting new organizations or revitalizing mature organizations, particularly new businesses (legally recognized organizations designed to provide goods and/or services to consumers or customers), generally in response to identified opportunities. Entrepreneurship is often a difficult undertaking, as it is commonly accepted that a vast majority of new businesses fail. Entrepreneurial activities are substantially different depending on the type of organization that is being started. Entrepreneurship ranges in scale from solo projects (even involving the entrepreneur only part time) to major undertakings creating many job opportunities. Many of these "high-profile" entrepreneurial ventures seek outside capital or funding in order to raise capital to attempt to build the business successfully.

Entrepreneurship is about taking risk. An entrepreneur is a kind of person willing to put his or her career and financial security on the line and take risks in the name of an idea, spending much time as well as capital on an uncertain venture. Interestingly, three types of uncertainty often are present:

1. **Risk**, which is measurable statistically (such as the probability of drawing a red ball from a jar containing five red balls and five white balls)

2. **Ambiguity**, which is hard to measure statistically (such as the probability of drawing a red ball from a jar containing five red balls and an unknown number of white balls)

3. **True uncertainty**, which is impossible to estimate or predict statistically (such as the probability of drawing a red ball from a jar whose total number of balls, red and of other colors, is unknown)

Acts of entrepreneurship often are associated with true uncertainty, particularly when they involve bringing something novel to the world, whose market has never previously existed. Before the Internet, nobody knew the market for Internet-related businesses such as Amazon, Google, YouTube, Yahoo!, and so forth. Only after the Internet emerged did people begin to see opportunities and market that technology.

It is the element of risk and uncertainty that has resulted in the evolution of business (corporate) structure. As entrepreneurs (1) looked for ways to limit their exposure (despite the fact that merely being an entrepreneur exposed them to risk at various levels) and (2) sought capital from persons who also desired to limit their risk both as an investor/funder (Will I get my money back and get paid for the risk?) and owner (How can I protect myself and my other assets if the business does, in fact, fail?), business structures evolved beyond proprietorships in order to better meet these diverse needs.

Consequently, the first decision (beyond "Will I start a business?") that must be faced—and often is decided inappropriately in forming a business—is the ultimate structure of the entity. This book guides the entrepreneur to select the most appropriate business entity, one that will maximize both the risk management objectives and the probability of successfully finding/raising necessary capital.

Once the entrepreneur has decided to start and form the business, there usually is a requirement for capital. Since we all know that "money doesn't grow on trees," the entrepreneur has to look for and obtain necessary funds with which to start and operate the business. This capital can take many forms and come from a variety of sources. Some are better than others, and some should be avoided at all costs. This book guides the entrepreneur through the myriad of capital choices and funding sources to maximize the probability not only of success at obtaining the necessary funds but also of having the funding source be a true contributor to the overall success of the enterprise, even if the only contribution is the capital.

Last, the issue of an exit strategy needs to be considered. How would the entrepreneur appropriately and successfully exit from the business at the appropriate point in time? Consideration of that question often directs the enterprise structure and the capital sought. This book helps guide the entrepreneur to appropriate decisions.

This book is aimed at a wide range of readers, from new entrepreneurs to corporate executives faced with first-time corporate formation or fundraising.

Chapter 1 deals with the various forms of corporate structures and should enable the reader to identify the advantages and disadvantages of each. Chapter 2 discusses the various forms of capital that may be raised upon an entity's formation. Chapter 3 identifies the various sources from which critical capital could be raised. Chapter 4 identifies and warns about various pitfalls that could be encountered in raising capital and could result in violations of securities laws. Chapters 5, 6, and 7 discuss the all-too-attractive public markets and ways to transition a private company to a public company. Chapter 8 introduces the concept of exit strategies for the entrepreneur, and Chapter 9 provides a summary of how to maximize success in the real world.

In addition, throughout the book are real-world exhibits that may be useful in corporate formation and capital raising. This book also includes a Web site, www.wiley.com/go/capitalformation, which includes downloadable copies of all the documents in the book as well as other examples of documents that are used in the real world and are critical for capital raising.

The greatest value from this book lies in the author's personal experiences, included in the chapters. During his 40+ year career, he has been described as being able to "finance the unfinanceable." Perhaps one of his greatest achievements was to be the CEO of a development-stage medical diagnostics company, where at one point, the most complicated footnote in the consolidated financial statements was "Debt." How does one raise millions of dollars of straight and convertible debt to finance a business that takes years through the development cycle to commercialization with no immediate apparent ability to repay that debt? Read on. You too can hold the world on your shoulders!

About the Web Site

This book includes a Web site, www.wiley.com/go/capitalformation. This Web site includes these documents:

Limited Liability Company Operating Agreement

Series B Convertible Preferred Stock Certificate of Designation

Business Plan

Investment Agreement

Investor Rights Agreement

Placement Agency Agreement

Finder's Fee Agreement

Underwriting Letter of Intent

SEC Comment Letter (and Responses)

Underwriting Agreement

Form S-1

Form 10

Super 8-K

In addition to these documents, the Web site also includes all of the exhibits contained in the book.

The password to enter this site is: Fater. The password is case-sensitive.

Acknowledgments

This book is the product of 40+ years in the corporate world, dealing with the public markets, and raising capital. It is for those people who suddenly find themselves in a position of corporate and capital formation with no practical knowledge as to how to proceed and where all the land mines are buried in the real world.

This knowledge base did not happen overnight or come by divine inspiration. Along the way, I have had the privilege of working with and learning from dedicated, knowledgeable, and ethical professionals, and I have gained their insight by listening to what they were saying along the way. These individuals included:

My business partner in ALDA & Associates International, Inc., Richard M. Cohen, who also suffered through the reading of this book as it was being developed and written and has to implement some of the wild strategies I devise.

My attorneys, Leonard Bloom and Laura Holm of Akerman Senterfitt, who provide me counsel, advice, and the knowledge that they are always covering my back. They have been invaluable to me as protectors and counsel.

Acknowledgments

Great investment bankers like John Chambers, whom I have known for 16 years (currently with Merriman, Curhan & Ford). John has always been a great sounding board and provided helpful suggestions on the capital markets and how to access them (especially when they are perceptibly closed), even when he (or his firm) was not directly involved with the transaction at hand.

Financial printers like Ken McClure, with whom I have worked for 16 years (currently with Bowne), who always puts the client's needs first and has worked with me through four public companies at several different printers because he is "my rep."

I also want to thank many other individuals who have been at my side along the way, because without them being part of my world, even for a brief time, this book would not have been possible.

CHAPTER 1

Corporate Structure

After reading this chapter, you will be able to:

- Understand the various structures by which an enterprise can be formed
- Decide which is best for your situation

The obvious structures available for the enterprise traditionally have been:

- Proprietorships
- Partnerships
- Limited partnerships
- Limited liability companies
- Corporations (S and C)

Let us examine the features of each and the appropriateness for various enterprises.

Proprietorships

The sole proprietorship is the oldest, most common, and simplest form of business organization. A sole proprietorship is a business entity owned and managed by one person. The sole proprietorship can be organized very informally, is not subject to much federal or state regulation, and is relatively simple to manage and control.

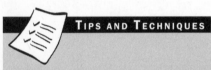

TIPS AND TECHNIQUES

The decision on which enterprise structure to use revolves around many factors, but the principal deciding factors involve:

- Willingness to assume risk
- Tax implications
- Need for capital
- Exit strategy

The prevalent characteristic of a sole proprietorship is that the owner is inseparable from the business. Because they are the same entity, the owner of a sole proprietorship has complete control over the business and its operations and is financially and legally responsible for all debts and legal actions against the business. Another aspect of the "same entity" situation is that taxes on a sole proprietorship are determined at the personal income tax rate of the owner. In other words, a sole proprietorship does not pay taxes separately from the owner.

A sole proprietorship is a good business organization for an individual starting a business that will remain small, does not have great exposure to liability, and does not justify the expenses of incorporating and ongoing corporate formalities.

Points to consider when considering a proprietorship include:

- It is the easiest type of business organization to establish. There are no formal requirements for starting a sole proprietorship.
- Decision making is in the direct hands of the owner.
- All profits and losses of the business are reported directly in the owner's income tax return.
- The start-up costs for a sole proprietorship are minimal.
- The owner has unlimited liability. Both the business and personal assets of the sole proprietor are subject to the claims of creditors.
- Because a sole proprietorship is not a separate legal entity, it usually terminates when the owner becomes disabled, retires, or dies. As a result, the sole proprietorship lacks continuity and does not have perpetual existence, as other business organizations do.
- It is difficult for a sole proprietorship to raise capital. Financial resources generally are limited to the owner's funds and any loans outsiders are willing to provide.
- An owner could spend an unlimited amount of time responding to business needs.

 TIPS AND TECHNIQUES

In looking at a proprietorship form of entity, the very aspects that make it attractive also make it potentially unsuitable. If you are

Partnerships

From the proprietorship structure evolved the partnership entity. A partnership as a business component (oftentimes referred to as a general partnership) is defined broadly, and, because "persons" can include individuals, groups of individuals, companies, and corporations, partnerships are highly adaptable in form and vary in complexity. Each partner shares directly in the organization's profits and shares control of the business operations. The consequence of this profit sharing is that partners are jointly and independently liable for the partnership's debts and liabilities. Creation, organization, and dissolution of partnerships are governed by state law. Many states have adopted the Uniform Partnership Act. A partner relationship is generally the result of a contract (either express or implied) with no formal requirements (such as a signed document). To determine whether a partnership exists, courts look at five areas:

1. Intention of the parties
2. Sharing of profits and losses
3. Joint administration and control of business operations
4. Capital investment by each partner
5. Common ownership of property

Under state agency law, partners are personally liable for torts committed by the partnership and its agents. (This is not the case for a limited partnership, in which one or more general partners manage business operations and assume personal liability for partnership debts while other contributing/profit-sharing partners take no part in running the business and incur no liability beyond contribution obligations. See the next section in this chapter, "Limited Partnerships." Limited partnerships are governed in many states by the Uniform Limited Partnership Act.) State property law also impacts partnerships by defining ownership in a partnership and determining how the death of a partner changes the partnership structure.

For state and federal tax purposes, a partnership is not a taxable entity. Partnership income is taxable to the partners in proportion to their share in the company's profits.

A partnership is a type of business entity in which partners share with each other the profits or losses of the business undertaking in which all have invested. Partnerships often are favored over corporations for taxation purposes, as the partnership structure generally does not incur a tax on profits before profits are distributed to the partners (i.e., no dividend tax is levied, so the issue of double taxation does not exist). However, depending on the partnership structure and the jurisdiction in which it operates, owners of a partnership may be exposed to greater personal liability than they would as shareholders of a corporation.

Again, in evaluating whether a partnership format is an appropriate structure for the entity, you have to revisit the initial four factors governing this important decision. From a risk standpoint, risk is shared jointly and severally by each of the partners, so a partnership structure does not provide the partners with any shield from liabilities or exposure to other risks. From a taxation standpoint, profits and losses "flow through" the partnership to the partners' individual tax returns. This eliminates the aspect of double taxation or provides a "shelter" against other taxable income if there is a taxable loss for the year. However, if the business is expected to be wildly profitable, it may not be advantageous to have that income included in partners' tax returns. There may not be cash distributions available for the partners to pay these tax liabilities, because the capital may be needed for additional growth plans. Also, if a business is organized to lose money (other than a real estate or similar investment), why are you even going into business if your objective is not to make money?

 TIPS AND TECHNIQUES

Because of liability and tax reasons, I generally discourage the use of a partnership structure for business ventures that will require capital and have a planned exit strategy.

Limited Partnerships

As the need to limit owner liability evolved and the need for investors grew, the limited partnership (LP) form of structure evolved, most notably in real estate ventures. In such ventures, the pass-through of the tax benefits was very attractive, as was the limitation of losses to the amount that each limited partner had invested.

Three distinctions between LPs and general partnerships are:

1. LPs are created by statute, not by intentions of the partners.

2. LPs may be able to override the partnership agreement.

3. There exists a difference in tax treatment: An LP normally has pass-through taxation, but must meet certain criteria to avoid being taxed as a corporation.

An LP consists of two or more persons, with at least one general partner and one limited partner. Although a general partner in an LP has unlimited personal liability, a limited partner's liability is limited to the amount of his or her investment in the company. LPs are creatures of statute; papers must be filed with the state in order to form an LP. Because of the limited liability of limited partnerships, they often are used as vehicles for raising capital. The LP is a separate entity and files taxes as a separate entity.

As in a general partnership (GP), the GPs have actual authority as agents of the firm to bind all the other partners in contracts with third parties that are in the ordinary course of the partnership's business. As with a GP, "An act of a general partner which is not apparently for carrying on in the ordinary course the limited partnership's activities or activities of the kind carried on by the limited partnership binds the limited partnership only if the act was actually authorized by all the other partners" (U.S. Uniform Limited Partnership Act § 402(b)).

Unlike GPs, LPs have limited liability, meaning they are liable only for debts incurred by the firm to the extent of their registered investment, and they have no management authority. The GPs pay the LPs a return on their investment (similar to a dividend), the nature and extent of which is usually defined in the partnership agreement.

In the United States, the LP organization is most common in the film industry and real estate investment projects or in types of businesses that focus on a single or limited-term project. They are also useful in "labor-capital" partnerships, in which one (or more) financial backer prefers to contribute money or resources while the other partner performs the actual work. In such situations, liability is the driving concern behind the choice of LP status. The LP is also attractive to firms wishing to provide shares to many individuals without the additional tax liability of a corporation. Private equity companies almost exclusively use a combination of general and limited partners for their investment funds.

In some states, an LP can elect to become a limited liability partnership (LLP). In this arrangement, the general partners are liable only for the business debts of the company, not for acts of malpractice or other wrongdoing done by the other partners in the course of the partnership's business.

TIPS AND TECHNIQUES

Limited partnerships may be an attractive vehicle for conducting a business that requires capital and has a defined exit strategy. As mentioned, LPs are widely used in real estate (or single-project ventures) and in investment funds. Keep LPs in mind as we explore several other corporate structures.

Limited Liability Companies

From the limited partnership structure evolved the limited liability company. A limited liability company (LLC) is a legal form of business company giving limited liability to its owners. Often incorrectly called a limited liability corporation (instead of company), it is a hybrid business entity having characteristics of both a corporation and a partnership. It is often more flexible than a corporation or partnership in that the owners have limited liability for the actions and debts of the company, and it is suitable for smaller companies with a single owner. The primary characteristic of a corporation is limited liability, and the primary characteristic of a partnership is the availability of pass-through income taxation.

Creation of an LLC requires several documents in addition to its formation documents. The most important of these is the operating agreement, which governs the manner in which the entity will be operated. Important terms in dealing with an LLC and their definitions follow.

Member

LLC members are the owners of the LLC, much as shareholders are the owners of a corporation or partners are the owners of a partnership. Like shareholders, a member's liability to repay the LLC's obligations is limited to his or her capital contribution. Members may be natural persons, corporations, partnerships, or other LLCs.

Membership Interest

A member's ownership interest in an LLC often is called a membership interest. Membership interests often are divided into

9

standardized units, which, in turn, often are called shares or units. Unless otherwise provided for in the operating agreement, a member's right to receive distributions or exercise member rights over the LLC is proportionate to his or her membership interest. Membership interests and member rights are regulated by state law.

Manager

LLCs may be managed by their members in proportion to their membership interests. Many LLC operating agreements, however, provide for a manager or board of managers to oversee or run the day-to-day operations of the LLC. The managers are elected or appointed by members. If it is so provided in the operating agreement, they also may be removed by members. A member may be a manager, often called a managing member.

Articles of Organization

All LLCs must file evidence of their existence with the secretary of state (or some governmental office) of the state where they choose to be organized. The articles of organization serve this purpose.

Operating Agreement

The operating agreement of an LLC is the document most important to its success, because it determines, defines, and apportions the rights of the members and the managers, if any. The operating agreement generally is not filed with the secretary of state (or other governmental office). A sample limited liability company operating agreement can be found on www.wiley.com/go/capitalformation.

Management

LLCs may be either member managed or manager managed. A member-managed LLC may be governed by a single class of members (in which case it approximates a partnership) or multiple classes of members (in which case it approximates a limited partnership). Choosing manager management creates a two-tiered management structure that approximates corporate governance, with the managers typically holding powers similar to corporate officers and directors. The LLC's operating agreement (the LLC version of a partnership agreement or a corporation's bylaws) determines how the LLC is managed. C corporations, S corporations, limited liability partnerships, limited partnerships, limited liability limited partnerships, and LLCs lie along a spectrum of flexibility, with LLCs being the most flexible, and thus preferable, for many businesses.

Income Taxation

For U.S. federal income tax purposes, LLCs that are treated as partnerships use IRS Form 1065. LLCs are organized with a document called the articles of organization or the rules of organization specified publicly by the state; additionally, it is common to have an operating agreement privately specified by the members. The operating agreement is a contract among the members of an LLC and the LLC, governing the membership, management, operation, and distribution of income of the company.

Under some circumstances, however, the members (the LLC version of shareholders or partners) may elect for the LLC to be taxed like a corporation (taxation of the entity's income prior to any dividends or distributions to the members and then taxation of the dividends or distributions once received as income by the members).

Operating as an LLC form of partnership does not mean that appropriate U.S. federal partnership tax forms are not necessary, or not complex. As a partnership, the entity's income and deductions attributed to each member are reported on that owner's tax return.

Advantages

Advantages of operating as an LLC include:

- Check-the-box taxation; an LLC can elect to be taxed as a sole proprietor, partnership, S corporation, or C corporation, providing much flexibility
- Limited liability; the owners of the LLC, called members, are protected from liability for acts and debts of the LLC
- Much less administrative paperwork and recordkeeping than a corporation
- Pass-through taxation (i.e., no double taxation), unless the LLC elects to be taxed as a C corporation
- Using default tax classification, profits are taxed personally at the member level, not at the LLC level
- LLCs in most states are treated as entities separate from their members; in some jurisdictions, case law has developed deciding

LLCs are not considered to have separate legal standing from their members

- LLCs in some states can be set up with just one natural person involved

- Membership interests of LLCs can be assigned, and the economic benefits of those interests can be separated and assigned, providing the assignee with the economic benefits of distributions of profits/losses (like a partnership), without transferring the title to the membership interest

- Unless the LLC has chosen to be taxed as a corporation, income of the LLC generally retains its character (e.g., as capital gains or as foreign-sourced income) in the hands of the members

Disadvantages

The disadvantages of the LLC structure include:

- Although there is no statutory requirement for an operating agreement in most states, members who operate without one may run into problems.

- It may be more difficult to raise financial capital for an LLC. Investors may be more comfortable investing funds in the better-understood corporate form, with a view toward an eventual initial public offering (IPO). One possible solution may be to form a new corporation and merge into it, dissolving the LLC and converting into a corporation.

- Many states, including Alabama, California, Kentucky, New York, Pennsylvania, Tennessee, and Texas, levy a franchise tax or capital values tax on LLCs. In essence, this franchise or business privilege tax is the "fee" the LLC pays the state for the benefit of limited liability. The franchise tax can be an amount based on revenue, on profits, or on the number of owners or the amount of capital employed in the state, or some combination of those factors, or simply a flat fee, as in Delaware. In most states, however, the fee is nominal. Only a handful charge a tax comparable to the tax imposed on corporations.

- Some creditors will require members of up-and-starting LLCs to personally guarantee the LLC's loans, thus making the members personally liable for the debt of the LLC.

- The management structure of an LLC may be unfamiliar to many. Unlike corporations, LLCs are not required to have a board of directors or officers.

- The LLC form of organization is relatively new. For that reason, some states do not treat LLCs like corporations for liability purposes but instead treat them more as disregarded entities. In this case, an individual operating a business as an LLC may be treated as operating it as a sole proprietorship, or a group operating as an LLC may be treated as a general partnership, which defeats the purpose of establishing an LLC: to have limited liability. (A sole proprietor has unlimited liability for the business; in a partnership, the partners have joint and several liability, meaning any and all of the partners can be held liable for the business's debts, no matter how small their investment or what their percentage of ownership is.)

- The principals of LLCs use many different titles (e.g., member, manager, managing member, managing director, chief executive officer, president, and partner). As such, it can be difficult to determine who actually has the authority to enter into a contract on the LLC's behalf.

TIPS AND TECHNIQUES

Applying the four factors to evaluate structure—willingness to assume risk, need for capital, tax objectives, and exit strategy— should enable you to evaluate whether the LLC structure makes sense for your enterprise.

Corporations

Last, we come to the corporate form of structure. This is perceived to be the most common form, and depending on the various objectives, it actually may make the most sense.

A corporation is a legal entity separate from the persons that form it. It is a legal entity owned by individual stockholders. In American and, increasingly, international usage, the term "corporation" denotes a body corporate (i.e., an entity separate and apart from a natural person) formed to conduct business.

Corporations exist as a product of corporate law, and their rules balance the interests of the shareholders who invest their capital and the employees who contribute their labor. People work together in corporations to produce value and generate income. In modern times, corporations have become an increasingly dominant part of economic life. People rely on corporations for employment, for their goods and services, for the value of the pensions, and for economic growth and social development.

The defining feature of a corporation is its legal independence from the people who created it. If a corporation fails, shareholders normally stand to lose only their investment, and employees will lose their jobs, but neither will be further liable for debts that remain owing to the corporation's creditors unless they have personally guaranteed certain indebtedness (not recommended by the author) or taken some other actions. This limited liability is similar to limited partnerships and limited liability companies and is perhaps the most attractive feature of a corporation.

Despite not being natural persons, corporations are recognized by the law to have rights and responsibilities like actual people. Corporations can exercise human rights against real individuals and the state, and they may be responsible for human rights violations. Just as they are "born" into existence through their founders obtaining a certificate of incorporation, they can "die" when they lose money and become insolvent. Corporations can even be convicted of criminal offenses, such as fraud and manslaughter (topics that are not contemplated in this book).

Five common characteristics of the modern corporation include:

1. Delegated management; in other words, control of the company is placed in the hands of a board of directors
2. Limited liability of the shareholders

3. Investor ownership, or, more clearly, ownership by shareholders

4. Separate legal personality of the corporation (the right to sue and be sued in its own name)

5. Transferrable shares (sometimes on a listed exchange)

Ownership of a corporation is complicated by increasing social and economic interdependence, as different stakeholders compete to have a say in corporate affairs. Company boards have representatives of both shareholders and employees to "codetermine" company strategy. Calls for increasing corporate social responsibility are made by consumers and by environmental and human rights activists, and this has led to larger corporations drawing up codes of conduct. The existence of a corporation requires a special legal framework and body of law that specifically grants the corporation legal personality and typically views a corporation as a fictional person, a legal person, or a moral person (as opposed to a natural person). As such, corporate statutes typically give corporations the ability to own property, sign binding contracts, and pay taxes in a capacity that is separate from that of its shareholders.

The legal personality has two economic implications:

1. It grants creditors priority over the corporate assets upon liquidation.

2. Corporate assets cannot be withdrawn by its shareholders, nor can the assets of the firm be taken by personal creditors of its shareholders. This feature requires special legislation and a special legal framework, as it cannot be reproduced via standard contract law.

See Exhibit 1.1 for a sample corporation article of incorporation and Exhibit 1.2 for an example of corporation bylaws.

Corporation Articles of Incorporation

CERTIFICATE OF INCORPORATION

OF

[name of corporation]

1. The name of the Corporation is:

   [name of corporation]

2. The address of its registered office in the State of Delaware is [1209 Orange Street, Wilmington, Delaware 19801, County of New Castle.] The name of its registered agent at such address is [The Corporation Trust Company].

3. The purpose of the Corporation is to engage in any lawful act or activity for which corporations may be organized under the General Corporation Law of the State of Delaware.

4. The Corporation is authorized to issue capital stock to the extent of:

   a. _____ Million (___0,000,000) Shares Common Stock, Par Value $.0001 per Share; and

   b. _____ Million (___0,000,000) Shares Preferred Stock, Par Value $.0001 Per Share (the "Preferred Stock").
   The Board of Directors of the Corporation shall have the authority to issue shares of Preferred Stock in series or subseries and to fix by resolution the designations, powers, preferences, rights, and the qualifications, limitations, or restrictions in respect of any such series or subseries by filing a certificate pursuant to the applicable law of the State of Delaware.

5. The Corporation is to have perpetual existence.
6. Directors.

a. <u>Number</u>. Except as otherwise fixed by or pursuant to provisions hereof relating to the rights of the holders of Preferred Stock to elect additional Directors under specified circumstances, the number of Directors of the Corporation shall be fixed from time to time by affirmative vote of a majority of the Directors then in office; provided, <u>however</u>, that the number of Directors shall not be reduced to shorten the term of any Director then in office.

b. <u>Elections And Terms</u>. The Board of Directors, other than those who may be elected by the holders of any series of Preferred Stock having a preference over the common stock as to dividends or upon liquidation, shall be classified, with respect to the time for which they severally hold office, into three classes, as nearly equal in number as possible, as shall be provided in the manner specified in the Bylaws of the Corporation, one class to be originally elected for a term expiring at the annual meeting of stockholders to be held in _____, another class to be originally elected for a term expiring at the annual meeting of stockholders to be held in _____, and another class to be originally elected for a term expiring at the annual meeting of the stockholders to beheld in _____, with each class to hold office until its successors are elected and qualified. At each annual meeting of the stockholders of the Corporation after fiscal year _____, the successors of the class of Directors whose term expires at that meeting shall be elected to hold office for a term expiring at the annual meeting of stockholders held in the third year following the year of their election.

c. <u>Newly Created Directorships And Vacancies</u>. Except as otherwise fixed by or pursuant to provisions hereof

(*continued*)

(continued)

relating to the rights of the holders of any series of Preferred Stock to elect additional Directors under specified circumstances, newly created directorships resulting from any increase in the number of directors and any vacancies on the Board of Directors resulting from death, resignation, disqualification, removal, or other cause shall be filled by the affirmative vote of a majority of the remaining Directors then in office, even though less than a quorum of the Board of Directors. Except as otherwise provided under Delaware law, newly created directorships and vacancies resulting from any cause may not be filled by any other person or persons. Any Director elected in accordance with this Paragraph 6(c) shall hold office for the remainder of the full term of the class of Directors in which the new directorship was created or the vacancy occurred and until such Director's successor shall have been elected and qualified.

d. <u>Removal</u>. Except as otherwise fixed by or pursuant to provisions hereof relating to the rights of the holders of any class or series of Preferred Stock to elect additional Directors under specified circumstances, any Director may be removed from office only for cause and only by the affirmative vote of the holders of [two-thirds] of the outstanding shares of stock entitled to vote generally in the election of Directors.

7. A director of the Corporation shall not be personally liable to the Corporation or its stockholders for monetary damages for breach of fiduciary duty as a director for any act or omission except to the extent such exemption from liability or limitation thereof is not permitted under the General Corporation Law of the State of Delaware as the same exists or may hereafter be amended. Any amendment, repeal, or modification of this Paragraph by the stockholders of the Corporation shall be prospective only, and shall not adversely affect any

limitation on the personal liability of a director of the Corporation in respect of any act or omission occurring prior to the time of such amendment, modification, or repeal.

8. Amendments to the Certificate of Incorporation of the Corporation shall require the affirmative vote of holders of [two-thirds] of the outstanding shares of stock entitled to vote on the proposed amendment to the Certificate of Incorporation. Notwithstanding the foregoing, in the event that a resolution to amend the Certificate of Incorporation of the Corporation is adopted by the affirmative vote of at least eighty percent (80%) of the members of the Board of Directors, approval of the amendment shall only require the affirmative vote of the holders of a majority of the outstanding shares of stock entitled to vote on the proposed amendment to the Certificate of Incorporation.

9. All of the powers of this Corporation, insofar as the same may be lawfully vested by this Certificate of Incorporation in the Board of Directors, are hereby conferred upon the Board of Directors of this Corporation. In furtherance and not in limitation of that power, the Board of Directors shall have the power to make, adopt, alter, amend, and repeal from time to time bylaws of this Corporation, subject to the right of the stockholders entitled to vote with respect thereto, to adopt, alter, amend, and repeal bylaws made by the Board of Directors; provided, however, that bylaws shall not be adopted, altered, amended, or repealed by the stockholders of the Corporation except by the affirmative vote of the holders of [two-thirds] of the outstanding shares of stock entitled to vote upon the election of directors.

10. No action required to be taken or which may be taken at any annual or special meeting of stockholders of the Corporation may be taken without a meeting, and the power of the stockholders to consent in writing, without a meeting, to the taking of any action is specifically denied.

(*continued*)

(*continued*)

11. Special meetings of stockholders for any purpose or purposes may be called by the Board of Directors, or by a committee of the Board of Directors that has been designated by the Board of Directors and whose powers and authority, as expressly provided in a resolution of the Board of Directors, include the power to call such meetings, and shall be held at such time, date, and place, either within or without the state of Delaware, as shall be designated by resolution of the Board of Directors or such committee. Special meetings of stockholders may not be called by any other person or persons.

12. The Corporation hereby elects to be governed by Section 203 of the General Corporation Law of the State of Delaware.

13. Elections of directors need not be by written ballot except and to the extent provided in the bylaws of the Corporation.

14. The name and mailing address of the Sole Incorporator is as follows:

[provide]

I, [name], being the Sole Incorporator hereinbefore named, for the purpose of forming a corporation pursuant to the General Corporation Law of the State of Delaware, do make this certificate, hereby declaring and certifying and this is my act and deed and the facts herein stated are true, and accordingly have hereunto set my hand this _____ day of _____, _____.

_____

_____ , Sole Incorporator

EXHIBIT 1.2

Corporation Bylaws

BYLAWS

OF

[name]
(a Delaware corporation)

ARTICLE I

Meetings of Stockholders and Other Stockholder Matters

SECTION 1.   Annual Meeting. An annual meeting of the stock-holders of [name] (hereinafter, the "Corporation") shall be held for the election of directors and for the transaction of such other proper business at such time, date, and place, either within or without the State of Delaware, as shall be designated by resolution of the Board of Directors from time to time.

SECTION 2.   Special Meetings. Special meetings of stockholders for any purpose or purposes may be called by the Board of Directors, or by a committee of the Board of Directors that has been designated by the Board of Directors and whose powers and authority, as expressly provided in a resolution of the Board of Directors, include the power to call such meetings, and shall be held at such time, date, and place, either within or without the state of Delaware, as shall be designated by resolution of the Board of Directors or such committee. The only business to be transacted at a special meeting of stockholders shall be that business set forth in the notice of meeting given pursuant to Section 3 of this Article I. Special meetings of stockholders may not be called by any other person or persons.

SECTION 3.   Notice of Meetings. Written notice of each meeting of the stockholders, which shall state the time, date, and place of the meeting and, in the case of a special meeting, the purpose or

(*continued*)

23

(*continued*)

purposes for which it is called, shall, unless otherwise provided by applicable law, the certificate of incorporation or these bylaws, be given not less than ten (10) nor more than sixty (60) days before the date of such meeting to each stockholder entitled to vote at such meeting, and, if mailed, it shall be deposited in the United States mail, postage prepaid, directed to the stockholder at such stockholder's address as it appears on the records of the Corporation. Whenever notice is required to be given, a written waiver thereof signed by the person entitled thereto, whether before or after the time stated therein, shall be deemed equivalent to notice. Neither the business to be transacted nor the purpose of any annual or special meeting of the stockholders need be specified in any written waiver of notice. Attendance of a person at a meeting shall constitute a waiver of notice of such meeting, except when the person attends a meeting for the express purpose of objecting, at the beginning of the meeting, to the transaction of any business because the meeting is not lawfully called or convened.

SECTION 4. Adjournments. Any meeting of the stockholders may adjourn from time to time to reconvene at the same or some other place, and notice need not be given of any such adjourned meeting if the time and place thereof are announced at the meeting at which the adjournment is taken. At any such adjourned meeting at which a quorum may be present, the Corporation may transact any business which might have been transacted at the original meeting. If the adjournment is for more than thirty (30) days, or if after the adjournment a new record date is fixed for the adjourned meeting, a notice of the adjourned meeting shall be given to each stockholder of record entitled to vote at the meeting.

SECTION 5. Quorum. Except as otherwise provided by Delaware law, the certificate of incorporation or these bylaws, at any meeting of the stockholders the holders of a majority of the shares of stock, issued and outstanding and entitled to vote, shall be present in person or represented by proxy in order to constitute a quorum for the transaction of any business. In the absence of a quorum, the holders of a majority of the shares present in person or represented by proxy and entitled to vote may adjourn the meeting from time to time in the manner described in Section 4 of this Article I.

SECTION 6. <u>Organization</u>. At each meeting of the stockholders, the Chairman of the Board, or in his absence or inability to act, the Chief Executive Officer or, in his absence or inability to act, the President, or in his absence or inability to act, a Vice President or, in the absence or inability to act of such persons, any person designated by the Board of Directors, or in the absence of such designation, any person chosen by a majority of those stockholders present in person or represented by proxy, shall act as chairman of the meeting. The Secretary or, in his absence or inability to act, any person appointed by the chairman of the meeting, shall act as secretary of the meeting and keep the minutes thereof.

SECTION 7. <u>Notice of Business</u>. At any annual meeting of the stockholders of the Corporation, only such business shall be conducted as shall have been brought before the meeting. To be properly brought before an annual meeting, such business must be (i) specified in the notice of meeting (or any supplement thereto) given by or at the direction of the Board of Directors; (ii) otherwise properly brought before the meeting by or at the direction of the Board of Directors; or (iii) otherwise properly brought before the meeting by any stockholder of the Corporation who is a stockholder of record at the time of giving of the notice provided for in this Section 7, who shall be entitled to vote at such meeting and who complies with the notice procedures set forth in this Section 7. For business to be properly brought before an annual meeting of the stockholders by a stockholder, the stockholder shall have given timely notice thereof in writing to the Secretary of the Corporation. To be timely, a stockholder's notice shall be delivered to or mailed and received by the Secretary at the principal executive

(*continued*)

(*continued*)

office of the Corporation not less than sixty (60) days nor more than ninety (90) days prior to the annual meeting; provided, however, that in the event that less than seventy (70) days' notice or prior public disclosure of the date of the annual meeting is given or made to stockholders, notice by the stockholder to be timely must be so received not later than the close of business on the tenth day following the day on which such notice of the date of the meeting was mailed or such public disclosure was made, whichever first occurs. Such stockholder's notice to the Secretary of the Corporation shall set forth as to each matter the stockholder proposes to bring before the annual meeting (a) a brief description of the business desired to be brought before the annual meeting, the reasons for conducting such business at the annual meeting and, in the event that such business includes a proposal to amend any document, including these bylaws, the language of the proposed amendment, (b) the name and address, as they appear on the Corporation's books, of the stockholder proposing such business, (c) the class and number of shares of capital stock of the Corporation which are beneficially owned by such stockholder and (d) any material interest of such stockholder in such business. Notwithstanding anything in these bylaws to the contrary, no business shall be conducted at any annual meeting of the stockholders except in accordance with the procedures set forth in this Section 7. The chairman of the annual meeting of the stockholders shall, if the facts warrant, determine and declare to the meeting that business was not properly brought before the meeting in accordance with the provisions of this Section 7, and if he should so determine, he shall so declare to the meeting and any such business not properly brought before the meeting shall not be transacted. Notwithstanding the foregoing provisions of this Section 7, a stockholder shall also comply with all applicable requirements of the Securities and Exchange Act of 1934, as amended, and the rules and regulations promulgated thereunder with respect to matters set forth in this Section 7.

SECTION 8. <u>Order of Business; Conduct of Meetings</u>. The order of business at all meetings of the stockholders shall be as determined by the chairman of the meeting.

SECTION 9. <u>Voting; Proxies</u>. Unless otherwise provided by Delaware law or in the certificate of incorporation, each stockholder entitled to vote at any meeting of stockholders shall be entitled to one vote for each share of capital stock which has voting power upon the matter in question held by such stockholder either (i) on the date fixed pursuant to the provisions of Section 10 of Article I of these bylaws as the record date for the determination of the stockholders to be entitled to notice of or to vote at such meeting; or (ii) if no record date is fixed, then at the close of business on the day next preceding the day on which notice is given. Each stockholder entitled to vote at any meeting of the stockholders may authorize another person or persons to act for him by proxy. Any such proxy shall be delivered to the secretary of such meeting at or prior to the time designated in the order of business for so delivering such proxies. At all meetings of the stockholders for the election of directors, a plurality of the votes cast shall be sufficient to elect. On all other matters, except as otherwise required by Delaware law or the certificate of incorporation, a majority of the votes cast at a meeting of the stockholders shall be necessary to authorize any corporate action to be taken by vote of the stockholders. Unless required by Delaware law, or determined by the chairman of the meeting to be advisable, the vote on any question other than the election of directors need not be by written ballot. On a vote by written ballot, each written ballot shall be signed by the stockholder voting, or by his proxy if there be such proxy, and shall state the number of shares voted.

SECTION 10. <u>Fixing of Record Date for Stockholder Meetings</u>. In order that the Corporation may determine the stockholders entitled to notice of or to vote at any meeting of stockholders or any adjournment thereof, the Board of Directors may fix a record date,

(continued)

(continued)

which record date shall not precede the date upon which the resolution fixing the record date is adopted by the Board of Directors, and which record date shall not be more than sixty (60) nor less than ten (10) days before the date of such meeting. If no record date is fixed by the Board of Directors, the record date for determining stockholders entitled to notice of or to vote at a meeting of stockholders shall be the close of business on the day next preceding the day on which notice is given or, if notice is waived, at the close of business on the day next preceding the day on which the meeting is held. A determination of stockholders of record entitled to notice of or to vote at a meeting of stockholders shall apply to any adjournment of the meeting; provided, however, that the Board of Directors may fix a new record date for the adjourned meeting.

SECTION 11.   Fixing a Record Date for Other Purposes. In order that the Corporation may determine the stockholders entitled to receive payment of any dividend or other distribution or allotment of any rights or the stockholders entitled to exercise any rights in respect of any change, conversion, or exchange of stock, or for the purposes of any other lawful action, the Board of Directors may fix a record date, which record date shall not precede the date upon which the resolution fixing the record date is adopted, and which record date shall not be more than sixty (60) days prior to such action. If no record date is fixed, the record date for determining stockholders for any such purpose shall be at the close of business on the day on which the Board of Directors adopts the resolution relating thereto.

SECTION 12.   List of Stockholders Entitled to Vote. The officer of the Corporation who has charge of the stock ledger of the Corporation shall prepare and make, at least ten (10) days before every meeting of the stockholders, a complete list of the stockholders entitled to vote at the meeting, arranged in alphabetical order, and showing the address of each stockholder and the number of shares registered in the name of each stockholder. Such list shall be open to the examination of any stockholder, for any purpose germane to the meeting, during ordinary business hours, for a period of at least ten (10) days prior to the meeting, either at a place within the city where the meeting is to be held, which place shall be specified in the notice of the meeting, or, if not so specified, at the place where the meeting is to be held. The list shall also be produced and kept at the time and place of the meeting during the whole time thereof, and may be inspected by any stockholder of the Corporation who is present.

SECTION 13.   Inspectors. The Board of Directors may, in advance of any meeting of stockholders, appoint one or more inspectors to act at such meeting or any adjournment thereof. If the inspectors shall not be so appointed or if any of them shall fail to appear or act, the chairman of the meeting shall appoint inspectors. Each inspector, before entering upon the discharge of his or her duties, shall take and sign an oath faithfully to execute the duties of inspector at such meeting with strict impartiality and according to the best of his or her ability. The inspectors shall determine the number of shares outstanding and the voting power of each, the number of shares represented at the meeting, the existence of a quorum, and the validity and effect of proxies, and shall receive votes, ballots, or consents, hear and determine all challenges and questions arising in connection with the right to vote, count, and tabulate all votes, ballots, or consents, determine the result, and do such acts as are proper to conduct the election or vote with fairness to all stockholders. On request of the chairman of the meeting or any stockholder entitled to vote thereat, the inspectors shall make a report in writing of any challenge, question, or matter determined by them and shall execute a certificate of any fact found by them. No director or candidate for the office of director shall act as an inspector of an election of directors. Inspectors need not be stockholders.

SECTION 14.   Stock Ledger. The stock ledger of the Corporation shall be the only evidence as to who are the stockholders entitled

(*continued*)

(*continued*)

to examine the stock ledger, the list required by Section 12 of this Article I, the books of the Corporation, or to vote in person or by proxy at any meeting of the stockholders.

ARTICLE II

Board of Directors

SECTION 1. <u>General Powers</u>. The business and affairs of the Corporation shall be managed by or under the direction of a Board of Directors. The Board of Directors may exercise all such authority and powers of the Corporation and do all such lawful acts and things as are not, by Delaware law or the certificate of incorporation, directed or required to be exercised or done by the stockholders.

SECTION 2. <u>Number, Qualification</u>. Except as otherwise fixed by or pursuant to provisions of the certificate of incorporation relating to the rights of the holders of any class or series of stock having a preference over common stock as to dividends or upon liquidation to elect additional directors under specified circumstances, the number of directors of the Corporation shall be fixed from time to time by affirmative vote of a majority of the directors then in office; <u>provided</u>, <u>however</u>, that the numbers of directors constituting the whole Board of Directors shall be an odd number. Directors need not be stockholders.

SECTION 3. <u>Elections And Terms</u>. The Board of Directors, other than those who may be elected by the holders of any classes or series of stock having a preference over the common stock as to dividends or upon liquidation, shall be classified, with respect to the time for which they severally hold office, into three class, as nearly equal in number as possible, one class to be originally elected for a term expiring at the annual meeting of stockholders to be held in _____, another class to be originally elected for a term expiring at the annual meeting of stockholders to be held in _____, and another class to be originally elected for a term

30

expiring at the annual meeting of the stockholders to be held in
_____, with each class to hold office until its successors are
elected and qualified. At each annual meeting of the stockholders
of the Corporation after fiscal year _____, the successors of the
class of directors whose term expires at that meeting shall be
elected to hold office for a term expiring at the annual meeting of
stockholders held in the third year following the year of their
election.

SECTION 4. Newly Created Directorships And Vacancies.
Except as otherwise fixed by or pursuant to provisions of the certificate of incorporation relating to the rights of the holders of any
class or series of stock having a preference over common stock
as to dividends or upon liquidation to elect additional directors
under specified circumstances, newly created directorships resulting from any increase in the number of directors and any
vacancies on the Board of Directors resulting from death, resignation, disqualification, removal, or other cause shall be filled by the
affirmative vote of a majority of the remaining directors then in
office, even though less than a quorum of the Board of Directors.
Except as otherwise provided under Delaware law, newly created
directorships and vacancies resulting from any cause may not be
filled by any other person or persons. Any director elected in accordance with the preceding sentence shall hold office for the remainder of the full term of the class of directors in which the new
directorship was created or the vacancy occurred and until such
director's successor shall have been elected and qualified. No decrease in the number of directors constituting the Board of Directors shall shorten the term of any director then in office.

SECTION 5. Removal and Resignation. Except as otherwise
fixed by or pursuant to provisions of the certificate of incorporation relating to the rights of the holders of any class or series of
stock having a preference over common stock as to dividends
or upon liquidation to elect additional directors under specified
(*continued*)

(*continued*)

circumstances, any director may be removed from office only for cause and only by the affirmative vote of the holders of [two-thirds] of the outstanding shares of stock entitled to vote generally in the election of directors. Any director may resign at any time upon written notice to the Corporation. Any such resignation shall take effect at the time specified therein or, if the time when it shall become effective shall not be specified therein, immediately upon its receipt; and, unless otherwise specified therein, the acceptance of such resignation shall not be necessary to make it effective.

SECTION 6. Nomination of Directors. Only persons who are nominated in accordance with the following procedures shall be eligible for election by the stockholders as directors of the Corporation. Nominations of persons for election as directors of the Corporation may be made at an annual meeting of stockholders (i) by or at the direction of the Board of Directors; (ii) by any nominating committee or persons appointed by the Board of Directors; or (iii) by any stockholder of the Corporation entitled to vote for the election of directors at the meeting who complies with the notice procedures set forth in this Section 6. Such nominations, other than those made by or at the direction of the Board of Directors, shall be made pursuant to timely notice in writing to the Secretary of the Corporation. To be timely, a stockholder's notice shall be delivered to or mailed and received at the principal executive office of the Corporation not less than sixty (60) days nor more than ninety (90) days prior to the annual meeting; provided, however, that in the event that less than seventy (70) days' notice or prior public disclosure of the date of the annual meeting is given or made to stockholders, notice by the stockholder to be timely must be so received not later than the close of business on the tenth day following the day on which such notice of the date of the meeting was mailed or such public disclosure was made, whichever first occurs. Such stockholder's notice to the Secretary of the Corporation shall set forth (a) as to each person whom the stockholder proposes to nominate for election or reelection as a director, (i) the name, age, business address, and residence address of the person, (ii) the principal occupation or employment of the person, (iii) the class and number of shares of capital stock of the Corporation which are beneficially owned by the person, and (iv) any other information relating to the person that is required to be disclosed in solicitations for proxies for election of directors pursuant to Regulation 14A under the Securities Exchange Act of 1934, as now or hereafter amended; and (b) as to the stockholder giving the notice, (i) the name and record address of such stockholder and (ii) the class and number of shares of capital stock of the Corporation which are beneficially owned by such stockholder. The Corporation may require any proposed nominee to furnish such other information as may reasonably be required by the Corporation to determine the eligibility of such proposed nominee to serve as a director of the Corporation. No person shall be eligible for election by the stockholders as a director of the Corporation unless nominated in accordance with the procedures set forth herein. The chairman of the annual meeting of the stockholders shall, if the facts warrant, determine and declare to the meeting that nomination was not made in accordance with the foregoing procedure, and if he should so determine, he shall so declare to the meeting and the defective nomination shall be disregarded.

SECTION 7.   Regular Meetings. Regular meetings of the Board of Directors may be held at such places within or without the State of Delaware and at such times as the Board of Directors may from time to time determine. Notice of regular meetings of the Board of Directors need not be given except as otherwise required by Delaware law or these bylaws.

SECTION 8.   Special Meetings. Special meetings of the Board of Directors may be held at any time or place within or without the State of Delaware whenever called by the Chairman of the Board

(*continued*)

(*continued*)

of Directors, by the Chief Executive Officer, or by a majority of the whole Board of Directors.

SECTION 9.   Notice of Meetings. Notice of each special meeting of the Board of Directors (and of each regular meeting for which notice shall be required) shall be given by the Secretary as hereinafter provided in this Section 9, in which notice shall be stated the time and place of the meeting. Except as otherwise required by Delaware law or these bylaws, such notice need not state the purpose (s) of such meeting. Notice of each such meeting shall be mailed, postage prepaid, to each director, addressed to such director at such director's residence or usual place of business, by registered mail, return receipt requested delivered at least two (2) days before the day on which such meeting is to be held, or shall be sent addressed to such director at such place by electronic mail, telegraph, telex, cable, or wireless, or be delivered to such director personally, by facsimile or by telephone, at least 24 hours before the time at which such meeting is to be held. A written waiver of notice, signed by the director entitled to notice, whether before or after the time stated therein, shall be deemed equivalent to notice. Notice of any such meeting need not be given to any director who shall, either before or after the meeting, submit a signed waiver of notice or who shall attend such meeting without protesting, prior to or at its commencement, the lack of notice to him. Neither the business to be transacted nor the purpose of any meeting of the Board of Directors need be specified in any written waiver of notice.

SECTION 10.   Quorum and Manner of Acting. Except as hereinafter provided, a majority of the whole Board of Directors shall be present in person or by means of a conference telephone or similar communications equipment which allows all persons participating in the meeting to hear each other at the same time at any meeting of the Board of Directors in order to constitute a quorum for the transaction of business at such meeting; and, except as otherwise required by Delaware law, the certificate of incorporation or these bylaws, the act of a majority of the directors present at any meeting at which a quorum is present shall be the act of the Board of Directors. Once a quorum for the transaction of business has been established at any meeting of the Board of Directors in accordance with this Section 10 it may not be broken by the departure of any director or directors. In the absence of a quorum at any meeting of the Board of Directors, a majority of the directors present thereat may adjourn such meeting to another time and place. Notice of the time and place of any such adjourned meeting shall be given to the directors who were not present at the time of the adjournment and, unless such time and place were announced at the meeting at which the adjournment was taken, to the other directors. At any adjourned meeting at which a quorum is present, any business may be transacted which might have been transacted at the meeting as originally called. The directors shall act only as a Board and the individual directors shall have no power as such.

SECTION 11.   Action Without a Meeting. Any action required or permitted to be taken at any meeting of the Board of Directors may be taken without a meeting if all members of the Board consent thereto in writing, and the writing or writings are filed with the minutes of the proceedings of the Board of Directors.

SECTION 12.   Telephonic Participation. Members of the Board of Directors may participate in a meeting of the Board by means of a conference telephone or similar communications equipment allowing all persons participating in the meeting to hear each other at the same time. Participation in such a meeting shall constitute presence in person at such meeting.

SECTION 13.   Organization. At each meeting of the Board, the Chairman of the Board or, in his absence or inability to act, the Chief Executive Officer or, in his absence or inability to act, another director chosen by a majority of the directors present shall act as chairman of the meeting and preside thereat. The Secretary or, in his absence or inability to act, any person appointed by the

(*continued*)

(*continued*)

chairman shall act as secretary of the meeting and keep the minutes thereof.

SECTION 14.   Compensation. The Board of Directors shall have authority to fix the compensation, including fees and reimbursement of expenses, of directors for services to the Corporation in any capacity.

ARTICLE III

Committees

SECTION 1.   Committees. The Board of Directors may, by resolution passed by a majority of the whole Board of Directors, designate one or more committees, each committee to consist of two (2) or more of the directors of the Corporation. The Board of Directors may fill vacancies in, change the membership of, or dissolve any such committee. The Board of Directors may designate one or more directors as alternate members of any committee who may replace any absent or disqualified member at any meeting of the committee. In the absence or disqualification of a member of the committee, the member or members thereof present at any meeting and not disqualified from voting, whether or not he or they constitute a quorum, may unanimously appoint another member of the Board of Directors to act at the meeting in place of such absent or disqualified member. Any such committee, to the extent provided by Delaware law and to the extent provided in the resolution of the Board of Directors, shall have and may exercise the powers of the Board of Directors in the management of the business and affairs of the Corporation, and may authorize the seal of the Corporation to be affixed to all papers which may require it. Each committee shall keep written minutes of its proceedings and shall report such minutes to the Board of Directors when required. All such proceedings shall be subject to revision or alteration by the Board of Directors; provided, however, that third parties shall not be prejudiced by such revision or alteration.

SECTION 2. Committee Rules. Unless the Board of Directors otherwise provides, each committee designated by the Board of Directors may make, alter, and repeal rules for the conduct of its business. In the absence of such rules, each committee shall conduct its business in the same manner as the Board of Directors conducts its business pursuant to Article II of these bylaws.

SECTION 3. Standing Committees. Notwithstanding anything contained in this Article III to the contrary, the Board of Directors shall maintain two (2) standing committees consisting of (a) a Corporate Governance Committee; and (b) an Audit Committee. The Corporate Governance Committee shall consist of at least three (3) members of the Board of Directors who are "non-employee directors" within the meaning of Rule 16b-3 promulgated under the Securities Exchange Act of 1934, as amended, and who are "outside directors" within the meaning of Section 162(m) of the Internal Revenue Code of 1986, as amended. The Corporate Governance Committee shall have the power and authority to recommend general compensation polices to the full Board of Directors, oversee the Corporation's compensation plans, establish the compensation levels for the Corporation's Chief Executive Officer and other Executive Officers, and advise the full Board of Directors on general compensation policies for the Company's Executive Officers. The Audit Committee shall consist of at least three (3) members of the Board of Directors, none of which shall also serve as an Executive Officer of the Corporation. The Audit Committee shall have the power and authority to review and report to the full Board of Directors with respect to the selection, retention, termination, and terms of engagement of the Corporation's independent public accountants and maintain communications among the Board of Directors, the independent public accountants, and the Corporation's internal accounting staff with respect to accounting and audit procedures. The Audit Committee shall also have the power and authority to

(continued)

(*continued*)

review the Corporation's processes, internal accounting and control procedures and policies, and related matters with the Corporation's management.

ARTICLE IV

Officers

SECTION 1. <u>Number</u>. The officers of the Corporation shall be elected by the Board of Directors and shall consist of a Chairman of the Board, a Chief Executive Officer, a President, one or more Vice Presidents, a Secretary, a Treasurer, and such other officers and assistant officers as may be deemed necessary or desirable by the Board of Directors. Any number of offices may be held by the same person. In its discretion, the Board of Directors may choose not to fill any office for any period that it may deem advisable unless otherwise required by Delaware law.

SECTION 2. <u>Election and Term of Office</u>. The officers of the Corporation shall be elected annually by the Board of Directors at its first meeting held after each annual meeting of stockholders or as soon thereafter as conveniently may be. The Chief Executive Officer shall appoint persons to other officers as he or she deems desirable, and such appointments, if any, shall serve at the pleasure of the Board of Directors. Each officer shall hold office until a successor is duly elected and qualified or until his or her earlier death, resignation or removal as hereinafter provided.

SECTION 3. <u>Resignations</u>. Any officer may resign at any time upon written notice to the Corporation. Any such resignation shall take effect at the time specified therein or, if the time when it shall become effective shall not be specified therein, immediately upon its receipt; and, unless otherwise specified therein, the acceptance of such resignation shall not be necessary to make it effective.

SECTION 4. <u>Removal</u>. Any officer or agent of the Corporation may be removed, either with or without cause, at any time, by the

Board of Directors at any meeting of the Board of Directors or, except in the case of an officer or agent elected or appointed by the Board of Directors, by the Chief Executive Officer, but any such removal shall be without prejudice to the contract rights, if any, of the person so removed.

SECTION 5.   Vacancies. Any vacancy occurring in any office of the Corporation by death, resignation, removal, or otherwise, may be filled for the unexpired portion of the term of the office which shall be vacant by the Board of Directors at any special or regular meeting.

SECTION 6.   Powers and Duties of Executive Officers. The officers of the Corporation shall have such powers and duties in the management of the Corporation as may be prescribed in a resolution by the Board of Directors and, to the extent not so provided, as generally pertain to their respective offices, subject to the control of the Board of Directors. The Board of Directors may require any officer, agent, or employee to give security for the faithful performance of his or her duties.

SECTION 7.   The Chairman of the Board. The Chairman of the Board shall be an officer of the Corporation for the purpose of executing agreements and other instruments on behalf of the Corporation but shall not be an employee of the Corporation. He shall, if present, preside at each meeting of the stockholders and of the Board of Directors and shall be an exofficio member of all committees of the Board of Directors. Such person shall perform all duties incident to the office of Chairman of the Board and such other duties as may from time to time be assigned to such person by the Board of Directors.

SECTION 8.   The Chief Executive Officer. The Chief Executive Officer shall have the general and active supervision and direction over the business operations and affairs of the Corporation and over the other officers, agents, and employees and shall see that

(*continued*)

(*continued*)

their duties are properly performed. At the request of the Chairman of the Board or in the case of his absence or inability to act, the Chief Executive Officer shall perform the duties of the Chairman of the Board and when so acting shall have all the powers of and be subject to all the restrictions upon the Chairman of the Board. Such person shall perform all duties incident to the office of Chief Executive Officer and such other duties as may from time to time be assigned to such person by the Board of Directors.

SECTION 9. The President. The President shall be the Chief Operating Officer of the Corporation and shall have general and active supervision and direction over the business operations and affairs of the Corporation and over its several officers, agents, and employees, subject, however, to the direction of the Chief Executive Officer and the control of the Board of Directors. In general, the President shall have such other powers and shall perform such other duties as usually pertain to the office of President or as from time to time may be assigned to him by the Board of Directors or the Chief Executive Officer.

SECTION 10. Vice Presidents. Each Vice President shall have such powers and perform such duties as from time to time may be assigned to him by the Board of Directors or the Chief Executive Officer.

SECTION 11. The Treasurer. The Treasurer shall (a) have charge and custody of, and be responsible for, all the funds and securities of the Corporation; (b) keep full and accurate accounts of receipts and disbursements in books belonging to the Corporation; (c) cause all monies and other valuables to be deposited to the credit of the Corporation in such depositories as may be designated by the Board; (d) receive, and give receipts for, monies due and payable to the Corporation from any source whatsoever; (e) disburse the funds of the Corporation and supervise the investment of its funds as ordered or authorized by the Board, taking proper vouchers therefor; and (f) in general, have all the powers and perform all the duties incident to the office of Treasurer and such other duties as from time to time may be assigned to him by the Board of Directors or the Chief Executive Officer.

SECTION 12.   The Secretary. The Secretary shall (a) record the proceedings of the meetings of the stockholders and directors in a minute book to be kept for that purpose; (b) see that all notices are duly given in accordance with the provisions of these bylaws and as required by law; (c) be custodian of the records and the seal of the Corporation and affix and attest the seal to all stock certificates of the Corporation (unless the seal of the Corporation on such certificates shall be a facsimile, as hereinafter provided) and affix and attest the seal to all other documents to be executed on behalf of the Corporation under its seal; (d) see that the books, reports, statements, certificates, and other documents and records required by law to be kept and filed are properly kept and filed; and (e) in general, have all the powers and perform all the duties incident to the office of Secretary and such other duties as from time to time may be assigned to him by the Board of Directors or the Chief Executive Officer.

SECTION 13.   Officers' Bonds or Other Security. The Board of Directors may secure the fidelity of any or all of its officers or agents by bond or otherwise, in such amount and with such surety or sureties as the Board of Directors may require.

SECTION 14.   Compensation. The compensation of the officers of the Corporation for their services as such officers shall be fixed from time to time by the Board of Directors; provided, however, that the Board of Directors may delegate to the Chief Executive Officer or the President the power to fix the compensation of officers and agents appointed by the Chairman of the Board or the President, as the case may be. An officer of the Corporation shall not be prevented from receiving compensation by reason of the fact that such person is also a director of the Corporation.

(continued)

(*continued*)

ARTICLE V

Shares of Stock

SECTION 1. <u>Stock Certificates</u>. Every holder of stock in the Corporation shall be entitled to have a certificate signed by or in the name of the Corporation by the Chairman of the Board or the Chief Executive Officer or the President or a Vice President, and by the Treasurer or an Assistant Treasurer, or the Secretary or an Assistant Secretary, certifying the number of shares owned by such holder in the Corporation. Any of or all the signatures on the certificate may be a facsimile. In case any officer, transfer agent, or registrar who has signed or whose facsimile signature has been placed upon such certificate shall have ceased to be such officer, transfer agent, or registrar before such certificate is issued, it may nevertheless be issued by the Corporation with the same effect as if he were such officer, transfer agent, or registrar at the date of issue.

SECTION 2. <u>Books of Account and Record of Stockholders</u>. The books and records of the Corporation may be kept at such places, within or without the State of Delaware, as the Board of Directors may from time to time determine. The stock record books and the blank stock certificate books shall be kept by the Secretary or by any other officer or agent designated by the Board of Directors.

SECTION 3. <u>Transfer of Shares</u>. Transfers of shares of stock of the Corporation shall be made on the stock records of the Corporation only upon authorization by the registered holder thereof, or by his attorney hereunto authorized by power of attorney duly executed and filed with the Secretary or with a transfer agent or transfer clerk, and on surrender of the certificate or certificates for such shares properly endorsed or accompanied by a duly executed stock transfer power and the payment of all taxes thereon. Except as otherwise provided by Delaware law, the Corporation shall be entitled to recognize the exclusive right of a person in whose name any share or shares stand on the record of stockholders as the owner of such share or shares for all purposes, including, without limitation, the rights to receive dividends or other distributions, and to vote as such owner, and the Corporation may hold any such stockholder of record liable for calls and assessments and the Corporation shall not be bound to recognize any equitable or legal claim to or interest in any such share or shares on the part of any other person whether or not it shall have express or other notice thereof. Whenever any transfers of shares shall be made for collateral security and not absolutely, and both the transferor and transferee request the Corporation to do so, such fact shall be stated in the entry of the transfer.

SECTION 4.   <u>Regulations</u>. The Board of Directors may make such additional rules and regulations, not inconsistent with these bylaws, as it may deem expedient concerning the issue, transfer, and registration of certificates for shares of stock of the Corporation. It may appoint, or authorize any officer or officers to appoint, one or more transfer agents or one or more transfer clerks and one or more registrars and may require all certificates for shares of stock to bear the signature or signatures of any of them.

SECTION 5.   <u>Lost, Stolen or Destroyed Stock Certificates</u>. The holder of any certificate representing shares of stock of the Corporation shall immediately notify the Corporation of any loss, destruction, or mutilation of such certificate, and the Corporation may issue a new certificate of stock in the place of any certificate theretofore issued by it, alleged to have been lost, stolen, or destroyed, and the Board of Directors may, in its discretion, require the owner of the lost, stolen, or destroyed certificate, or his legal representative, to give the Corporation a bond sufficient, as the Board in its absolute discretion shall determine, to indemnify the Corporation against any claim that may be made against it on account of the alleged loss, theft, or destruction of any such certificate or the issuance of such new certificate. Anything herein to the contrary notwithstanding, the Board of Directors, in its absolute discretion, may refuse to issue any such new certificate,

(continued)

(*continued*)

except pursuant to judicial proceedings under the laws of the State of Delaware.

ARTICLE VI

Contracts, Checks, Drafts, Bank Accounts, Etc.

SECTION 1.   Execution of Contracts. Except as otherwise required by statute, the certificate of incorporation or these bylaws, any contract or other instrument may be executed and delivered in the name and on behalf of the Corporation by such officer or officers (including any assistant officer) of the Corporation as the Board of Directors may from time to time direct. Such authority may be general or confined to specific instances as the Board of Directors may determine. Unless authorized by the Board of Directors or expressly permitted by these bylaws, no officer or agent or employee shall have any power or authority to bind the Corporation by any contract or engagement or to pledge its credit or to render it pecuniary liable for any purpose or to any amount.

SECTION 2.   Loans. Unless the Board of Directors shall otherwise determine, the Chief Executive Officer, President, or any Vice President may effect loans and advances at any time for the Corporation from any bank, trust company, or other institution, or from any firm, corporation, or individual, and for such loans and advances may make, execute, and deliver promissory notes, bonds, or other certificates or evidences of indebtedness of the Corporation, but no officer or officers shall mortgage, pledge, hypothecate, or transfer any securities or other property of the Corporation other than in connection with the purchase of chattels for use in the Corporation's operations, except when authorized by the Board of Directors.

SECTION 3.   Checks, Drafts, Bank Accounts, Etc. All checks, drafts, bills of exchange, or other orders for the payment of money out of the funds of the Corporation, and all notes or other evidence of indebtedness of the Corporation, shall be signed in the name and on behalf of the Corporation by such persons and in such manner as shall from time to time be authorized by the Board of Directors.

SECTION 4.   Deposits. All funds of the Corporation not otherwise employed shall be deposited from time to time to the credit of the Corporation in such banks, trust companies, or other depositaries as the Board of Directors may from time to time designate or as may be designated by any officer or officers of the Corporation to whom such power of designation may from time to time be delegated by the Board of Directors. For the purpose of deposit and for the purpose of collection for the account of the Corporation, checks, drafts, and other orders for the payment of money which are payable to the order of the Corporation may be endorsed, assigned, and delivered by any officer or agent of the Corporation.

SECTION 5.   General and Special Bank Accounts. The Board of Directors may from time to time authorize the opening and keeping of general and special bank accounts with such banks, trust companies, or other depositaries as the Board of Directors may designate or as may be designated by any officer or officers of the Corporation to whom such power of designation may from time to time be delegated by the Board of Directors. The Board of Directors may make such special rules and regulations with respect to such bank accounts, not inconsistent with the provisions of these bylaws, as it may deem expedient.

ARTICLE VII

Indemnification

SECTION 1.   Right to Indemnification. The Corporation shall indemnify and hold harmless to the fullest extent permitted by applicable law as it presently exists or may hereafter be amended, any person who was or is a party or is threatened to be made a party or is otherwise involved in any threatened, pending, or completed action, suit or proceeding, whether civil, criminal, administrative, or investigative, or by or in the right of the Corporation to procure a

(*continued*)

(*continued*)

judgment in its favor (a "Proceeding"), by reason of the fact that such person is or was a director, officer, employee, or agent of the Corporation, or is or was serving at the request of the Corporation as a director, officer, employee, or agent of another corporation, partnership, joint venture, trust, enterprise, or nonprofit entity, including serving with respect to employee benefit plans, against all liability and loss suffered and expenses (including attorneys' fees), judgments, fines, and amounts paid in settlement actually and reasonably incurred by such person in connection with such action, suit, or proceeding if such person acted in good faith and in a manner such person reasonably believed to be in or not opposed to the best interests of the Corporation; provided, however, with respect to a Proceeding involving the right of the Corporation to procure judgment in its favor, such indemnification shall only cover expenses (including attorney fees) and shall only be made if such person acted in good faith and in a manner such person reasonably believed to be in the best interests of the Corporation and shall not be made with respect to any Proceeding as to which such person has been adjudged to be liable to the Corporation unless and only to the extent that the Court of Chancery of the State of Delaware or the court in which such Proceeding was brought shall determine upon application that, despite the adjudication of liability but in view of all the circumstances of the case, such person is fairly and reasonably entitled to indemnity for such expenses which the Court of Chancery of the State of Delaware or such other court shall deem proper. The Corporation shall be required to indemnify a person in connection with a Proceeding (or part thereof) initiated by such person only if the Proceeding (or part thereof) was authorized by the Board of Directors of the Corporation.

SECTION 2.   Prepayment of Expenses. Expenses incurred in defending any Proceeding may be paid by the Corporation in advance of the final disposition of such action, suit, or proceeding as authorized by the Board of Directors in the specific case upon receipt of an undertaking by or on behalf of the director or officer to repay such amount if it should be ultimately determined that such person is not entitled to be indemnified by the Corporation as authorized in this Article VII or otherwise.

SECTION 3. Claims. If a claim for indemnification or payment of expenses under this Article VII is not paid in full within sixty (60) days after a written claim therefor has been received by the Corporation, the claimant may file suit to recover the unpaid amount of such claim and, if successful in whole or in part, shall be entitled to be paid the expense of prosecuting such claim. In any such action the Corporation shall have the burden of proving that the claimant was not entitled to the requested indemnification or payment of expenses under applicable Delaware law.

SECTION 4. Non-Exclusivity of Rights. The indemnification provided by this Article VII shall not be deemed exclusive of any other rights to which those seeking indemnification may be entitled under these bylaws or any agreement or vote of stockholders or disinterested directors or otherwise, both as to action in such person's official capacity and as to action in another capacity while holding such office, and shall continue as to a person who has ceased to be a director, officer, employee, or agent and shall inure to the benefit of the heirs, executors, and administrators of such a person.

SECTION 5. Other Indemnification. The Corporation's obligation, if any, to indemnify any person who was or is serving at its request as a director, officer, employee, or agent of another corporation, partnership, joint venture, trust, enterprise, or nonprofit entity be reduced by any amount such person may collect as indemnification from such other corporation, partnership, joint venture, trust, enterprise, or nonprofit enterprise.

SECTION 6. Insurance. The Corporation may purchase and maintain insurance on behalf of any person who is or was a director, officer, employee, or agent of the Corporation, or is or was serving at the request of the Corporation as a director, officer, employee, or agent of another corporation, partnership, joint venture, trust,

(*continued*)

(*continued*)

or other enterprise against any liability asserted against such person and incurred by such person in any such capacity, or arising out of such person's status as such, whether or not the Corporation would have the power to indemnify such person against such liability under the provisions of Delaware law, the certificate of incorporation or of this Article VII.

SECTION 7. Amendment or Repeal. Any repeal or modification of the foregoing provisions of this Article VII shall not adversely effect any right or protection hereunder of any person respective of any act or omission occurring prior to the time of such repeal or modification.

ARTICLE VIII

General Provisions

SECTION 1. Registered Office. The registered office and registered agent of the Corporation will be as specified in the certificate of incorporation of the Corporation.

SECTION 2. Other Offices. The Corporation may also have such offices, both within or without the State of Delaware, as the Board of Directors may from time to time determine or the business of the Corporation may require.

SECTION 3. Fiscal Year. The fiscal year of the Corporation shall be so determined by the Board of Directors.

SECTION 4. Seal. The seal of the Corporation shall be circular in form, shall bear the name of the Corporation and shall include the words and numbers "Corporate Seal," "Delaware," and the year of incorporation.

SECTION 5. Voting Securities Owned By Corporation. Voting securities in any other corporation held by the Corporation shall be voted by the Chairman of the Board, unless the Board of Directors specifically confers authority to vote with respect thereto, which authority may be general or confined to specific instances, upon some other person or officer. Any person authorized to vote securities shall have the power to appoint proxies, with general power of substitution.

SECTION 6. <u>Inspection of Books and Records</u>. Any stockholder of record, in person or by attorney or other agent, shall, upon written demand under oath stating the purpose thereof, have the right during the usual hours for business to inspect for any proper purpose the Corporation's stock ledger, a list of its stockholders, and its other books and records, and to make copies or extracts therefrom. A proper purpose shall mean any purpose reasonably related to such person's interest as a stockholder. In every instance where an attorney or other agent shall be the person who seeks the right to inspection, the demand under oath shall be accompanied by a power of attorney or such other writing which authorizes the attorney or other agent to so act on behalf of the stockholder. The demand under oath shall be directed to the Corporation at its registered office in the State of Delaware or at its principal place of business.

SECTION 7. <u>Section Headings</u>. Section headings in these bylaws are for convenience of reference only and shall not be given any substantive effect in limiting or otherwise construing any provision herein.

SECTION 8. <u>Inconsistent Provisions</u>. In the event that any provision of these bylaws is or becomes inconsistent with any provision of the certificate of incorporation, the general corporation law of the State of Delaware or any other applicable law, the provision of these bylaws shall not be given any effect to the extent of such inconsistency but shall otherwise be given full force and effect.

ARTICLE X

<u>Amendment</u>

These bylaws may be adopted, amended, or repealed, and new bylaws made, by the Board of Directors of the Corporation, but the

(*continued*)

(*continued*)

stockholders of the Corporation may make additional bylaws and may alter and repeal any bylaws, whether adopted by them or otherwise, by affirmative vote of the holders of [two-thirds] of the outstanding shares of stock entitled to vote upon the election of directors.

Some of the advantages of corporate structure are:

- **Limited liability.** Unlike in a partnership or sole proprietorship, shareholders of a modern business corporation have "limited" liability for the corporation's debts and obligations. As a result, their potential losses cannot exceed the amount that they contributed to the corporation in payment for shares. Limited liability further allows corporations to raise much more funds for enterprises by combining funds from the stock owners. This in turn greatly reduces the individual risk for potential shareholders and increases both the number of willing shareholders and the amount they are likely to invest.

- **Perpetual lifetime.** Another favorable regulation is that the assets and structure of the corporation exist beyond the lifetime of any of its shareholders, bondholders, or employees. This allows for stability and accumulation of capital, which thus becomes available for investment in projects of a larger size and over a longer term than if the corporate assets remained subject to dissolution and distribution. It is important to note that the "perpetual lifetime" feature is an indication of the unbounded potential duration of the corporation's existence and its accumulation of wealth and thus power.

- **Ownership and control.** Persons and other legal entities composed of persons (such as trusts and other corporations) can have the right to vote or share in the profit of corporations. In the case of for-profit corporations, these voters hold shares of stock and are thus called shareholders or stockholders.

There are two principal types of corporations utilized, the S corporation and the C corporation.

An S corporation is taxed like a partnership; it pays no taxes as an entity, but its earnings or losses flow through to the owners' individual tax returns. Restrictions exist regarding how many stockholders there may be in an S corporation, as well as what kinds of stockholders may exist without jeopardizing the S election. S shareholders do enjoy limited liability. There are advantages to operating a business as an S corporation, in that income is taxed only once while enjoying limited liability. However, the consideration of an exit strategy may influence this type of structure; when an S election is terminated, there may be adverse tax consequences.

A C corporation is the most common form of corporation and affords its stockholders limited liability and the most flexibility in being able to operate and raise capital. While as an entity, the C corporation is subject to paying tax on its profits before shareholders receive a return (which then gets taxed again at the shareholder level), this is the predominant corporate structure for someone who is interested in:

- Minimizing personal risk
- Ignoring the minimum consequences of taxation at both a corporate and an individual level
- Raising necessary capital with which to grow the business

- Having a clearly executable exit strategy with an organization structure that will facilitate its execution

TIPS AND TECHNIQUES

It is always the author's recommendation to form a C corporation to conduct meaningful business, especially when additional outside capital will be required. Such a structure facilitates the flexibility by which this capital can be sought and raised, as discussed in later chapters.

Summary

Various structures exist for the formation of a business. After considering the advantages and disadvantages of the various structures (and considering the title of this book and the author's built-in bias), you can logically decide that a corporation makes the most sense for a venture that is to be formed to protect the entrepreneur and raise capital.

CHAPTER 2

Initial Capital Formation

After reading this chapter, you will be able to:

- Differentiate the features of debt and equity from both a business and an accounting standpoint.

- Gain an understanding of the various types of debt available to you, such as straight debt, small business loans, and convertible debt.

- Gain an understanding of the various types of equity instruments that may be utilized, such as preferred stock, convertible preferred stock, and common stock.

- Be in a position to select the most appropriate capital structure for your situation.

Debt

Simplistically, "debt" represents an obligation for which repayment is expected. Interestingly enough, there are financial debts, debts for goods and services, and other debts (i.e., moral obligations). So while debt has numerous connotations in life and society, here we will presume it to mean the receipt of money by a "borrower" with intent to repay those funds to the "lender" with some remuneration for the use of the money and the implicit risk that repayment is not assured.

The reasons an entity might want to borrow and incur debt include to:

- Reduce or eliminate the amount of equity investment required to be sold by the company, thus decreasing potential dilution to owners and investors (more about this later when we explore equity)
- Provide working capital
- Raise the funds to finance the acquisition of another business
- Refinance existing debt with a new lender
- Restructure the company's balance sheet
- Raise funds for product expansion
- Accommodate a lender's request for loan repayment

In initial formation situations, the only reason for debt that really applies is the first one—that is, reducing the amount of the entity being given away at formation. However, due to the entity's business, debt may not be available to a start-up enterprise because of serious limitations on its ability to repay that debt. There are situations where money could be borrowed by the entity but only if the principals "guarantee" the repayment of the loan.

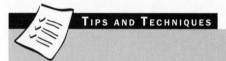

TIPS AND TECHNIQUES

It is my recommendation (with very few exceptions) to *never* personally guarantee such debt. As discussed in the preface, one of the reasons to select a structure for an entity is to control the risks to the entrepreneur. Why would you form an entity that protects your personal assets and then violate that principle by personally guaranteeing the debt? Not very smart.

The simplest form of debt is what is referred to as straight debt. It is simply an agreement (in the form of a note, as shown in Exhibit 2.1) to repay funds advanced, together with interest, on either a set repayment schedule or at a fixed point in time. The simplest debt is "unsecured" (meaning all the lender is receiving is your promise to repay). As situations change and riskier loans are sought, the lenders may introduce security interest in which they have access to assets to protect them in the event of nonpayment. They may also introduce the concept of "covenants," which are conditions that, if they occur, enable the lender to have certain pre-emptive rights, including declaring the loan/debt in default.

Covenants are not a desirable consequence and may have very adverse effects for the entity. Consequently, care must be taken when negotiating covenants to minimize the risk that the entity may breach them.

EXHIBIT 2.1

15% Promissory Note

THIS 15% NOTE HAS NOT BEEN REGISTERED UNDER THE SECU-RITIES ACT OF 1933, AS AMENDED (THE "SECURITIES ACT") OR UNDER THE SECURITIES LAWS OF ANY STATE. THE SECURITIES REPRESENTED HEREBY ARE RESTRICTED AND MAY NOT BE OFFERED, RESOLD, PLEDGED, OR TRANSFERRED EXCEPT IF SUCH TRANSACTION IS REGISTERED UNDER THE SECURITIES ACT AND APPLICABLE STATE SECURITIES LAWS OR IF SUCH TRANSACTION IS EXEMPT FROM SUCH REGISTRATION, AS CON-FIRMED BY AN OPINION OF COUNSEL TO THE COMPANY.

No. 15%PN-___   US $_____

_____ , **INC.**

15% PROMISSORY NOTE DUE ____, 2007

FOR VALUE RECEIVED, _____, INC., a Delaware corporation (the "Company"), promises to pay to _____ (the "Holder"), the principal sum of _____ (US$_____) and unpaid accrued interest on the principal sum at the rate of 15% per annum on _____, 2007 (the "Maturity Date"). Interest will be calculated on the basis of a 360-day year consisting of twelve 30-day months and be paid monthly. Accrual of interest shall commence on the first such business day to occur after the date hereof and continue until payment in full of the principal sum has been made in cash or this Note is converted as provided herein. The Company shall pay the principal of and interest upon this Note, less any amounts re-quired by law to be deducted, to the Holder of this Note at the address of such Holder, which is the last address appearing on the Note register of the Company for such Holder.

This Note is subject to the following additional provisions:

1. <u>Withholding</u>. The Company shall be entitled to withhold from all payments of principal and interest on this Note any amounts required to be withheld under the applicable provisions of the United States income tax laws or other applicable laws at the time of such payments, and the Holder shall execute and deliver all required documentation in connection therewith.

2. <u>Restrictions on Transfer</u>. This Note has been issued subject to investment representations of the original purchaser hereof and may be transferred or exchanged only in compliance with the Securities Act of 1933, as amended (the "Securities Act"), and applicable state securities laws. In the event of any proposed transfer of this Note, the Company may require, prior to issuance of a new Note in the name of such other person, that it receive reasonable transfer documentation including opinions of counsel that the issuance of the Note in such other name does not and will not cause a violation of the Securities Act or any applicable state securities laws. Prior to due presentment for transfer of this Note, the Company may treat the person in whose name this Note is duly registered on the Company's Note register as the owner hereof for the purpose of receiving payment as herein provided and for all other purposes, whether or not this Note is overdue, and the Company shall not be affected by notice to the contrary.

3. <u>Interest Rate</u>. The Company shall pay the Holder interest at the rate of 15% per annum, payable monthly.

4. <u>Warrant Issuance</u>. Simultaneously with the purchase of the 15% Note, the Company will issue a warrant to purchase, for five years from date of issuance, common stock of the Company in an amount equal to 50% of the principal amount of the Note at an exercise price equal to $2.50.

5. <u>Reservation of Common Stock Issuable Upon Conversion</u>. The Company shall at all times reserve and keep available out of its authorized but unissued shares of Common Stock,

(continued)

(*continued*)

such number of its shares of Common Stock as shall from time to time be sufficient to effect the exercise of the then outstanding Warrant.

6. Call Feature. This Note shall be callable for redemption by the Company, at its option, anytime after two (2) months from the date of issuance. The Company shall provide formal notice of its intent to call the Notes to the Holder. Upon receipt of the notice, the Holder shall present the Note to the Company for repayment of principal plus accrued and unpaid interest up to and through the date of such notice.

7. Unsecured Obligation. This Note shall be unsecured. The Holder shall have no recourse against any specific assets of the Company in the event of nonpayment of the Note.

8. Direct Obligation. No provision of this Note shall alter or impair the obligation of the Company, which is absolute and unconditional, to pay the principal of, and interest on, this Note at the time, place, and rate, and in the manner herein prescribed. This Note is a direct obligation of the Company.

9. Investment Representations. The Holder of the Note, by acceptance hereof, represents that the Holder is an ''accredited investor'' as defined in the Securities Act and the rules promulgated thereunder, and agrees that this Note is being acquired for investment and not with a view to the distribution thereof, and that such Holder will not offer, sell, or otherwise dispose of this Note except under circumstances which will not result in a violation of the Securities Act or any applicable state ''blue sky'' laws or similar state laws relating to the sale of securities.

10. Governing Law; Jurisdiction. This Note shall be governed by and construed in accordance with the laws of the State of _____. Each of the parties consents to the jurisdiction of the federal courts whose districts encompass any part of

_____ County, _____ or the state courts of the State of _____ sitting in _____ County in connection with any dispute arising under this Note and hereby waives, to the maximum extent permitted by law, any objection, including any objection based on *forum non conveniens*, to the bringing of any such proceeding in such jurisdictions.

11. Default. Each of the following shall constitute an "Event of Default":

a. the Company fails to pay the principal or accrued interest on this Note on the Maturity Date;

b. the Company commences any voluntary proceeding under any bankruptcy, reorganization, insolvency, readjustment of debt, receivership, dissolution, or liquidation law or statute, of any jurisdiction, whether now or subsequently in effect; or the Company is adjudicated insolvent or bankrupt by a court of competent jurisdiction; or the Company petitions or applies for, acquiesces in, or consents to, the appointment of any receiver or trustee of the Company for all or substantially all of its property or assets; or the Company makes an assignment for the benefit of its creditors; or the Company is unable to pay its debts as they mature;

c. there is commenced against the Company any proceeding relating to the Company under any bankruptcy, reorganization, insolvency, readjustment of debt, receivership, dissolution, or liquidation law or statute, of any jurisdiction, whether now or subsequently in effect, and the proceeding remains undismissed for a period of sixty (60) days or the Company by any act indicates its consent to, approval of, or acquiescence in, the proceedings; or a receiver or trustee is appointed for the Company for all or substantially all of its property or assets, and the receivership or trusteeship remains undischarged for a period of sixty (60) days; or a

(continued)

(*continued*)

warrant of attachment, execution, or similar process is issued against any substantial part of the property or assets of the Company, and the warrant or similar process is not dismissed or bonded within sixty (60) days after the levy;

d. the Company shall fail to perform or observe, in any material respect, any covenant, term, provision, condition, agreement, or obligation of the Company under this Note and such failure shall continue uncured for a period of thirty (30) days after notice from the Holder of such failure;

e. any governmental agency or any court of competent jurisdiction at the instance of any governmental agency shall assume custody or control of the whole or substantially all of the properties or assets of the Company; then, or at any time thereafter, and in each and every such case, unless such Event of Default shall have been waived in writing by the Holder (which waiver shall not be deemed to be a waiver of any subsequent default), this Note shall bear interest at the maximum lawful rate of interest permitted by applicable laws and at the option of the Holder and in the Holder's sole discretion, the Holder may consider this Note immediately due and payable, without presentment, demand, protest, or notice of any kind, all of which are hereby expressly waived, anything herein or in any other instruments to the contrary notwithstanding, and the Holder may immediately enforce any and all of the Holder's rights and remedies provided herein or any other rights or remedies afforded by law.

12. Collection Costs. In the event an Event of Default has occurred and has not been waived by Holder, the Holder shall be entitled to collect from the Company all costs and expenses incurred by Holder in enforcing its rights hereunder, including reasonable attorneys' fees.

[SIGNATURES FOLLOW ON NEXT PAGE]

IN WITNESS WHEREOF, the Company has caused this instrument to be duly executed by an officer thereunto duly authorized.

Effective as of this _____ day of _____, 20___.

_____ , **INC.**

By: _____

Name: _____

Title: <u>Chief Executive Officer</u>

Other Forms of Straight Debt

Since we are exploring the whole concept of debt, which could apply to growing established businesses as well, let us explore some traditional types of straight debt and sources. The traditional sources of debt capital for growing businesses historically have been banks and finance companies. Finance companies offer forms of financing similar to banks but typically are willing to assume more risk.

More recently, the definition of "lender" has become more complex, especially in the high-growth market niche. In an active financial market, there are cash-flow lenders, secured lenders, asset-based lenders, and hybrid lenders. These terms refer as much to the lender's market niche as they do to primary repayment sources and credit criteria. Within each of these categories, lending can be further defined by specific lending criteria, such as:

- Minimum and maximum loan size
- Credit agreements (cash-flow lender) versus demand contract agreements (secured and asset-based lender)

- Pricing considerations
- Industry preferences
- Geographic preferences
- Purpose of loans (i.e., to finance receivables, inventory, equipment, fixtures, real estate, expansions, acquisitions, buyouts, or growth)
- Types of loans (i.e., lines of credit, term loans, mezzanine loans, or subordinated debt)

A "cash-flow lender" of today is the traditional handshake lender of yesterday. This lender generally is part of a commercial bank and is likely to be the most conservative of the lenders discussed here. The cash-flow lender may or may not require security but does look primarily to the continuation of *historical* profits to repay the loan. *The reliance on past profitability limits the attractiveness of cash-flow debt to early-stage companies.* Credit criteria focuses heavily on the use of the proceeds, leverage considerations (total liabilities to total net worth), and cash-flow coverage available to repay the principal and interest when due. The loan generally is monitored by a credit agreement with negotiated covenants and specified definitions and remedies for default of a loan. For the most part, the company remains in control of its cash.

A "secured lender" tends to be either the asset-based lending department within a commercial bank or a regional bank. This department is a cross between the cash-flow lender and the hard-asset lender, because loan repayment from cash flow and profits remains an aspect of the credit decision, as does asset coverage for the loan. Less consideration generally is given to leverage issues because greater reliance is placed on the value of the assets and their collateral coverage. Pricing for secured loans tends to be higher than for cash–flow loans, as secured loans are perceived to have more risk and require more administrative attention to monitor the collateral. The increased risk generally is defined by a lack of strong operating trend, higher leverage, perceived industry difficulties, and so on.

Secured loans tend to be structured using a borrowing-base formula. This formula allows outstanding loans to be monitored against assets, with a typical borrowing base of 75% to 80% of eligible accounts receivable and 25% to 50% of raw material and/or finished-goods inventory. Secured-lender loans tend to be governed by demand agreements that generally allow the lender to control the receipt and disbursement of company cash.

The lender receives checks and cash daily from either a lockbox or a blocked account with a depository bank, or directly from the company. These proceeds are used to reduce the debt. Simultaneously, readvances are made available at the company's request according to availability under the borrowing-base formula. The loan contract typically specifies that the loan is outstanding for a one- to three-year time period, with prepayment penalties. While these secured-lending departments exist within commercial banks and tend to assume more risk in their lending activities, it is important to remember that these departments, like the bank itself, are subject to high levels of government regulatory scrutiny. Therefore, the "regulated" secured lender typically will have less flexibility in its lending practices than will unregulated commercial financing companies, often known as asset-based lenders.

Asset-based debt represents funding from the typical commercial finance company. Similar to the secured loan from a commercial bank, an asset-based loan is secured with collateral provided by the borrower, such as accounts receivable, inventory, or plant and equipment, to support general working-capital needs, inventory buildup, loan refinancings, asset acquisitions, or a leveraged buyout.

The major differences between the secured-lending departments at a bank and at a commercial finance company are the criteria by which borrowers are evaluated and the level of risk the institutions are willing to assume. Unlike asset-based departments of commercial banks, finance companies are not heavily regulated by the government. Consequently they have the ability to assume more risk in their loan portfolios and are paid accordingly. In granting secured loans, finance companies rely more on strength of the company's collateral than on its operating track record or profit potential. Finance companies focus primarily on the liquidation value of the assets with little consideration for leverage.

Many small- and medium-size businesses have found that finance companies provide an important source of funds that are not widely available through commercial banking channels. The typical finance company borrower is a company with erratic performance or one whose growth has outstripped its net worth and available working capital, and is unable to increase its bank borrowing. These tend to be highly leveraged companies. In many cases, asset-based lending is the sole source of working capital for these companies.

Finance companies charge higher interest rates than commercial banks and somewhat higher interest rates than secured lenders. This results from three factors:

1. The increased level of risk associated with highly leveraged and undercapitalized borrowers

2. The greater amount of administrative time and costs required to monitor collateral

3. A higher cost of funds to the finance company, since a substantial part of its lendable dollars often are borrowed rather than in the form of depository balances

TIPS AND TECHNIQUES

By now you should have an appreciation for the various types of straight debt and recognize that it is unlikely that an early-stage entity can secure capital in this manner.

Another source for early-stage companies is an SBA (Small Business Administration) loan. The Small Business Administration offers numerous loan programs to assist small businesses. It is important to note, however, that the SBA is primarily a guarantor of loans made by private and other institutions. These loans are covered by the Basic 7(a) Loan Guaranty program, which serves as the SBA's primary business loan program to help qualified small businesses obtain financing when they might not be eligible for business loans through normal lending channels. It is also the agency's most flexible business loan program, since financing under this program can be guaranteed for a variety of general business purposes.

Loan proceeds can be used for most sound business purposes, including working capital, machinery and equipment, furniture and fixtures, land and building (including purchase, renovation, and new construction), leasehold improvements, and debt refinancing (under special conditions). Loan maturity is up to 10 years for working capital and generally up to 25 years for fixed assets. Potential customers for such a program are start-up and existing small businesses. The loans are delivered through commercial lending institutions but guaranteed by the SBA, which is how these loans can be made.

 TIPS AND TECHNIQUES

I have little experience with SBA loans and understand that they may require guarantees and personal asset collateralization to the SBA, thereby reducing their desirability under ''Fater's Rules,'' the first of which is guarantee nothing.

Convertible Debt

Now that we have discussed the concept of straight debt, let us explore an attractive alternative: convertible debt. Convertible debt is a promissory note (much like straight debt) but has other features that provide the lender (or purchaser) with the potential for a much higher return than the simple interest because of its ability to be converted into equity rather than simply be repaid. For example, if an entity were to issue a convertible note that bears interest at 12% *and* also can be converted at the holder's option into shares of common stock (equity) of the entity, the value of the stock may exceed the principal amount of the loan and thus provide the lender with a much higher return for providing the capital to the entity. (See Exhibit 2.2.)

EXHIBIT 2.2

12% Convertible Note

NEITHER THIS BRIDGE NOTE NOR THE COMMON STOCK ISSU-ABLE UPON CONVERSION HEREOF HAS BEEN REGISTERED UN-DER THE SECURITIES ACT OF 1933, AS AMENDED (THE "SECURITIES ACT") OR UNDER THE SECURITIES LAWS OF ANY STATE. THE SECURITIES REPRESENTED HEREBY ARE RE-STRICTED AND MAY NOT BE OFFERED, RESOLD, PLEDGED, OR TRANSFERRED EXCEPT IF SUCH TRANSACTION IS REGISTERED UNDER THE SECURITIES ACT AND APPLICABLE STATE SECURI-TIES LAWS OR IF SUCH TRANSACTION IS EXEMPT FROM SUCH REGISTRATION, AS CONFIRMED BY AN OPINION OF COUNSEL TO THE COMPANY.

No. CBPN-1 US $ _____

_____, INC.

12% CONVERTIBLE PROMISSORY NOTE DUE _____, 20____

FOR VALUE RECEIVED, _____, INC., a Delaware corporation (the "Company"), promises to pay to _____ (the "Holder"), the principal sum of _____ (US$_____) and unpaid accrued interest on the principal sum at the rate of 10% per annum on _____, 20___ (the "Maturity Date"). Interest will be calculated on the basis of a 360-day year consisting of twelve 30-day months and be paid monthly. Accrual of interest shall commence on the first such business day to

(*continued*)

(*continued*)

occur after the date hereof and continue until payment in full of the principal sum has been made in cash or this Note is converted as provided herein. The Company shall pay the principal of and interest upon this Note, less any amounts required by law to be deducted, to the Holder of this Note at the address of such Holder which is the last address appearing on the Note register of the Company for such Holder.

This Note is subject to the following additional provisions:

1. <u>Withholding</u>. The Company shall be entitled to withhold from all payments of principal and interest on this Note any amounts required to be withheld under the applicable provisions of the United States income tax laws or other applicable laws at the time of such payments, and the Holder shall execute and deliver all required documentation in connection therewith.

2. <u>Restrictions on Transfer</u>. This Note has been issued subject to investment representations of the original purchaser hereof and may be transferred or exchanged only in compliance with the Securities Act of 1933, as amended (the "Securities Act"), and applicable state securities laws. In the event of any proposed transfer of this Note, the Company may require, prior to issuance of a new Note in the name of such other person, that it receive reasonable transfer documentation, including opinions of counsel that the issuance of the Note in such other name does not and will not cause a violation of the Securities Act or any applicable state securities laws. Prior to due presentment for transfer of this Note, the Company may treat the person in whose name this Note is duly registered on the Company's Note register as the owner hereof for the purpose of receiving payment as herein provided and for all other purposes, whether or not this Note

is overdue, and the Company shall not be affected by notice to the contrary.

3. Interest Rate. The Company shall pay the Holder interest at the rate of 12% per annum, payable monthly.

4. Conversion.

   A. Voluntary Conversion. The Holder of this Note is entitled to convert the face value of this Note or any portion thereof, plus any accrued but unpaid interest on the date of conversion, into shares of the Company's common stock, par value $.0001 per share ("Common Stock"), at a conversion price equal to 33½% below the price (the "Offering Price") at which Common Stock is first offered to the public in an offering underwritten by _____during the term of this Note. If this Offering is not consummated during the term of this Note, the Holder will have no right to convert this Note into Common Stock.

   B. Notice of Conversion. In order to convert the Note into Common Stock, the Holder must deliver a Notice of Conversion (the "Notice of Conversion") to the Company, in the form attached hereto as Exhibit A. Notices of Conversion shall be deemed delivered on the date sent, if personally delivered or sent by facsimile (with confirmation of transmission) to the Company, to the Company's Chief Executive Officer at the Company's principal place of business, or when actually received if sent by another method. The Notice of Conversion shall be accompanied by either a copy of (which shall be followed by an original within one (1) business day) or the original Note to be converted.

   C. Conversion Procedure. The Company shall instruct the Transfer Agent to issue the Common Stock within six (6) business days after the Company receives a fully executed Notice of Conversion and original Note. The

(continued)

(*continued*)

> Common Stock shall be issued with a restrictive legend indicating that it was issued in a transaction which is exempt from registration under the Securities Act and that it cannot be transferred unless it is so registered, or an exemption from registration is available in the opinion of counsel to the Company. The Common Stock shall be issued in the same name as the person who is the Holder of this Note unless, in the opinion of counsel to the Company, such transfer can be made in compliance with applicable securities laws. The person in whose name the certificates of Common Stock are so registered shall be treated as a common stockholder of the Company on the date the Common Stock certificates are so issued.

> D. Warrant Issuance. If the Holder elects to be repaid in full, the Company will issue a warrant to purchase, for five (5) years from date of issuance, Common Stock of the Company in the total principal amount of the Note at an exercise price equal to the Offering Price which shares will be offered to the public by _____.

5. Reservation of Common Stock Issuable Upon Conversion. The Company shall at all times reserve and keep available out of its authorized but unissued shares of Common Stock such number of its shares of Common Stock as shall from time to time be sufficient to effect the conversion of all then outstanding Notes.

6. Call Feature. This Note shall be callable for redemption by the Company, at its option, anytime after six (6) months from the date of issuance. The Company shall provide formal notice of its intent to call the Notes to the Holder. Upon receipt of the notice, the Holder shall either (i) present the Note to the Company for repayment of principal plus accrued and unpaid interest up to and through the date of such notice or (ii) provide the Company notice of conversion to convert the Note plus accrued and unpaid interest into shares of common stock, as outlined in Section 4 above.

7. <u>Unsecured Obligation</u>. This Note shall be unsecured. The Holder shall have no recourse against any specific assets of the Company in the event of nonpayment of the Note.

8. <u>Direct Obligation</u>. Subject to prior conversion, no provision of this Note shall alter or impair the obligation of the Company, which is absolute and unconditional, to pay the principal of, and interest on, this Note at the time, place, and rate, and in the manner herein prescribed. This Note is a direct obligation of the Company.

9. <u>Investment Representations</u>. The Holder of the Note, by acceptance hereof, represents that the Holder is an "accredited investor" as defined in the Securities Act and the rules promulgated thereunder, and agrees that this Note is being acquired for investment and not with a view to the distribution thereof, and that such Holder will not offer, sell, or otherwise dispose of this Note or the shares of Common Stock issuable upon conversion thereof except under circumstances which will not result in a violation of the Securities Act or any applicable state "blue sky" laws or similar state laws relating to the sale of securities. Unless the issuance of the shares of Common Stock issuable upon conversion of this Note shall have been registered under the Securities Act, the Holder of this Note, by tendering notice to the Company of the Holder's intent to convert all or part of this Note pursuant to Section 4A hereof, shall be deemed to represent to the Company that the Holder is acquiring such shares of Common Stock for investment and not with a view to the distribution thereof.

10. <u>Governing Law; Jurisdiction</u>. This Note shall be governed by and construed in accordance with the laws of the State of _____. Each of the parties consents to the jurisdiction of the federal courts whose districts encompass any part of _____ County, _____ or the state courts of the State of _____ sitting in _____ County in connection with

(continued)

(*continued*)

any dispute arising under this Note and hereby waives, to the maximum extent permitted by law, any objection, including any objection based on *forum non conveniens*, to the bringing of any such proceeding in such jurisdictions.

11. <u>Default</u>. Each of the following shall constitute an "Event of Default":

a. the Company fails to pay the principal or accrued interest on this Note on the Maturity Date;

b. the Company commences any voluntary proceeding under any bankruptcy, reorganization, insolvency, readjustment of debt, receivership, dissolution, or liquidation law or statute, of any jurisdiction, whether now or subsequently in effect; or the Company is adjudicated insolvent or bankrupt by a court of competent jurisdiction; or the Company petitions or applies for, acquiesces in, or consents to the appointment of any receiver or trustee of the Company for all or substantially all of its property or assets; or the Company makes an assignment for the benefit of its creditors; or the Company is unable to pay its debts as they mature;

c. there is commenced against the Company any proceeding relating to the Company under any bankruptcy, reorganization, insolvency, readjustment of debt, receivership, dissolution, or liquidation law or statute, of any jurisdiction, whether now or subsequently in effect, and the proceeding remains undismissed for a period of sixty (60) days or the Company by any act indicates its consent to, approval of, or acquiescence in, the proceedings; or a receiver or trustee is appointed for the Company for all or substantially all of its property or assets, and the receivership or trusteeship remains undischarged for a period of sixty (60) days; or a warrant of attachment, execution, or similar process is issued against any substantial part of the property or assets of the Company, and the warrant or similar process is not dismissed or bonded within sixty (60) days after the levy;

d. the Company shall fail to perform or observe, in any material respect, any covenant, term, provision, condition, agreement, or obligation of the Company under this Note and such failure shall continue uncured for a period of thirty (30) days after notice from the Holder of such failure;

e. any governmental agency or any court of competent jurisdiction at the instance of any governmental agency shall assume custody or control of the whole or substantially all of the properties or assets of the Company; then, or at any time thereafter, and in each and every such case, unless such Event of Default shall have been waived in writing by the Holder (which waiver shall not be deemed to be a waiver of any subsequent default), this Note shall bear interest at the maximum lawful rate of interest permitted by applicable laws and at the option of the Holder and in the Holder's sole discretion, the Holder may consider this Note immediately due and payable, without presentment, demand, protest, or notice of any kind, all of which are hereby expressly waived, anything herein or in any other instruments to the contrary notwithstanding, and the Holder may immediately enforce any and all of the Holder's rights and remedies provided herein or any other rights or remedies afforded by law.

12. Collection Costs. In the event an Event of Default has occurred and has not been waived by Holder, the Holder shall be entitled to collect from the Company all costs and expenses incurred by Holder in enforcing its rights hereunder, including reasonable attorneys' fees.

[SIGNATURES FOLLOW ON NEXT PAGE]

IN WITNESS WHEREOF, the Company has caused this instrument to be duly executed by an officer thereunto duly authorized.

Effective as of this ___ day of _____, 20___.

_____ , INC.

By:_____

Name: _____

Title: Chief Executive Officer_____

EXHIBIT A

NOTICE OF CONVERSION

(To be executed by the registered Holder in order to convert the Note)

The undersigned hereby irrevocably elects to convert $_____ of the principal and accrued interest of the above Note No. _____ into shares of Common Stock of _____, INC., (the "Company") according to the conditions hereof, as of the date written below.

Date of Conversion* _____

Signature _____

Name _____

Social Security No. _____

Address _____

_____

Let us assume XYZ Company borrows $1 million from ABC for a two-year term. The note pays interest at 12% and, at the option of ABC, could be converted into shares of common stock of XYZ at a fixed price of $2.00 per share. If, after a year and a half, XYZ received an offer to sell the company for $5.00 per share, ABC could convert the note prior to the sale transaction and receive 500,000 shares of common stock, which then get sold in the acquisition transaction for $2.5 million. This would provide ABC a total return of 168% of both interest and principal. If, however, at the end of two years, XYZ was still just operating the business, it would presumably repay the loan and, together with the interest for two years, ABC would have a return of 24%. ABC made the loan with the intent of receiving 12% per year for the risk involved and was provided a "sweetener" with the conversion feature so that if things went really well, it could share in the reward of being an "owner" of XYZ.

Because of the conversion feature and significant upside potential for convertible instruments, lenders are willing to charge lower annual interest rates, especially if they believe that a significant liquidity event may occur to increase their reward.

Convertible notes are an attractive type of capital for many businesses, especially those in the early stages of development, because lenders appreciate the upside potential. As long as they believe they can ultimately be repaid in a worst-case scenario, lenders are keenly interested in the high reward offered by conversion.

Another feature to consider with convertible notes is to let the interest be payment-in-kind, or PIK, interest. With this provision in the notes (see Exhibit 2.3), no interest would be paid until the notes either were repaid (at which time the accrued interest to that date would be paid as well) or were converted, at which point the accrued interest would be converted into additional shares of common stock. This method also reduces the cash drain on the borrower by eliminating the need for monthly cash interest payments.

EXHIBIT 2.3

10% Convertible Note

NEITHER THIS NOTE NOR THE COMMON STOCK ISSUABLE UPON CONVERSION HEREOF HAS BEEN REGISTERED UNDER THE SECURITIES ACT OF 1933, AS AMENDED (THE "SECURITIES ACT") OR UNDER THE SECURITIES LAWS OF ANY STATE. THE SECURITIES REPRESENTED HEREBY ARE RESTRICTED AND MAY NOT BE OFFERED, RESOLD, PLEDGED, OR TRANSFERRED EXCEPT IF SUCH TRANSACTION IS REGISTERED UNDER THE SECURITIES ACT AND APPLICABLE STATE SECURITIES LAWS OR IF SUCH TRANSACTION IS EXEMPT FROM SUCH REGISTRATION, AS CONFIRMED BY AN OPINION OF COUNSEL TO THE COMPANY.

No. N-1   US $ _____

_____, INC.

10% CONVERTIBLE PROMISSORY NOTE DUE _____, 20____

FOR VALUE RECEIVED, _____, INC., a Delaware corporation (the "Company"), promises to pay to _____ (the "Holder"), the principal sum of _____ (US$_____) and accrued interest on the principal sum at the rate of 10% per annum, accruing from the date hereof, on _____, 20___ (the "Maturity Date"). Interest will be calculated on the basis of a 360-day year consisting of twelve 30-day months. Accrual of

---

interest shall commence on the first such business day to occur after the date hereof and continue until payment in full of the principal sum has been made in cash or this Note is converted as provided herein. The Company shall pay the principal of and interest upon this Note, less any amounts required by law to be deducted, to the Holder of this Note at the address of such Holder which is the last address appearing on the Note register of the Company for such Holder.

This Note is subject to the following additional provisions:

1. Withholding. The Company shall be entitled to withhold from all payments of principal and interest on this Note any amounts required to be withheld under the applicable provisions of the United States income tax laws or other applicable laws at the time of such payments, and the Holder shall execute and deliver all required documentation in connection therewith.

2. _Restrictions on Transfer_. This Note has been issued subject to investment representations of the original purchaser hereof and may be transferred or exchanged only in compliance with the Securities Act of 1933, as amended (the "Securities Act"), and applicable state securities laws. In the event of any proposed transfer of this Note, the Company may require, prior to issuance of a new Note in the name of such other person, that it receive reasonable transfer documentation, including opinions of counsel that the issuance of the Note in such other name does not and will not cause a violation of the Securities Act or any applicable state securities laws. Prior to due presentment for transfer of this Note, the Company may treat the person in whose name this Note is duly registered on the Company's Note register as the owner hereof for the purpose of receiving payment as herein provided and for all other purposes, whether or not this Note is overdue, and the Company shall not be affected by notice to the contrary.

(continued)

(*continued*)

3. Interest Rate. The Company shall pay the Holder interest at the rate of 10% per annum, payable on the Maturity Date *together with principal.*

4. Conversion.

   A. Voluntary Conversion. The Holder of this Note is entitled to convert, at any time, the face value of this Note or any portion thereof, plus any accrued but unpaid interest on the date of conversion, into shares of the Company's common stock, par value $.0001 per share ("Common Stock"), at a conversion rate equal to (i) $4.50 per share.

   B. Notice of Conversion. In order to convert the Note into Common Stock, the Holder must deliver a notice of conversion (the "Notice of Conversion") to the Company, in the form attached hereto as Exhibit A. Notices of Conversion shall be deemed delivered on the date sent, if personally delivered or sent by facsimile (with confirmation of transmission) to the Company, to the Company's Chief Executive Officer at the Company's principal place of business, or when actually received if sent by another method. The Notice of Conversion shall be accompanied by either a copy of (which shall be followed by an original within one (1) business day) or the original Note to be converted.

   C. Conversion Procedure. The Company shall issue the Common Stock within six (6) business days after the Company receives a fully executed Notice of Conversion and original Note. The Common Stock shall be issued with a restrictive legend indicating that it was issued in a transaction which is exempt from registration under the Securities Act and that it cannot be transferred unless it is so registered, or an exemption from registration is available in the opinion of counsel to the Company. The Common Stock shall be issued in the same name as the person who is the Holder of this Note unless, in the opinion of counsel to the Company, such transfer can be made in compliance with applicable securities laws. The person in whose name the certificates of Common Stock are so registered shall be treated as a common stockholder of the Company on the date the Common Stock certificates are so issued.

5. Reservation of Common Stock Issuable Upon Conversion. The Company shall at all times reserve and keep available out of its authorized but unissued shares of Common Stock such number of its shares of Common Stock as shall from time to time be sufficient to effect the conversion of all then outstanding Notes.

6. Call Feature. This Note shall be callable for redemption by the Company, at its option, anytime after six months from the date of issuance. The Company shall provide formal notice of its intent to call the Notes to the Holder. Upon receipt of the notice, the Holder shall either (i) present the Note to the Company for repayment of principal plus accrued and unpaid interest up to and through the date of such notice or (ii) provide the Company notice of conversion to convert the Note plus accrued and unpaid interest into shares of common stock as outlined in Section 4 above.

7. Unsecured Obligation. This Note shall be unsecured. The Holder shall have no recourse against any specific assets of the Company in the event of nonpayment of the Note.

8. Direct Obligation. Subject to prior conversion, no provision of this Note shall alter or impair the obligation of the Company, which is absolute and unconditional, to pay the principal of, and interest on, this Note at the time, place, and rate, and in the manner herein prescribed. This Note is a direct obligation of the Company.

(*continued*)

(*continued*)

9. Investment Representations. The Holder of the Note, by acceptance hereof, represents that the Holder is an "accredited investor" as defined in the Securities Act and the rules promulgated thereunder, and agrees that this Note is being acquired for investment and not with a view to the distribution thereof, and that such Holder will not offer, sell, or otherwise dispose of this Note or the shares of Common Stock issuable upon conversion thereof except under circumstances which will not result in a violation of the Securities Act or any applicable state "blue sky" laws or similar state laws relating to the sale of securities. Unless the issuance of the shares of Common Stock issuable upon conversion of this Note shall have been registered under the Securities Act, the Holder of this Note, by tendering notice to the Company of the Holder's intent to convert all or part of this Note pursuant to Section 4A hereof, shall be deemed to represent to the Company that the Holder is acquiring such shares of Common Stock for investment and not with a view to the distribution thereof.

10. Governing Law; Jurisdiction. This Note shall be governed by and construed in accordance with the laws of the State of _____. Each of the parties consents to the jurisdiction of the federal courts whose districts encompass any part of _____ County, _____ or the state courts of the State of _____ sitting in _____ County in connection with any dispute arising under this Note and hereby waives, to the maximum extent permitted by law, any objection, including any objection based on *forum non conveniens*, to the bringing of any such proceeding in such jurisdictions.

11. Default. Each of the following shall constitute an "Event of Default":

a. the Company fails to pay the principal or accrued interest on this Note on the Maturity Date;

b. the Company commences any voluntary proceeding under any bankruptcy, reorganization, insolvency, readjustment of debt, receivership, dissolution, or liquidation law or statute, of any jurisdiction, whether now or subsequently in effect; or the Company is adjudicated insolvent or bankrupt by a court of competent jurisdiction; or the Company petitions or applies for, acquiesces in, or consents to the appointment of any receiver or trustee of the Company for all or substantially all of its property or assets; or the Company makes an assignment for the benefit of its creditors; or the Company is unable to pay its debts as they mature;

c. there is commenced against the Company any proceeding relating to the Company under any bankruptcy, reorganization, insolvency, readjustment of debt, receivership, dissolution, or liquidation law or statute, of any jurisdiction, whether now or subsequently in effect, and the proceeding remains undismissed for a period of sixty (60) days or the Company by any act indicates its consent to, approval of, or acquiescence in the proceedings; or a receiver or trustee is appointed for the Company for all or substantially all of its property or assets, and the receivership or trusteeship remains undischarged for a period of sixty (60) days; or a warrant of attachment, execution, or similar process is issued against any substantial part of the property or assets of the Company, and the warrant or similar process is not dismissed or bonded within sixty (60) days after the levy;

d. the Company shall fail to perform or observe, in any material respect, any covenant, term, provision, condition, agreement, or obligation of the Company under this Note and such failure shall continue uncured for a period of thirty (30) days after notice from the Holder of such failure;

(continued)

e. any governmental agency or any court of competent jurisdiction at the instance of any governmental agency shall assume custody or control of the whole or substantially all of the properties or assets of the Company; then, or at any time thereafter, and in each and every such case, unless such Event of Default shall have been waived in writing by the Holder (which waiver shall not be deemed to be a waiver of any subsequent default), this Note shall bear interest at the maximum lawful rate of interest permitted by applicable laws and at the option of the Holder and in the Holder's sole discretion, the Holder may consider this Note immediately due and payable, without presentment, demand, protest, or notice of any kind, all of which are hereby expressly waived, anything herein or in any other instruments to the contrary notwithstanding, and the Holder may immediately enforce any and all of the Holder's rights and remedies provided herein or any other rights or remedies afforded by law.

12. Collection Costs. In the event an Event of Default has occurred and has not been waived by Holder, the Holder shall be entitled to collect from the Company all costs and expenses incurred by Holder in enforcing its rights hereunder, including reasonable attorneys' fees.

[SIGNATURES FOLLOW ON NEXT PAGE]

IN WITNESS WHEREOF, the Company has caused this instrument to be duly executed by an officer thereunto duly authorized.

Effective as of this _____ day of _____, 20___.

_____ , **INC.**

By: _____

Name: _____

Title: ___Chief Executive Officer___

EXHIBIT A
NOTICE OF CONVERSION

(To be executed by the registered Holder in order to convert the Note)

The undersigned hereby irrevocably elects to convert $_____ of the principal and accrued interest of the above Note No._____ into shares of Common Stock of _____ INC., (the "Company") according to the conditions hereof, as of the date written below.

Date of Conversion* _____

Signature _____

Name _____

Social Security No. _____

Address _____

_____

TIPS AND TECHNIQUES

Always use methods that reduce the outflow of cash for a start-up or growing business. Having convertible notes with a PIK interest feature accomplishes this.

IN THE REAL WORLD

In the real world, start-up and early-stage corporations can make extremely effective use of convertible instruments, including those with no cash payment provisions. Investors in these types of securities (even if they are unsecured) view them as more secure, because if the company fails, the ownership of debt, even unsecured, enables the holders to move up the food chain in a worst-case scenario of liquidation, in which the real ownership would be transferred to the note holders rather than to the equity holders. If all goes according to plan and the business is wildly successful, the holders convert their notes and get to participate as owners *when success has been achieved*. Thus, the holders of convertible notes get the best of both worlds. Therefore, despite a start-up or early-stage company's perceived inability to repay any debt, investors are willing to purchase this type of instrument. Start-ups should use convertible instruments aggressively.

Mezzanine or Hybrid Debt

Although this book primarily deals with early-stage companies, their formation, and obtaining capital, a third type of debt should be considered. This is the "hybrid" or "mezzanine" debt. While mezzanine debt more closely resembles straight debt, the pricing mechanism includes features that make it somewhere between straight debt and equity, thus earning it the "mezzanine" category.

The hybrid lender represents a cross between a cash-flow lender, a secured lender, and an equity investor. This type of lender typically represents a one-stop shop from which a borrower may obtain both secured and unsecured debt as well as revolving term debt and equity financing. These lenders are trained to assess cash-flow and equity risks and receive the appropriate compensation for debt or equity funding.

This category of lender has developed as the result of high-priced leveraged buyout transactions of the 1980s. The high purchase prices exceeded the comfortable credit limits of cash-flow lenders, and the purchase prices exceeded the lendable asset base. Many of the companies being acquired, such as those within the service industry, had little or no assets. This resulted in a layer of financing beneath senior debt but above equity, which typically is called mezzanine debt.

Generally, mezzanine debt is repaid within two to four years, whereas subordinated debt is long term by definition, with repayment beginning after other debt has been retired. Mezzanine or subordinated debt may be structured with features similar to equity and, over time, may be able to command an equity interest in the company, typically in the form of warrants or options.

Warrants or options permit the holder to purchase shares of common stock at a fixed price for a period of time. They represent a sweetener for straight debt, because unlike convertible debt, which provides the lender an either/or situation, mezzanine debt provides for full repayment and an opportunity to participate from an equity perspective.

Hybrid lenders consider cash flow and asset values but focus most heavily on the inherent value of the business enterprise and the ultimate rate of return on their investment. The repayment source in this case may be the sale of the company in order to receive a value for the stock.

Hybrid lenders represent a blurring of lender categories, since various types of financing institutions operate within this area. Hybrid lenders can be found among large commercial finance companies, commercial banks, insurance companies, pension funds, public and private investment funds, and venture capital firms.

Equity

Equity represents an ownership interest in the entity. It can be either in the form of common stock or preferred stock.

Securities representing common stock represent equity ownership in a corporation, usually have voting rights, and entitle the holder to a share of the company's success through dividends and/or capital appreciation. Typically, common stockholders receive one vote per share to elect the company's board of directors (although the number of votes is not always directly proportional to the number of shares owned). The board of directors is the group of individuals who represent the owners of the corporation and oversee major decisions for the company. Common shareholders also receive voting rights regarding other company matters, such as stock splits and company objectives.

Capital stock that provides a specific dividend paid before any dividends are paid to common stockholders and that takes precedence over common stock in the event of a liquidation is referred to as preferred stock. Like common stock, preferred stock represents partial ownership in a company, although preferred stock shareholders usually do not enjoy any of the voting rights of common stockholders. Also unlike common stock, a preferred stock pays a fixed dividend that does not fluctuate, although the company does not have to pay this dividend if it lacks the financial ability to do so. The main benefit to owning preferred stock is that the investor has a greater claim on the company's assets than common stockholders. Preferred shareholders always receive their dividends first and, in the event the company fails, preferred shareholders receive distributions before common stockholders. In general, there are four different types of preferred stock: cumulative preferred, noncumulative, participating, and convertible.

We should also identify warrants and options here, as they represent additional forms of equity. As mentioned earlier in this chapter, warrants typically are issued in connection with mezzanine debt. A warrant is a security that enables the holder to purchase shares of common stock for a fixed period of time in the future at a fixed price. It is this fixed price that provides for the future value. An option is identical to a warrant in the rights that it gives the holder; however, options typically are issued to employees and directors subject to an option plan approved by the stockholders, and warrants typically are issued or sold to nonemployees.

Securities such as warrants and options have a value, and these values (typically determined by a method such as the Black-Scholes method) have to be accounted for in a certain manner, depending on the individual transaction. Since they ultimately are subject to being converted into an ownership position, warrants and options also are considered a part of the "equity" of an entity.

Common Stock

Common stock represents the most common form of equity issued by corporations. Common shares of companies represent the bulk of the shares traded on the various exchanges. It may be unusual for a corporation to issue more than one class of common stock or any class or series of preferred stock. Decisions to do so generally revolve around control issues and the need for capital, which may dictate that a preferred stock be issued in lieu of common stock.

The number of authorized shares of common stock that can be issued is determined in the incorporation papers. Any increase to this number can be authorized by amending the certificate of incorporation but will require stockholder approval.

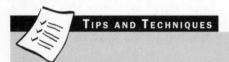

TIPS AND TECHNIQUES

When forming a business, it is best to provide for a large enough number of authorized shares, even if that number seems impossibly large. They do not have to be issued, but it is easier to authorize them at the time an entity is formed than later on, when all the other stockholders have to vote on the increase.

Common stockholders all share equally in the success or failure of a business. When raising capital in the form of equity, the most common type of capital to utilize is common shares.

Preferred Stock

Preferred stock is senior to common stock and generally includes an annual dividend that can be paid in cash or can accumulate. Such accumulation is often referred as cumulative preferred stock. Preferred stock participates in the success of the entity only to the extent of its stated value or liquidation preference. Companies utilize preferred stock because investors prefer the dividend as an annual return and enjoy the "security" that the liquidation preference provides them if something negative should happen to the entity. Preferred stocks are authorized in the articles of incorporation and created through certificate of designations filed with the secretary of state.

Convertible Preferred Stock

Preferred stock that can be converted into shares of common stock offers an investor two unique opportunities in one investment.

1. Convertible preferred stock has the implicit security of a preferred stock and its annual dividend return with certain seniority preferences.

2. Convertible preferred stock also can be converted into shares of common stock, thus allowing the investor to share in the absolute success of the corporation. (Some convertible preferred stocks can be converted mandatorily by the company/entity, but this usually occurs only upon the occurrence of a favorable event, such as a major financing or the sale of the entity.)

Convertible preferred stocks are attractive to issue because the dividend rate usually is lower than straight preferred stock and "accrues"; thus, the entity does not have to make an annual cash payment. This accrued dividend can be converted into additional common shares of the company at the same price that the preferred is able to convert. (See "Certificate of Designations" for a convertible preferred stock on www.wiley.com/go/capitalformation.)

Convertible preferred stock is an attractive blend and is usually the form that many early-stage investors want to see because of the liquidation preference and the ability to convert if and when the entity becomes successful.

Mandatory Redeemable Preferred Stock

Mandatory redeemable preferred stock is a form of preferred stock that contains terms that require the company to redeem the shares at a set price and specified time. This hybrid preferred stock was created to bolster balance sheets by portraying debt as equity. The Securities and Exchange Commission and the Financial Accounting Standards Board finally took issue with this method and now require this type of preferred stock to be treated as debt rather than equity in the balance sheet.

IN THE REAL WORLD

Because of the required accounting and financial statement presentation, there is almost no reason to issue mandatory redeemable preferred stock. If these are the terms, there may be better reasons to bite the bullet and just issue straight debt with a fixed term.

Dilution

The concept of dilution should be discussed now, as every business-person tries to avoid it like the plague. Because of this, there is a lot of confusion as to what dilution really is. There are really two kinds of dilution: percentage dilution and economic dilution. Percentage dilution usually is unavoidable; economic dilution is best avoided (if possible).

Percentage dilution occurs each time an additional investment in the enterprise is made that represents equity securities or that ultimately can be converted into an equity ownership. (Examples include convertible debt, convertible preferred stock, warrants, options, and common stock.) So, if I form a business (corporation) and take an investor for 10% of the entity, I have incurred a percentage dilution because I now own only 90% of the business. Let us assume that the investor paid $10,000 for that 10% interest. The business, at that point, has a postmoney valuation of $100,000. Let us assume four months go by, and the business takes in another investor who acquires a 10% investment for $50,000. More percentage dilution has occurred because I own less of the business; However, because that next investor has come in with a valuation of $500,000, my smaller ownership percentage is worth more money. My 80% is now worth $400,000 as opposed to the $90,000 my 90% was worth before the last investor.

Consequently, percentage dilution is not always bad and usually is unavoidable. Generally, the reduction in ownership percentage is offset by an increase in the value of the business. The opposite of this is economic dilution.

Economic dilution occurs when the value of the enterprise has gone down (through lack of performance, perception in the marketplace, or any other reason that creates a dire need for investment capital at any cost). Let us look at the example from the preceding paragraph. Instead of the first investor investing $10,000, let us assume he was the one who invested $50,000 for 10%. My 90% is now worth $450,000. However, let us assume the business did not execute on its business plan and needed another $50,000, but at this time, the valuation (postmoney) was only $100,000. Now the second investor invests his $50,000 but receives 50% of the business. Not only have I suffered percentage dilution from 90% down to 45%, but I have also suffered severe economic dilution because my share of the business is now only worth $45,000. This dilution is to be avoided at all costs and generally can be by the successful execution of the business plan, thereby always creating shareholder value at each step.

Summary

Based on all the parameters discussed in this chapter, for an early-stage enterprise, the most desirable initial capital is clearly equity, whether it is common or some type of preferred equity. Debt clearly does not impinge on the ownership of the entity, but in early stages of development, debt may not be able to be raised because of the entity's limited prospects for repayment.

CHAPTER 3

Finding the Capital

After reading this chapter, you will be able to:

- Identify the various sources from which to raise capital and the times that may be the most appropriate to access each source.
- Gain an understanding of the different kinds of private placements and why they are exempt from registering with the Securities and Exchange Commission (SEC).

Are There Really Angels in Heaven?

Angel investors (sometimes referred to as "friends and family") often provide the initial capital for an enterprise. They do so for obvious reasons. Friends and family know you and are confident that if you are starting an enterprise, it will be successful. Consequently, they are more apt to assist in providing the formative capital.

Additionally, these investors also subscribe to one of the fundamental rules of investing—*greed*. Consequently, whenever capital is being raised, apply two fundamental rules, which can be summed up as *fear and greed*. Always take advantage of investors' (1) fears that they will (a) miss out on something valuable if they do not invest and (b) lose their original investment if they do not invest more and (2) greed in convincing them that your enterprise will be able to provide them a multi-multiple return on their investment with minimal risk.

IN THE REAL WORLD

If the original amount being sought is less than $2 million to $3 million, then friends and family and/or angel investors are the place to start. They require much less work than a formal private placement (as described later in the chapter), and venture capital and private equity funds are not interested in investing such small amounts. You have to remember, however, that any time capital is raised, the appropriate documents have to be completed to protect you, the company, and the investor, and to stay within the confines of the securities laws. (See Exhibit 3.1 for a simple set of subscription documents.)

Angel investors are typically high-net-worth individuals who enjoy the ability to provide capital to early-stage enterprises. Beside

EXHIBIT 3.1

Simple Subscription Documents

SUBSCRIPTION AGREEMENT

_____, Inc

_____

_____

_____

Gentlemen:

1. <u>Subscription</u>. (a) The undersigned, intending to be legally bound, hereby irrevocably subscribes to purchase from _____, Inc., a Delaware corporation (the "Company"), that amount of Convertible Bridge Promissory Notes (the "Bridge Notes") set forth on the signature page hereof. Each Note is in a minimum principal amount of $10,000 (with incremental amounts of $5,000) and will mature twelve (12) months from the date of purchase, bears interest at a rate of 10%, and can be convertible into shares (the "Conversion Shares") of the Company's common stock, par value $.0001 per share (the "Common Stock") at a conversion price equal to 33 1/3% below the price which shares will be offered to the public by _____. The Bridge Note and Common Stock are sometimes referred to herein as the "Securities". (A copy of the Bridge Note is attached hereto as Exhibit A.) This subscription is submitted to you in accordance with and subject to the terms and conditions described in this Subscription Agreement (the "Agreement"), and the Note.

   The Company is offering the Bridge Notes for sale solely to its shareholders who are "accredited investors" as defined in Regulation D promulgated under the Securities Act of 1933 (the "Securities Act"). <u>Shareholders can acquire more than one Bridge Note.</u>

   (*continued*)

(*continued*)

b. Subscription payments should be made payable to the Company and should be delivered together with two executed and properly completed copies of this Agreement. If this subscription is not accepted in whole or in part by the Company, the full or ratable amount, as the case may be, of any subscription payment received will be promptly refunded to the subscriber without deduction therefrom or interest thereon.

c. Funds received from subscribers for the Notes offered hereby will not be placed in escrow. The Company will receive and has the right to expend the proceeds from the sale of the Bridge Notes upon receipt.

d. The undersigned may not withdraw this subscription or any amount paid pursuant thereto except as otherwise provided below.

e. The Company shall have the right to accept or reject this subscription in whole or in part, with or without reason.

2. <u>Representations and Warranties of the Company</u>. The Company represents and warrants to, and agrees with the undersigned as follows:

a. The Company is a corporation duly organized, validly existing, and in good standing under the laws of Delaware with full power and authority to own, lease, license, and use its properties and assets and to carry out the businesses in which it is engaged. The Company is duly qualified to transact the business in which it is engaged in the State of Delaware and _____.

b. The Company has all requisite power and authority to (i) execute, deliver and perform its obligations under this Agreement; and (ii) to issue and sell the Bridge Notes. All necessary corporate proceedings of the Company have been duly taken to authorize the execution, delivery, and performance of this Agreement. This Agreement has been duly authorized by the Company and, when executed and delivered by the Company, will constitute the legal, valid, and binding obligation of the Company, enforceable against the Company in accordance with its terms, except (i) as such enforceability may be limited by bankruptcy, insolvency, reorganization, moratorium, fraudulent conveyance, or similar laws affecting creditors' rights generally; (ii) as enforceability of any indemnification, contribution, or exculpation provision may be limited under applicable federal and state securities laws; and (iii) that the remedy of specific performance and injunctive and other forms of equitable relief may be subject to the equitable defenses and to the discretion of the court before which any proceeding therefor may be brought.

3. <u>Representations, Warranties, and Covenants of the Subscriber</u>. The undersigned hereby represents and warrants to, and agrees with, the Company as follows:

a. The undersigned is a shareholder of the Company and is an "accredited investor" as that term is defined in Rule 501(a) of Regulation D promulgated under the Securities Act. Specifically, the undersigned is (check appropriate items(s)):

_____ (i) A bank as defined in Section 3(a)(2) of the Securities Act, or a savings and loan association or other institution as defined in Section 3(a)(5)(A) of the Securities Act, whether acting in its individual or fiduciary capacity; a broker or dealer registered pursuant to Section 15 of the Securities Exchange Act of 1934; an insurance company as defined in Section 2(13) of the Securities Act; an investment company registered under the Investment Company Act of 1940 (the "Investment Company Act") or a business development company as defined in

(*continued*)

(continued)

Section 2(a)(48) of the Investment Company Act; a Small Business Investment Company licensed by the U.S. Small Business Administration under Section 301(c) or (d) of the Small Business Investment Act of 1958; a plan established and maintained by a state, its political subdivisions, or any agency or instrumentality of a state or its political subdivisions for the benefit of its employees, if such plan has total assets in excess of $5,000,000; an employee benefit plan within the meaning of Title I of the Employee Retirement Income Securities Act of 1974 (ERISA), if the investment decision is made by a plan fiduciary, as defined in Section 3(21) of ERISA, which is either a bank, savings and loan association, insurance company, or registered investment advisor, or if the employee benefit plan has total assets in excess of $5,000,000 or, if a self-directed plan, with investment decisions made solely by persons that are accredited investors.

_____ (ii) A private business development company as defined in Section 202(a)(22) of the Investment Advisers Act of 1940.

_____ (iii) An organization described in Section 501(c) (3) of the Internal Revenue Code or similar business trust, or partnership, not formed for the specific purpose of acquiring the Units, with total assets in excess of $5,000,000.

_____ (iv) A director or executive officer of the Company.

_____ (v) A natural person whose individual net worth, or joint net worth with that person's spouse, at the time of his or her purchase exceeds $1,000,000.

_____ (vi) A natural person who had an individual income in excess of $200,000 in each of the two most recent years or joint income with that person's spouse in excess of $300,000 in each of those years and has a reasonable expectation of reaching the same income level in the current year.

_____ (vii) A trust, with total assets in excess of $5,000,000, not formed for the specific purpose of acquiring the Units, whose purchase is directed by a sophisticated person as described in Rule 506(b)(2)(ii) (i.e., a person who has such knowledge and experience in financial and business matters that he is capable of evaluating the merits and risks of the prospective investment).

_____ (viii) An entity in which all of the equity owners are accredited investors (if this alternative is checked, the undersigned must identify each equity owner and provide statements signed by each demonstrating how each is qualified as an accredited investor).

b. If a natural person, the undersigned is: a bona fide resident of the state contained in the address set forth on the signature page of this Agreement as the undersigned's home address; at least 21 years of age; and legally competent to execute this Agreement. If an entity, the undersigned is duly authorized to execute this Agreement, and this Agreement constitutes the legal, valid, and binding obligation of the undersigned enforceable against the undersigned in accordance with its terms.

c. The undersigned has received, read carefully, and is familiar with this Agreement and the Informational Document. The undersigned is familiar with the Company's business, plans, and financial condition, the terms of the Offering, and any other matters relating to the Offering; the undersigned has received all materials that have been requested by the undersigned; the undersigned has had a reasonable opportunity to ask questions of the Company and its representatives; and the Company has

(continued)

(*continued*)

answered all inquiries that the undersigned or the under-signed's representatives have put to it. The undersigned has had access to all additional nonconfidential informa-tion necessary to verify the accuracy of the information set forth in this Agreement and the Informational Docu-ment and any other materials furnished herewith, and has taken all the steps necessary to evaluate the merits and risks of an investment as proposed hereunder. The undersigned acknowledges receiving a copy of the Com-pany's audited financial statements for the year ended at December 31, 20___.

d. The undersigned has such knowledge and experience in finance, securities, investments, and other business mat-ters so as to be able to protect the interests of the under-signed in connection with this transaction, and the undersigned's investment in the Company hereunder is not material when compared to the undersigned's total financial capacity.

e. The undersigned understands the various risks of an in-vestment in the Company as proposed herein and can af-ford to bear such risks, including, without limitation, the risks of losing the entire investment.

f. The undersigned acknowledges that no market for the Se-curities currently exists and none may develop in the fu-ture and that the undersigned may find it impossible to liquidate the investment at a time when it may be desir-able to do so, or at any other time.

g. The undersigned has been advised by the Company that none of the Securities have been registered under the Se-curities Act, that the Securities will be issued on the ba-sis of the statutory exemption provided by Section 4(2) of the Securities Act or Regulation D promulgated thereunder, or both, relating to transactions by an issuer not involving any public offering and under exemptions under certain state securities laws, that this transaction has not been reviewed by, passed on, or submitted to any federal or state agency or self-regulatory organization where an exemption is being relied upon, and that the Company's reliance thereon is based in part upon the representations made by the undersigned in this Agreement. The undersigned acknowledges that the undersigned has been informed by the Company of, or is otherwise familiar with, the nature of the limitations imposed by the Securities Act and the rules and regulations thereunder on the transfer of the Securities. In particular, the undersigned agrees that the Company shall not be required to give any effect to sale, assignment or transfer, unless (i) the sale, assignment, or transfer of such Securities is registered under the Securities Act, it being understood that the Securities are not currently registered for sale and that the Company has no obligation or intention to so register the Securities, or (ii) such Securities are sold, assigned, or transferred in accordance with all the requirements and limitations of Rule 144 under the Securities Act, it being understood that Rule 144 is not available at the present time for the sale of the Securities, or (iii) such sale, assignment, or transfer is otherwise exempt from registration under the Securities Act. The undersigned further understands that an opinion of counsel and other documents may be required to transfer the Securities. The undersigned acknowledges that the Securities shall be subject to stop transfer orders and the certificate or certificates evidencing any Securities shall bear the following or a substantially similar legend or such other legend as may appear on the forms of

(*continued*)

(*continued*)

Securities and such other legends as may be required by state blue sky laws:

"THE SECURITIES REPRESENTED BY THIS CERTIFICATE HAVE NOT BEEN REGISTERED UNDER THE SECURITIES ACT OF 1933, AS AMENDED (THE SECURITIES ACT), OR ANY STATE OR FOREIGN SECURITIES LAWS, AND NEITHER SUCH SECURITIES NOR ANY INTEREST THEREIN MAY BE OFFERED, SOLD, PLEDGED, ASSIGNED, OR OTHERWISE TRANSFERRED UNLESS (1) A REGISTRATION STATEMENT WITH RESPECT THERETO IS EFFECTIVE UNDER THE SECURITIES ACT AND ANY APPLICABLE STATE OR FOREIGN SECURITIES LAWS, OR (2) THE COMPANY RECEIVES AN OPINION OF COUNSEL TO THE HOLDER OF SUCH SECURITIES, WHICH COUNSEL AND OPINION ARE REASONABLY SATISFACTORY TO THE COMPANY, THAT SUCH SECURITIES MAY BE OFFERED, SOLD, PLEDGED, ASSIGNED, OR TRANS-FERRED IN THE MANNER CONTEMPLATED WITHOUT AN EFFEC-TIVE REGISTRATION STATEMENT UNDER THE SECURITIES ACT OR APPLICABLE STATE OR FOREIGN SECURITIES LAWS."

h. The undersigned will acquire the Securities for the under-signed's own account (or for the joint account of the under-signed and the undersigned's spouse, either in joint tenancy, tenancy by the entirety, or tenancy in common) for investment and not with a view to the sale or distribution thereof or the granting of any participation therein, and has no present intention of distributing or selling to others any of such interest or granting any participation therein.

i. No representations have been made other than as stated herein and no oral or written information furnished to the undersigned or the undersigned's advisor(s) in connection with the Offering were in any way inconsistent with the in-formation stated herein or in the Informational Document.

j. The undersigned is not subscribing for Securities as a re-sult of or subsequent to any advertisement, article, notice, or other communication published in any newspaper, mag-azine, or similar media or broadcast over television or radio, or presented at any seminar or meeting, or any solicitation of a subscription by a person other than a representative of the Company with which the under-signed had a pre-existing relationship as a shareholder.

k. The undersigned is not relying on the Company with re-spect to the tax and other economic considerations of this investment.

l. The undersigned understands that the proceeds from all subscriptions paid and accepted pursuant to the Offering (after deduction for expenses of the Offering) will be used in all material respects for the purposes set forth in the Informational Document.

m. Without limiting any of the undersigned's other representa-tions and warranties hereunder, the undersigned acknowl-edges that the undersigned has reviewed and is aware of the risk factors described in the Informational Document.

n. The undersigned acknowledges that the representations, warranties, and agreements made by the undersigned herein shall survive the execution and delivery of this Agreement and the purchase of the Bridge Note(s).

o. Blue sky matters:

THE SECURITIES HAVE NOT BEEN REGISTERED UNDER THE SECURITIES ACT OR THE SECURITIES LAWS OF ANY STATE AND ARE BEING OFFERED AND SOLD IN RELIANCE ON EXEMPTIONS FROM THE REGISTRATION REQUIREMENTS OF THE SECURITIES ACT AND SUCH LAWS. THE SECURITIES HAVE NOT BEEN APPROVED OR DISAPPROVED BY THE SECURITIES AND EXCHANGE COMMISSION, ANY STATE SECURITIES COMMISSION, OR OTHER REGULATORY AUTHORITY, NOR HAVE ANY OTHER FOREGOING AUTHORI-TIES PASSED UPON OR ENDORSED THE MERITS OF THIS OFFERING OR THE ACCURACY OR ADEQUACY OF THE INFORMATIONAL DOCUMENT. ANY REPRESENTATION TO THE CONTRARY IS UNLAWFUL.

THE SECURITIES ARE SUBJECT TO RESTRICTIONS ON TRANSFERABILITY AND RESALE AND MAY NOT BE TRANS-FERRED OR RESOLD EXCEPT AS PERMITTED UNDER THE SECURITIES ACT AND APPLICABLE STATE SECURITIES LAWS,

(continued)

(*continued*)

PURSUANT TO REGISTRATION OR EXEMPTION THEREFROM. SUBSCRIBERS SHOULD BE AWARE THAT THEY MAY BE REQUIRED TO BEAR THE FINANCIAL RISKS OF THIS INVESTMENT FOR AN INDEFINITE PERIOD OF TIME.

p. The undersigned has consulted his own financial, legal, and tax advisors with respect to the economic, legal, and tax consequences of an investment in the Bridge Note(s) and has not relied on the Informational Document or the Company, its officers, directors, or professional advisors for advice as to such consequences.

4. Indemnification. The undersigned acknowledges that the undersigned understands the meaning and legal consequences of the representations and warranties contained in Section 3 hereof, and agrees to indemnify and hold harmless the Company and each officer, director, employee, agent, and controlling person of the Company from and against any and all loss, damage or liability due to or arising out of a breach of any such representation or warranty.

5. Transferability. Neither this Agreement, nor any interest of the undersigned herein, shall be assignable or transferable by the undersigned in whole or in part except by operation of law. Any attempt to assign or transfer this Agreement or any interest therein other than by operation of law shall be void.

6. Miscellaneous.

a. This Agreement, together with the Bridge Note, sets forth the entire understanding of the parties with respect to the subject matter hereof, supersedes all existing agreements between them concerning such subject matter, and may be modified only by a written instrument duly executed by each of the parties hereto.

b. Except as otherwise specifically provided herein, any notice or other communication required or permitted to be given hereunder shall be in writing and shall be mailed by certified mail, return receipt requested, or by Federal Express, Express Mail, or similar overnight delivery or courier service, or delivered (in person or by telecopy, telex or similar telecommunications equipment) against receipt to the party to whom it is to be given, (i) if to the Company, at the address set forth on the first page hereof, (ii) if to the undersigned, at the address set forth on the signature page hereof, or (iii) in either case, to such other address as the party shall have furnished in writing in accordance with the provisions of this Section 6(b). Notice to the estate of any party shall be sufficient if addressed to the party as provided in this Section 6(b). Any notice or other communication given by certified mail shall be deemed given at the time of certification thereof, except for a notice changing a party address, which shall be deemed given at the time of receipt thereof. Any notice given by other means permitted by this Section 6(b) shall be deemed given at the time of receipt thereof.

c. This Agreement shall be binding upon and inure to the benefit of the parties hereto, the successors and assigns of the Company, and the permitted successors, assigns, heirs, and personal representatives of the undersigned.

d. The headings in this Agreement are solely for convenience of reference and shall be given no effect in the construction or interpretation of this Agreement.

e. This Agreement may be executed in any number of counterparts, each of which shall be deemed an original, but all of which together shall constitute one and the same instrument.

f. This Agreement shall be governed by and construed in accordance with the laws of the State of Florida, without giving effect to principles governing conflicts of law.

(*continued*)

(*continued*)

g. This Agreement does not create, and shall not be construed as creating, any rights enforceable by any person not a party to this Agreement (except as provided in Sections 3, 4, 6(c) and 6(g)).

h. The parties hereto irrevocably consent to the jurisdiction of the courts of the State of _____, _____ County, and of any federal court located in _____ County in connection with any action or proceeding arising out of or relating to this Agreement, any document or instrument delivered pursuant to, in connection with, or simultaneously with this Agreement, or a breach of this Agreement or any such document or instrument. In any such action or proceeding, each party hereto waives personal service of any summons, complaint, or other process and agrees that service thereof may be made in accordance with Section 6 (b). Within thirty (30) days after such service, or such other time as may be mutually agreed upon in writing by the attorneys for the parties to such action or proceeding, the party so served shall appear or answer such summons, complaint, or other process.

i. Unless otherwise defined herein, capitalized terms shall have the meanings assigned to them in the Informational Document.

[SIGNATURES FOLLOW ON NEXT PAGE]

IN WITNESS WHEREOF, the parties hereto have executed this Agreement as of the day and year this subscription has been accepted by the Company as set forth below.

Number of Bridge Note(s)
Being Purchased:

_____

Aggregate Purchase Price:

_____

Print Name of Subscriber

_____

_____

(Signature of Subscriber or Authorized Signatory)

Social Security Number or other Taxpayer Identification Number:

_____

Address: _____

_____

If the Bridge Note(s) will be held as joint tenants, tenants in common, or community property, please complete the following:

_____

Print name of spouse or other co-subscriber

_____

Signature of spouse or other co-subscriber

_____

Print manner in which Bridge Note(s) will be held

_____

Social Security Number

ACCEPTED BY:

_____, Inc.

By: _____

Name: _____

Title: Chief Executive Officer

Date: _____

the reward of a successful investment, they thrive on the cocktail-party chatter that surrounds telling others that they have gotten in on the ground floor of the next Apple or Microsoft. Angel investors typically do some due diligence, but not as much as other investor types.

Until recently, angel investors were regarded as detached from the companies they backed, wealthy amateurs who dropped in between rounds of golf to cut checks and rub elbows with entrepreneurs. No more. Increasing numbers of angels around the United States are forming organized investment groups, while others are starting formal funds.

The Angel Capital Association (ACA), a trade group for these investment networks, has continued to grow and now has approximately 140 member organizations. Only a small number of its members have separate investment funds, although a large number have shown increasing interest in starting up such a fund.

Although angel groups structure their funds differently, a sidecar fund generally consists of a separate investment vehicle funded by the individual angels to make investments alongside the angel network. Sidecar funds in the United States today contain more than $100 million under management.

One of the oldest sidecar funds (a $50 million fund—the Band of Angels—founded in Silicon Valley in 1999) operates like a venture capital firm (discussed later in the chapter), with the fund overseen by a professional manager who makes investments alongside individual deals struck by participating angels.

By contrast, CommonAngels, a group in Boston with two funds totaling $20 million, invests with a hybrid approach. The funds automatically make first-round investments in companies, but a full-time manager decides whether to make follow-on investments and works with individual portfolio companies, helping to get them off the ground, successfully execute their business plan, and create value.

Silicon Valley venture capital investors are not shy about funneling hot investments to their friends through the sidecar fund that gets to ride along on a transaction, even in tight deals in which the firm's main stake is scaled down. The justification is well honed: The people they include in their funds are often movers and shakers who help the fund back. Except that is pretty much the same justification that Frank Quattrone (the notorious Silicon Valley investment banker) used to justify allocations of hot initial public offering (IPO) stock to Valley bigwigs, the Friends of Frank, back in the 1990s. Every possible profit siphoned off by an investor's personal contacts comes at the expense of the university endowments and other institutions that invest in venture capital funds. Quattrone's legal travails showed that routine Silicon Valley practice, complacently accepted by the insiders who benefit, can come off to others as borderline corrupt. The beneficiaries of sidecar generosity or hedge funds that worm their way into hot deals may turn out to be random friends of key investors or even relatives. This boom is providing venture capitalists with quite a ride, but they should be careful whom they take along.

In southern Florida, the most prominent two angel groups are the New World Angels (NWA) and the Angel Investment Forum of Florida (AIFFL). Neither of these groups has a formal sidecar fund. NWA is a group of private investors dedicated to providing equity capital to early- and mid-stage entrepreneurial companies. The primary focus is on companies based in South Florida. Members of NWA have extensive experience in founding, building, and managing companies in a wide variety of industries. In addition to providing funding, NWA members make their expertise and resource networks available to portfolio companies. They work closely with other regional and national venture firms. In addition, NWA is supported by such leading institutions as the Enterprise Development Corporation, Florida Atlantic University, and Florida International University. AIFFL is a nonprofit organization that facilitates interaction between individual investors and local entrepreneurs through periodic member meetings to showcase emerging and expanding local businesses seeking angel investment and periodic meetings to educate members about entrepreneurial investing, organizations, and programs supporting local business development. AIFFL is a forum to promote interaction by and between its members. It does not make, endorse, or derive benefit from any specific investments.

Driving the trend among angel groups to start sidecar funds is a wish to diversify their investments. On average, angel investors put money toward only two deals annually. Sidecar funds might make 10 or more investments in a given year, reducing portfolio risk and exposing investors to a wider range of opportunities. Angel investing is definitely a plus for many entrepreneurial companies. Care should be taken as to whom the angels bring along in the event, as they may really be devils in disguise. Thus the question: Are there really angels in heaven?

Allowing that any capital raised is a private placement, the next source of capital after family and friends/angel investors

Assuming you want to fly with the angels, how do you find them?

- Ask your local chamber of commerce.
- Find a local Small Business Development Center and ask the executive director.
- Ask your accountant. (If he or she does not know, check with a local office of one of the larger accounting firms in your city.)
- Ask your attorney.
- Call a venture capitalist in the area and ask if he or she is aware of an angel group in the area.
- Ask the regional or state economic development agency if they know of a local angel group.
- Call the editor of a local business publication and ask if he or she knows of local angel groups.
- Ask your banker.
- Ask other entrepreneurs in the area if they are aware of a local angel group.

could be either a venture capital fund, a private equity fund, or a formal private placement. The primary difference in dealing with a venture capital fund and a formal private placement lies in the sophistication of the investors and the nature of the related paperwork. Although legal documents will be required in either case to protect all parties, raising capital from a venture capital fund requires a different set documents that are much more focused. We examine that source of capital next.

Venture Capital

In addition to experienced management, a good forecast, and a solid business plan, what are venture capitalists typically looking for today?

- **Size.** A venture capital firm will rarely look at a deal below $3 million. Such smaller financing typically is provided by families and friends or angel investors.

- **Risks.** Identifiable and understandable business risks.

- **Growth.** Business with large upside possibility—the ability to grow very large in a short period of time.

- **Product.** A product that has completed the development stage and is ready for distribution, or a product in development for which the need and market are obvious.

- **Uniqueness.** A "niche" business—one with a product or service that has some sort of competitive edge, a sustainable strategic excellence position (SEP).

- **Market.** A company with potential sales and profits significant for its industry and likely to provide venture capitalists their required return on investment (generally five to eight times its investment).

- **Exit.** Venture investors require some strategy to facilitate liquidity in the future for their stake through either an IPO or an acquisition.

Now that you have decided to seek capital from a venture capital fund, how do you accomplish this? Unfortunately, venture funds receive hundreds of business plans daily, so their appetite for deal flow is restricted. The restrictions many funds place start with things such as geographic area and industry. Your search for an appropriate venture fund can be facilitated by research. The National Venture Capital Association maintains a comprehensive Web site (www.nvca.org). Information on venture capital funds can be obtained through that association, which facilitates the search for the right fund. However, generally speaking, these funds do not look at business plans submitted by anyone they do not already know. Thus, to get access to most venture funds, you need a door opener who can introduce your company to one of the fund's partners, who will at least take the time to read through the company information.

TIPS AND TECHNIQUES

Another suggestion is to speak to at least one chief executive in your industry who has raised venture capital. Ask about their experiences and the pitfalls and successes. This information also will help you decide whether it is worth pursuing institutional venture capital.

Without this door opener, the probability of successfully raising capital in this manner falls precipitously. Let us assume that you are successful in getting an audience through the doorman. Then what?

As the economy and capital markets have changed dramatically over the past several years and in light of the current financial crisis, one aspect of venture funds that has evolved is their desire to see revenues in a company in which they invest. Being pre-revenue substantially lowers a company's probability of securing funding, as many venture capitalists have in essence become late-stage private equity investors. The questions arise: Who is going to fund future innovation in this country? Will we lose our technological advantage?

What Do Venture Capitalists Expect?

Venture capitalists expect a detailed and meticulously accurate account in writing. This is usually done through the preparation of a business plan. The business plan spells out such basics as:

- A succinct history of the company
- The opportunity
- An estimate of how much capital is needed
- The state of the market, as the company sees it, today and in the near future
- The company's assessment of present and potential competitors
- New technologies and products that might affect the competitive environment

- The company's management team (Have they been there, seen it, and done it before?)
- Financial calculations, including cash flow for a number of years, expected profits, expected capital requirements, how this money would be used (use of proceeds), and any other relevant facts
- The company's short- and long-term goals

Obviously, this list would change somewhat from one company to another, but it illustrates the kind of information needed. Committing all this to writing serves two good purposes: It helps company management think things through in a careful, orderly manner, and it helps venture capitalists evaluate management's competence and weigh the risks that underlie their decisions. It also enables the company to transform the business plan into a strategy plan for execution. (See an example of a typical business plan on www.wiley.com/go/capitalformation.)

As you might expect, a company's business plan, no matter how thorough, is bound to raise questions. Management probably will have to go back to supply further facts, address new problems that came to light in the meeting with the venture capitalists, and maybe even recast the plan. There is a good chance a venture capitalist will use outsiders more expert than he or she in judging certain aspects of the plan. Thus, the process of getting to know each other goes on, often stretching into weeks and even months before an investment is structured that meets the objectives of both parties. These negotiations frequently involve attorneys and accountants for both sides to supply objective expertise in this delicate effort to create a relationship that will be fair and effective.

Major Concentration Points

A few features of the business plan deserve special emphasis. Many venture capitalists believe the most important ingredient is the management team. Accordingly, they carefully scrutinize the backgrounds of the key managers for assurance that these people have the intelligence, experience, and temperament to carry the business through the crucial years ahead when their money is on the line. They look for entrepreneurial skills and technical training; sophistication in research and development as well as production, distribution, marketing, finance, and administration; and any other qualifications that pertain to the specific type of business. They do expect to find enthusiasm and competitive spirit. All too often, the basic business plan tends to focus overwhelmingly on technical matters and neglects the human factor. This is almost always a mistake.

In creating the plan, another point of emphasis should be the size and attractiveness of the market. How big is the market? Is it completely saturated, or can it be expanded? How do you rate your competitors? Have many new competitors entered the market recently and gained a foothold? No matter how good the company's product may be, success will depend largely on how well its management understands the dynamics of the market, so the venture capitalist looks for signs that management is thoroughly and realistically up to date on the state of the market.

The business plan must address a third significant issue: Exactly how is this venture unique? Does the company have a unique product advantage? A unique packaging advantage? A unique method of distribution? A unique marketing edge? The venture capitalist expects management to define that element of uniqueness that sets it apart from the competition and gives it the jump on the field. Winners usually have such an edge, and it deserves to be a major feature of the business plan.

There is much to consider when preparing a business plan. Some types of information will be applicable to each situation, and some will not.

Valuation

Valuation is like beauty—it is in the eye of the beholder. The key ingredient of valuation is how much of the company is, in effect, being sold through this venture capital investment. Venture capitalists always have a lower valuation beginning point than the entrepreneur, which allows them to generate the significant returns they are looking for as compensation for taking the early risk. The rule of thumb is that venture capitalists expect a 30% to 40% annual return on total investments. In order to achieve this, they follow the 2-6-2 rule. Out of 10 investments made, 2 will generate high returns (in excess of 40% to 50% annually), 6 will merely enable them to get their money back, and 2 will be total write-offs.

Entrepreneurs, however, always believe their streets are paved with gold. The result has to be a negotiated answer. However, the intensity of the need for the money often dictates who has to compromise more.

Especially in today's financial markets, entrepreneurs should not reject a funding offer solely based on the perception that the valuation is too low. Capital is too difficult to come by, and without it, failure almost becomes a certainty. Be flexible on valuation, but do not give away the store away.

The two most important documents typically found in an institutional raise—the investment agreement and the investor rights agreement—can be found on www.wiley.com/go/capitalformation.

For whatever reason, you have decided that venture capital/institutional capital is not the route that you would like to take at this time. Are there any alternatives? The answer is yes.

Private Placements

Many entrepreneurs at the head of small and growing companies dream of going public not only as a means of raising capital for growth but for two other enticing advantages: the prestige of being a public company and the considerable financial gain earlier investors often can realize. But what if this is not the time? Three factors typically prevent IPOs:

1. The company does not yet have the financial strength or reputation to attract enough investors for a public offering.

2. The company cannot afford the expense of going through the public offering process.

3. The company needs the money now and cannot wait for the lengthy IPO process to run its course.

Going public will be feasible eventually, but how can the company obtain needed financing now? The answer may be an exempt offering, commonly called a private placement.

If a private placement is "exempt," the company (the offeror) does not have to file a registration statement with the SEC, a significant advantage because it cuts down paperwork and saves precious time and considerable expense. A private placement is so called because the company can offer the stock or debt to a few private investors instead of the public at large. Generally, this means the investment can involve no more than 35 nonaccredited investors and an "unlimited number" (usually assumed to be less than 100) of accredited investors and cannot involve advertising or general solicitation. Accredited investors are considered sophisticated investors with a net a worth of at least $1 million or income of at least $200,000 (2 years).

Saving time and money for small companies in need of growth capital was exactly what Congress had in mind when it spelled out these exemptions in the Securities Act of 1933. The aim was to simplify compliance with securities laws and make it easier for companies to raise capital. The Small Business Investment Incentive Act of 1980 expanded exempt-offering opportunities, and the resulting changes in SEC regulations have made private placements an increasingly popular method of raising capital. The SEC's 1992 Small Business Initiatives further simplified and expanded the exempt-offering process.

While "exemptions" is the key word, the company does not have a completely free hand—far from it. For one thing, although the private placement may be exempt from federal registration, it may not be exempt from registration under state laws. Some states require registration; some do not. *Note that private placements are not exempt from the antifraud provisions of the securities laws.* This means that the company must give potential investors the necessary information about the company so that they can make a well-informed decision. The company must exercise meticulous care not to omit or misstate the facts or give the facts a rosier hue than they deserve—a common pitfall! IPO or not, there are still risk factors to any investment.

Chapter 4 is devoted to the common pitfalls of private placements and exempt offerings, with the intent of ensuring that you keep your chances of running afoul of the securities laws and invoking the ire of the SEC to a minimum. However, despite the information and materials are provided in this book, attorneys should always be involved in the process.

When to Consider a Private Placement

Broadly defined, the private placement market includes a wide variety of larger corporate finance transactions, including senior and subordinated debt, asset-backed securities, and equity issues. This sophisticated, highly developed market is dominated by institutional investors (including insurance companies, pension funds, and money or management funds), larger corporate issuers, and investment bankers or other corporate finance intermediaries.

As privately negotiated transactions, private placements can be designed to meet the specific situation the company faces. Debt securities can have amortization schedules tailored to match anticipated cash flow. By attaching warrants or other equity "kickers," returns on debt securities for investors can be improved while not causing any immediate dilution or control implications for current ownership. Equity financing has the advantage of requiring no current debt service, thus conserving the company's cash flow for investment in the business. Creative securities can be structured to minimize the transfer of control to outside investors. Private placements can involve debt, equity, or both.

Private Placement Capital Sources

Compared with a public offering, a private placement probably will involve only a few investors. The job of finding investors usually is placed in the hands of a broker or financial advisor, who makes a business of keeping track of investors who are willing to take risks with small companies.

TIPS AND TECHNIQUES

There are other issues in dealing with brokers, financial advisors, consultants, and "finders" that we address in Chapter 4.

In all, there are at least three different groups of investors that might have a special interest in private placements:

1. People who know and respect the company. Moreover, they may depend on the company to supply the product they sell. They might consider it to be in their own self-interest to buy the company's stock if they believe it will help ensure continuation of product supply and perhaps give them favored treatment if you bring out a new product or product improvement.

These professional investors often are focused on a particular industry, a specific geographic area, or companies at a defined development stage. Examples are prominent in fields such as high technology or biotechnology. Many professional investors of funds invest in companies that have developed products but need to build manufacturing capacity. If the company's situation matches the investors' criteria, and the management team is strong enough to stand up to the intensive scrutiny that is typical of professional investors, this may be a good source of private capital for the company.

2. Other investors who are searching for opportunities to buy shares of small growth companies in the expectation that the company will soon go public and they will benefit as new investors bid the price up, as often happens. For such investors, news of a private placement is a tip-off that a company is on the move and worth investigating. These investors usually have no interest in taking a hand in running the company, so there is less reason to be concerned about losing control or suffering their interference.

3. Venture capitalists who hope to benefit when the company goes public or when it is sold. To help ensure that happy development, these investors get intimately involved at the board of directors level, where their skill and experience can help the company reach its potential.

Whatever the source of private capital, it is critical for the future growth and development of the company that the current management/owner and the new investors share a common outlook on the eventual exit strategy for the investors. Shared expectations with respect to the timing and structure of an IPO, recapitalization financing, or the sale of the company to a larger corporation are as important to both the entrepreneur and the investors as the terms and condition of the private placement.

Private Placement Memorandum

To best present the company information to potential investors, a private placement memorandum (PPM) will be prepared. At a minimum, it should include enough disclosure information to ensure compliance with the antifraud provisions—enough information for investors to make a well-informed decision, with no omissions, misstatements, or enhancements of material facts. The contents of a PPM parallel the contents of a full business plan, and should be tailored to meet the circumstances of the company and the purposes of the offering. For example, a new venture or the launching of a new product probably would require the most detailed memorandum. The raising of second- and third-round capital may require only information on funds required and their uses, historical and projected financial data, and a description of the company and its history.

Most PPMs also should include certain disclaimers regarding the type of securities being offered, the confidentiality of information, the accuracy of any projections, and the like. As discussed previously, certain information must be contained in an offering circular. The company's financial advisor and legal counsel can best advise the company in developing an effective and thorough PPM. Their input is critical both as the deal is sold and to protect everyone from legal liability.

Rules and Law

The rules covering private placements are contained primarily in Regulation D of the Securities Act of 1933. Regulation D (or Reg D, as it is affectionately called) is entitled "Rules Governing the Limited Offer and Sale of Securities Without Registration Under the Securities Act of 1933."

Certain definitions used in Reg D that are pertinent include:

"Accredited Investor" shall mean any person who the issuer reasonably believes comes within any of the following categories:

A. A bank,

B. Any private business development company, as defined,

C. Any organization described in Section 501(c)(3) of the Internal Revenue Code,

D. Any director, executive officer, or general partner of the issuer,

E. Any natural person whose individual net worth exceeds $1,000,000,

F. Any natural person who had income in excess of $200,000 in each of the two most recent years,

G. Any trust with total assets in excess of $5,000,000, or

H. Any entity in which all of the equity owners are accredited investors.

"Executive Officer" shall mean the president, any vice president in charge of a business unit or any other officer who performs a policy making function.

The information requirements involved in a private placement vary depending on the size of the offering and the sophistication of the investors. Care must be taken about the information being provided, since despite it being a private placement, the antifraud provisions of the Securities Act of 1933 apply.

TIPS AND TECHNIQUES

If the investor is a nonaccredited investor, the information requirements are more stringent. Also remember that in addition to the federal securities laws, each state has its own set of securities laws. That is why it is always beneficial to include your counsel on the team.

Three important exemptions from registration under the securities laws are contained in Reg D. They are:

1. Rule 504. This rule is the least restrictive of all the rules and allows companies to raise up to $1 million during a 12-month period, with no restrictions on the number or qualifications of investors. Additionally, there are no information

Briefly, by using Rule 504, a company can sell securities to any-one without providing any information and still not violate federal securities laws. Despite this, however, I always recommend having some documents and disclosure materials to prevent against litigation and problems. Even though you are always enamored by the romance, it is best to plan for the divorce. That is why there are prenuptial agreements in matrimony and subscription documents (see Exhibit 3.1 earlier in this chapter) and disclosure materials in private placements.

requirements, and general solicitation and advertising are permitted.

2. **Rule 505.** This rule allows companies to raise up to $5 million during a 12-month period from 35 "nonaccredited investors" and an unlimited number of accredited investors. This rule imposes information disclosure requirements.

3. **Rule 506.** This rule is sometimes referred to as unlimited private placements, because it can be used to raise any amount of capital. It too allows purchasers to include up to (and not more than) 35 nonaccredited investors and an unlimited number of accredited investors. This rule also imposes some sophistication requirements on the nonaccredited investors. Specifically, the company (offeror) must believe that the nonaccredited investors have the experience or advisors

("purchaser representatives") to properly evaluate the merits and risk of the offering.

TIPS AND TECHNIQUES

Rule 506 represents the greatest opportunity because of the lack of a limitation on the amount of capital that can be raised. However, no matter what rule is used to execute a private placement, I always strongly advise using good and complete disclosure materials and adequate subscription documents that include accredited investor questionnaires. Nothing will place a company afoul of the securities laws faster than selling to more than 35 nonaccredited investors. Ignorance and stupidity do not provide any defense.

Form D

Despite private placements being exempt from the federal securities laws, there is a requirement to file electronically a notice on Form D with the SEC within 15 days after the first sale of securities (see Exhibit 3.2). If sales are made under Rule 505, the SEC staff can request in writing and the company must provide the information furnished by the company to any nonaccredited investor.

It is always best to have complete disclosure documents, private placement memoranda, and other materials and to provide these to all investors, regardless of status.

EXHIBIT 3.2

You may not send a completed printout of this form to the SEC to satisfy a filing obligation. You can only satisfy an SEC filing obligation by submitting the information required by this form to the SEC in electronic format online at https://www.onlineforms.edgarfiling.sec.gov.

FORM D

Notice of Exempt Offering of Securities

U.S. Securities and Exchange Commission
Washington, DC 20549

(See instructions beginning on page 5)

Intentional misstatements or omissions of fact constitute federal criminal violations. See 18 U.S.C. 1001.

OMB APPROVAL
OMB Number: 3235-0076
Expires: June 30, 2012
Estimated average burden hours per response: 4.00

Item 1. Issuer's Identity

Name of Issuer

Previous Name(s) ☐ None

Entity Type (Select one)
☐ Corporation
☐ Limited Partnership
☐ Limited Liability Company
☐ General Partnership
☐ Business Trust
☐ Other (Specify)

Jurisdiction of Incorporation/Organization

Year of Incorporation/Organization
(Select one)
○ Over Five Years Ago   ○ Within Last Five Years (specify year)   ○ Yet to Be Formed

(If more than one issuer is filing this notice, check this box ☐ *and identify additional issuer(s) by attaching Items 1 and 2 Continuation Page(s).)*

Item 2. Principal Place of Business and Contact Information

Street Address 1

Street Address 2

City

State/Province/Country

ZIP/Postal Code

Phone No.

Item 3. Related Persons

Last Name

First Name

Middle Name

Street Address 1

Street Address 2

City

State/Province/Country

ZIP/Postal Code

Relationship(s):   ☐ Executive Officer   ☐ Director   ☐ Promoter

Clarification of Response (if Necessary)

(Identify additional related persons by checking this box ☐ *and attaching Item 3 Continuation Page(s).)*

Item 4. Industry Group   (Select one)

○ **Agriculture**

Banking and Financial Services
○ Commercial Banking
○ Insurance
○ Investing
○ Investment Banking
○ Pooled Investment Fund

If selecting this industry group, also select one fund type below and answer the question below:
○ Hedge Fund
○ Private Equity Fund
○ Venture Capital Fund
○ Other Investment Fund

Is the issuer registered as an investment company under the Investment Company Act of 1940?   ○ Yes   ○ No

○ Other Banking & Financial Services

○ **Business Services**

Energy
○ Electric Utilities
○ Energy Conservation
○ Coal Mining
○ Environmental Services
○ Oil & Gas
○ Other Energy

Health Care
○ Biotechnology
○ Health Insurance
○ Hospitals & Physcians
○ Pharmaceuticals
○ Other Health Care

○ **Manufacturing**

Real Estate
○ Commercial

○ Construction
○ REITS & Finance
○ Residential
○ Other Real Estate

○ **Retailing**
○ **Restaurants**

Technology
○ Computers
○ Telecommunications
○ Other Technology

Travel
○ Airlines & Airports
○ Lodging & Conventions
○ Tourism & Travel Services
○ Other Travel

○ **Other**

SEC1972 (09/08)

Form D   1

FORM D

U.S. Securities and Exchange Commission
Washington, DC 20549

Item 5. Issuer Size   (Select one)

Revenue Range (for issuer not specifying "hedge" or "other investment" fund in Item 4 above)

- ○ No Revenues
- ○ $1 - $1,000,000
- ○ $1,000,001 - $5,000,000
- ○ $5,000,001 - $25,000,000
- ○ $25,000,001 - $100,000,000
- ○ Over $100,000,000
- ○ Decline to Disclose
- ○ Not Applicable

OR

Aggregate Net Asset Value Range (for issuer specifying "hedge" or "other investment" fund in Item 4 above)

- ○ No Aggregate Net Asset Value
- ○ $1 - $5,000,000
- ○ $5,000,001 - $25,000,000
- ○ $25,000,001 - $50,000,000
- ○ $50,000,001 - $100,000,000
- ○ Over $100,000,000
- ○ Decline to Disclose
- ○ Not Applicable

Item 6. Federal Exemptions and Exclusions Claimed   (Select all that apply)

- ☐ Rule 504(b)(1) (not (i), (ii) or (iii))
- ☐ Rule 504(b)(1)(i)
- ☐ Rule 504(b)(1)(ii)
- ☐ Rule 504(b)(1)(iii)
- ☐ Rule 505
- ☐ Rule 506
- ☐ Securities Act Section 4(6)

Investment Company Act Section 3(c)

- ☐ Section 3(c)(1)
- ☐ Section 3(c)(2)
- ☐ Section 3(c)(3)
- ☐ Section 3(c)(4)
- ☐ Section 3(c)(5)
- ☐ Section 3(c)(6)
- ☐ Section 3(c)(7)

- ☐ Section 3(c)(9)
- ☐ Section 3(c)(10)
- ☐ Section 3(c)(11)
- ☐ Section 3(c)(12)
- ☐ Section 3(c)(13)
- ☐ Section 3(c)(14)

Item 7. Type of Filing

○ New Notice   **OR**   ○ Amendment

Date of First Sale in this Offering: _____   **OR**   ☐ First Sale Yet to Occur

Item 8. Duration of Offering

Does the issuer intend this offering to last more than one year?   ☐ Yes   ☐ No

Item 9. Type(s) of Securities Offered   (Select all that apply)

- ☐ Equity
- ☐ Debt
- ☐ Option, Warrant or Other Right to Acquire Another Security
- ☐ Security to be Acquired Upon Exercise of Option, Warrant or Other Right to Acquire Security

- ☐ Pooled Investment Fund Interests
- ☐ Tenant-in-Common Securities
- ☐ Mineral Property Securities
- ☐ Other (Describe)

Item 10. Business Combination Transaction

Is this offering being made in connection with a business combination transaction, such as a merger, acquisition or exchange offer?   ☐ Yes   ☐ No

Clarification of Response (if Necessary)

Form D   2

FORM D   U.S. Securities and Exchange Commission
Washington, DC 20549

Item 11. Minimum Investment

Minimum investment accepted from any outside investor $ [   ]

Item 12. Sales Compensation

Recipient
[   ]

Recipient CRD Number
[   ]   ☐ No CRD Number

(Associated) Broker or Dealer   ☐ None
[   ]

(Associated) Broker or Dealer CRD Number
[   ]   ☐ No CRD Number

Street Address 1
[   ]

Street Address 2
[   ]

City
[   ]

State/Province/Country
[   ]

ZIP/Postal Code
[   ]

States of Solicitation   ☐ All States

☐ AL	☐ AK	☐ AZ	☐ AR	☐ CA	☐ CO	☐ CT	☐ DE	☐ DC	☐ FL	☐ GA	☐ HI	☐ ID
☐ IL	☐ IN	☐ IA	☐ KS	☐ KY	☐ LA	☐ ME	☐ MD	☐ MA	☐ MI	☐ MN	☐ MS	☐ MO
☐ MT	☐ NE	☐ NV	☐ NH	☐ NJ	☐ NM	☐ NY	☐ NC	☐ ND	☐ OH	☐ OK	☐ OR	☐ PA
☐ RI	☐ SC	☐ SD	☐ TN	☐ TX	☐ UT	☐ VT	☐ VA	☐ WA	☐ WV	☐ WI	☐ WY	☐ PR

(Identify additional person(s) being paid compensation by checking this box ☐ and attaching Item 12 Continuation Page(s).)

Item 13. Offering and Sales Amounts

(a) Total Offering Amount $ [   ]   **OR** ☐ Indefinite

(b) Total Amount Sold $ [   ]

(c) Total Remaining to be Sold $ [   ]   **OR** ☐ Indefinite
(Subtract (a) from (b))

Clarification of Response (If Necessary)
[   ]

Item 14. Investors

Check this box ☐ if securities in the offering have been or may be sold to persons who do not qualify as accredited investors, and enter the number of such non-accredited investors who already have invested in the offering: [   ]

Enter the total number of investors who already have invested in the offering: [   ]

Item 15. Sales Commissions and Finders' Fees Expenses

Provide separately the amounts of sales commissions and finders' fees expenses, if any. If an amount is not known, provide an estimate and check the box next to the amount.

Sales Commissions $ [   ]   ☐ Estimate

Finders' Fees $ [   ]   ☐ Estimate

Clarification of Response (If Necessary)
[   ]

Form D 3

FORM D

U.S. Securities and Exchange Commission

Washington, DC 20549

Item 16. Use of Proceeds

Provide the amount of the gross proceeds of the offering that has been or is proposed to be used for payments to any of the persons required to be named as executive officers, directors or promoters in response to Item 3 above. If the amount is unknown, provide an estimate and check the box next to the amount.

$ [   ] ☐ Estimate

Clarification of Response (if Necessary)

[   ]

Signature and Submission

Please verify the information you have entered and review the Terms of Submission below before signing and submitting this notice.

Terms of Submission. In Submitting this notice, each identified issuer is:

Notifying the SEC and/or each State in which this notice is filed of the offering of securities described and undertaking to furnish them, upon written request, in accordance with applicable law, the information furnished to offerees.[*]

Irrevocably appointing each of the Secretary of the SEC and the Securities Administrator or other legally designated officer of the State in which the issuer maintains its principal place of business and any State in which this notice is filed, as its agents for service of process, and agreeing that these persons may accept service on its behalf, of any notice, process or pleading, and further agreeing that such service may be made by registered or certified mail, in any Federal or state action, administrative proceeding, or arbitration brought against the issuer in any place subject to the jurisdiction of the United States, if the action, proceeding or arbitration (a) arises out of any activity in connection with the offering of securities that is the subject of this notice, and (b) is founded, directly or indirectly, upon the provisions of: (i) the Securities Act of 1933, the Securities Exchange Act of 1934, the Trust Indenture Act of 1939, the Investment Company Act of 1940, or the Investment Advisers Act of 1940, or any rule or regulation under any of these statutes; or (ii) the laws of the State in which the issuer maintains its principal place of business or any State in which this notice is filed.

Certifying that, if the issuer is claiming a Rule 505 exemption, the issuer is not disqualified from relying on Rule 505 for one of the reasons stated in Rule 505(b)(2)(iii).

[*] This undertaking does not affect any limits Section 102(a) of the National Securities Markets Improvement Act of 1996 ("NSMIA") [Pub. L. No. 104-290, 110 Stat. 3416 (Oct. 11, 1996)] imposes on the ability of States to require information. As a result, if the securities that are the subject of this Form D are "covered securities" for purposes of NSMIA, whether in all instances or due to the nature of the offering that is the subject of this Form D, States cannot routinely require offering materials under this undertaking or otherwise and can require offering materials only to the extent NSMIA permits them to do so under NSMIA's preservation of their anti-fraud authority.

Each identified issuer has read this notice, knows the contents to be true, and has duly caused this notice to be signed on its behalf by the undersigned duly authorized person. (Check this box ☐ and attach Signature Continuation Pages for signatures of issuers identified in Item 1 above but not represented by signer below.)

Issuer(s)

[   ]

Name of Signer

[   ]

Signature

[   ]

Title

[   ]

Date

Number of continuation pages attached: [   ]

[   ]

Persons who respond to the collection of information contained in this form are not required to respond unless the form displays a currently valid OMB number.

Form D   4

FORM D

U.S. Securities and Exchange Commission
Washington, DC 20549

Instructions for Submitting a Form D Notice

General Instructions

Who must file: Each issuer of securities that sells its securities in reliance on an exemption provided in Regulation D or Section 4(6) of the Securities Act of 1933 must file this notice containing the information requested with the U.S. Securities and Exchange Commission (SEC) and with the state(s) requiring it. If more than one issuer has sold its securities in the same transaction, all issuers should be identified in one filing with the SEC, but some states may require a separate filing for each issuer or security sold.

When to file:

o An issuer must file a new notice with the SEC for each new offering of securities no later than 15 calendar days after the "date of first sale" of securities in the offering as explained in the Instruction to Item 7. For this purpose, the date of first sale is the date on which the first investor is irrevocably contractually committed to invest, which, depending on the terms and conditions of the contract, could be the date on which the issuer receives the investor's subscription agreement or check. An issuer may file the notice at any time before that if it has determined to make the offering. An issuer must file a new notice with each state that requires it at the time set by the state. For state filing information, go to www.NASAA.org. A mandatory capital commitment call does not constitute a new offering, but is made under the original offering, so no new Form D filing is required.

o An issuer may file an amendment to a previously filed notice at any time.

o An issuer must file an amendment to a previously filed notice for an offering:

- to correct a material mistake of fact or error in the previously filed notice, as soon as practicable after discovery of the mistake or error;

- to reflect a change in the information provided in the previously filed notice, except as provided below, as soon as practicable after the change; and

- annually, on or before the first anniversary of the most recent previously filed notice, if the offering is continuing at that time.

When amendment is not required: An issuer is not required to file an amendment to a previously filed notice to reflect a change that occurs after the offering terminates or a change that occurs solely in the following information:

- the address or relationship to the issuer of a related person identified in response to Item 3;

- an issuer's revenues or aggregate net asset value;

- the minimum investment amount, if the change is an increase, or if the change, together with all other changes in that amount since the previously filed notice, does not result in a decrease of more than 10%;

- any address or state(s) of solicitation shown in response to Item 12;

- the total offering amount, if the change is a decrease, or if the change, together with all other changes in that amount since the previously filed notice, does not result in an increase of more than 10%;

- the amount of securities sold in the offering or the amount remaining to be sold;

- the number of non-accredited investors who have invested in the offering, as long as the change does not increase the number to more than 35;

- the total number of investors who have invested in the offering; and

- the amount of sales commissions, finders' fees or use of proceeds for payments to executive officers, directors or promoters, if the change is a decrease, or if the change, together with all other changes in that amount since the previously filed notice, does not result in an increase of more than 10%.

Saturdays, Sundays and holidays: If the date on which a notice or an amendment to a previously filed notice is required to be filed falls on a Saturday, Sunday or holiday, the due date is the first business day following.

Amendment content: An issuer that files an amendment to a previously filed notice must provide current information in response to all items of this Form D, regardless of why the amendment is filed.

How to file: Issuers must file this notice with the SEC in electronic format. For state filing information, go to www.NASAA.org.

Filing fee: There is no federal filing fee. For information on state filing fees, go to www.NASAA.org.

Definitions of terms: Terms used but not defined in this form that are defined in Rule 405 and Rule 501 under the Securities Act of 1933, 17 CFR 230.405 and 230.501, have the meanings given to them in those rules.

Form D 5

FORM D

Item-by-Item Instructions

Item 1. Issuer's Identity. Identify each legal entity issuing any securities being reported as being offered by entering its full name; any previous name used within the past five years; and its jurisdiction of incorporation or organization, type of legal entity, and year of incorporation or organization within the past five years or status as formed over five years ago or not yet formed. If more than one entity is issuing the securities, identify a primary issuer in the first fields shown on the first page of the form, checking the box provided, and identify additional issuers by attaching Items 1 and 2 continuation page(s).

Item 2. Principal Place of Business and Contact Information. Enter a full street address of the issuer's principal place of business. Post office box numbers and "In care of" addresses are not acceptable. Enter a contact telephone number for the issuer. If you identified more than one issuer in response to Item 1, enter the requested information for the primary issuer you identified in response to that item and, at your option, for any or all of the other issuers you identified on your Item 1 and 2 continuation page(s).

Item 3. Related Persons. Enter the full name and address of each person having the specified relationships with any issuer and identify each relationship:

    • Each executive officer and director of the issuer and person performing similar functions (title alone is not determinative) for the issuer, such as the general and managing partners of partnerships and managing members of limited liability companies; and

    • Each person who has functioned directly or indirectly as a promoter of the issuer within the past five years of the later of the first sale of securities or the date upon which the Form D filing was required to be made.

If necessary to prevent the information supplied from being misleading, also provide a clarification in the space provided.

Identify additional persons having the specified relationships by checking the box provided and attaching Item 3 continuation page(s).

Item 4. Industry Group. Select the issuer's industry group. If the issuer or issuers can be categorized in more than one industry group, select the industry group that most accurately reflects the use of the bulk of the proceeds of the offering. For purposes of this filing, use the ordinary dictionary and commonly understood meanings of the terms identifying the industry group.

Item 5. Issuer Size.

• **Revenue Range** (for issuers that do not specify "Hedge Fund" or "Other Investment Fund" in response to Item 4): Enter the revenue range of the issuer or of all the issuers together for the most recently completed fiscal year available, or, if not in existence for a fiscal year, revenue range to date. Domestic SEC reporting companies should state revenues in accordance with Regulation S-X under the Securities Exchange Act of 1934. Domestic non-reporting companies should state revenues in accordance with U.S. Generally Accepted Accounting Principles (GAAP). Foreign issuers should calculate revenues in U.S. dollars and state them in accordance with U.S. GAAP, home country GAAP or International Financial Reporting Standards. If the issuer(s) declines to disclose its revenue range, enter "Decline to Disclose." If the issuer's(s') business is intended to produce revenue but did not, enter "No Revenues." If the business is not intended to produce revenue (for example, the business seeks asset appreciation only), enter "Not Applicable."

• **Aggregate Net Asset Value** (for issuers that specify "Hedge Fund" or "Other Investment Fund" in response to Item 4): Enter the aggregate net asset value range of the issuer or of all the issuers together as of the most recent practicable date. If the issuer(s) declines to disclose its aggregate net asset value range, enter "Decline to Disclose."

Item 6. Federal Exemption(s) and Exclusion(s) Claimed. Select the provision(s) being claimed to exempt the offering and resulting sales from the federal registration requirements under the Securities Act of 1933 and, if applicable, to exclude the issuer from the definition of "investment company" under the Investment Company Act of 1940. Select "Rule 504(b)(1) (not (i), (ii) or (iii))" only if the issuer is relying on the exemption in the introductory sentence of Rule 504 for offers and sales that satisfy all the terms and conditions of Rules 501 and 502(a), (c) and (d).

Item 7. Type of Filing. Indicate whether the issuer is filing a new notice or an amendment to a notice that was filed previously. If this is a new notice, enter the date of the first sale of securities in the offering or indicate that the first sale has "Yet to Occur." For this purpose, the date of first sale is the date on which the first investor is irrevocably contractually committed to invest, which, depending on the terms and conditions of the contract, could be the date on which the issuer receives the investor's subscription agreement or check.

Item 8. Duration of Offering. Indicate whether the issuer intends the offering to last for more than one year.

FORM D
Item-by-Item Instructions (Continued)

Item 9. Type(s) of Securities Offered. Select the appropriate type or types of securities offered as to which this notice is filed. If the securities are debt convertible into other securities, however, select "Debt" and any other appropriate types of securities except for "Equity." For purposes of this filing, use the ordinary dictionary and commonly understood meanings of these categories. For instance, equity securities would be securities that represent proportional ownership in an issuer, such as ordinary common and preferred stock of corporations and partnership and limited liability company interests; debt securities would be securities representing money loaned to an issuer that must be repaid to the investor at a later date; pooled investment fund interests would be securities that represent ownership interests in a pooled or collective investment vehicle; tenant-in-common securities would be securities that include an undivided fractional interest in real property other than a mineral property; and mineral property securities would be securities that include an undivided interest in an oil, gas or other mineral property.

Item 10. Business Combination Transaction. Indicate whether or not the offering is being made in connection with a business combination, such as an exchange (tender) offer or a merger, acquisition, or other transaction of the type described in paragraph (a)(1), (2) or (3) of Rule 145 under the Securities Act of 1933. Do not include an exchange (tender) offer for a class of the issuer's own securities. If necessary to prevent the information supplied from being misleading, also provide a clarification in the space provided.

Item 11. Minimum Investment. Enter the minimum dollar amount of investment that will be accepted from any outside investor. If the offering provides a minimum investment amount for outside investors that can be waived, provide the lowest amount below which a waiver will not be granted. If there is no minimum investment amount, enter "0." Investors will be considered outside investors if they are not employees, officers, directors, general partners, trustees (where the issuer is a business trust), consultants, advisors or vendors of the issuer, its parents, its majority owned subsidiaries, or majority owned subsidiaries of the issuer's parent.

Item 12. Sales Compensation. Enter the requested information for each person that has been or will be paid directly or indirectly any commission or other similar compensation in cash or other consideration in connection with sales of securities in the offering, including finders. Enter the CRD number for every person identified and any broker and dealer listed that has a CRD number. CRD numbers can be found at http://brokercheck.finra.org. A person that does not have a CRD number need not obtain one in order to be listed, and must be listed when required regardless of whether the person has a CRD number. In addition, check the State(s) in which the named person has solicited or intends to solicit investors. If more than five persons to be listed are associated persons of the same broker or dealer, enter only the name of the broker or dealer, its CRD number and street address, and the State(s) in which the named person has solicited or intends to solicit investors.

Item 13. Offering and Sales Amounts. Enter the dollar amount of securities being offered under a claim of federal exemption identified in Item 6 above. Also enter the dollar amount of securities sold in the offering as of the filing date. Select the "Indefinite" box if the amount being offered is undetermined or cannot be calculated at the present time, such as if the offering includes securities to be acquired upon the exercise or exchange of other securities or property and the exercise price or exchange value is not currently known or knowable. If an amount is definite but difficult to calculate without unreasonable effort or expense, provide a good faith estimate. The total offering and sold amounts should include all cash and other consideration to be received for the securities, including cash to be paid in the future under mandatory capital commitments. In offerings for consideration other than cash, the amounts entered should be based on the issuer's good faith valuation of the consideration. If necessary to prevent the information supplied from being misleading, also provide a clarification in the space provided.

Item 14. Investors. Indicate whether securities in the offering have been or may be sold to persons who do not qualify as accredited investors as defined in Rule 501(a), 17 CFR 230.501(a), and provide the number of such investors who already have already invested in the offering. In addition, regardless whether securities in the offering have been or may be sold to persons who do not qualify as accredited investors, specify the total number of investors who already have invested.

Item 15. Sales Commission and Finders' Fees Expenses. The information on sales commissions and finders' fees expenses may be given as subject to future contingencies.

Item 16. Use of Proceeds. No additional instructions.

Signature and Submission. An individual who is a duly authorized representative of each issuer identified must sign, date and submit this notice for the issuer. The capacity in which the individual is signing should be set forth in the "Title" field underneath the individual's name.

The name of the issuer(s) on whose behalf the notice is being submitted should be set forth in the "Issuer" field beside the individual's name; if the individual is signing on behalf of all issuers submitting the notice, the word "All" may be set forth in the "Issuer" field. Attach signature continuation page(s) to have different individuals sign on behalf of different issuer(s). Enter the number of continuation pages attached and included in the filing. If no continuation pages are attached, enter "0".

FORM D

U.S. Securities and Exchange Commission
Washington, DC 20549
Items 1 and 2 Continuation Page

Item 1 and 2. Issuer's Identity and Contact Information (Continued)

Name of Issuer

Jurisdiction of Incorporation/Organization

Year of Incorporation/Organization
(Select one)
○ Over Five Years Ago ○ Within Last Five Years (specify year) ○ Yet to Be Formed

Previous Name(s) ☐ None

Entity Type (Select one)
○ Corporation
○ Limited Partnership
○ Limited Liability Company
○ General Partnership
○ Business Trust
○ Other (Specify)

At your option, supply separate contact information for this issuer:

Street Address 1

Street Address 2

City

State/Province/Country

ZIP/Postal Code

Phone No.

Name of Issuer

Jurisdiction of Incorporation/Organization

Year of Incorporation/Organization
(Select one)
○ Over Five Years Ago ○ Within Last Five Years (specify year) ○ Yet to Be Formed

Previous Name(s) ☐ None

Entity Type (Select one)
○ Corporation
○ Limited Partnership
○ Limited Liability Company
○ General Partnership
○ Business Trust
○ Other (Specify)

At your option, supply separate contact information for this issuer:

Street Address 1

Street Address 2

City

State/Province/Country

ZIP/Postal Code

Phone No.

Name of Issuer

Jurisdiction of Incorporation/Organization

Year of Incorporation/Organization
(Select one)
○ Over Five Years Ago ○ Within Last Five Years (specify year) ○ Yet to Be Formed

Previous Name(s) ☐ None

Entity Type (Select one)
○ Corporation
○ Limited Partnership
○ Limited Liability Company
○ General Partnership
○ Business Trust
○ Other (Specify)

At your option, supply separate contact information for this issuer:

Street Address 1

Street Address 2

City

State/Province/Country

ZIP/Postal Code

Phone No.

(Copy and use additional copies of this page as necessary.)
Form D 8

FORM D

U.S. Securities and Exchange Commission
Washington, DC 20549

Item 3 Continuation Page

Item 3. Related Persons (Continued)

Last Name

First Name

Middle Name

Street Address 1

Street Address 2

City

State/Province/Country

ZIP/Postal Code

Relationship(s): ☐ Executive Officer ☐ Director ☐ Promoter

Clarification of Response (if Necessary)

- -

Last Name

First Name

Middle Name

Street Address 1

Street Address 2

City

State/Province/Country

ZIP/Postal Code

Relationship(s): ☐ Executive Officer ☐ Director ☐ Promoter

Clarification of Response (if Necessary)

- -

Last Name

First Name

Middle Name

Street Address 1

Street Address 2

City

State/Province/Country

ZIP/Postal Code

Relationship(s): ☐ Executive Officer ☐ Director ☐ Promoter

Clarification of Response (if Necessary)

- -

Last Name

First Name

Middle Name

Street Address 1

Street Address 2

City

State/Province/Country

ZIP/Postal Code

Relationship(s): ☐ Executive Officer ☐ Director ☐ Promoter

Clarification of Response (if Necessary)

(Copy and use additional copies of this page as necessary.)

Form D 9

FORM D

U.S. Securities and Exchange Commission

Washington, DC 20549

Item 12 Continuation Page

Item 12. Sales Compensation (Continued)

Recipient

Recipient CRD Number

☐ No CRD Number

(Associated) Broker or Dealer ☐ None

(Associated) Broker or Dealer CRD Number

☐ No CRD Number

Street Address 1

Street Address 2

City

State/Province/Country

ZIP/Postal Code

States of Solicitation ☐ All States

☐ AL	☐ AK	☐ AZ	☐ AR	☐ CA	☐ CO	☐ CT	☐ DE	☐ DC	☐ FL	☐ GA	☐ HI	☐ ID
☐ IL	☐ IN	☐ IA	☐ KS	☐ KY	☐ LA	☐ ME	☐ MD	☐ MA	☐ MI	☐ MN	☐ MS	☐ MO
☐ MT	☐ NE	☐ NV	☐ NH	☐ NJ	☐ NM	☐ NY	☐ NC	☐ ND	☐ OH	☐ OK	☐ OR	☐ PA
☐ RI	☐ SC	☐ SD	☐ TN	☐ TX	☐ UT	☐ VT	☐ VA	☐ WA	☐ WV	☐ WI	☐ WY	☐ PR

- - - - - - - - - - - - - -

Recipient

Recipient CRD Number

☐ No CRD Number

(Associated) Broker or Dealer ☐ None

(Associated) Broker or Dealer CRD Number

☐ No CRD Number

Street Address 1

Street Address 2

City

State/Province/Country

ZIP/Postal Code

States of Solicitation ☐ All States

☐ AL	☐ AK	☐ AZ	☐ AR	☐ CA	☐ CO	☐ CT	☐ DE	☐ DC	☐ FL	☐ GA	☐ HI	☐ ID
☐ IL	☐ IN	☐ IA	☐ KS	☐ KY	☐ LA	☐ ME	☐ MD	☐ MA	☐ MI	☐ MN	☐ MS	☐ MO
☐ MT	☐ NE	☐ NV	☐ NH	☐ NJ	☐ NM	☐ NY	☐ NC	☐ ND	☐ OH	☐ OK	☐ OR	☐ PA
☐ RI	☐ SC	☐ SD	☐ TN	☐ TX	☐ UT	☐ VT	☐ VA	☐ WA	☐ WV	☐ WI	☐ WY	☐ PR

- - - - - - - - - - - - - -

(Copy and use additional copies of this page as necessary.)

Form D 10

FORM D

U.S. Securities and Exchange Commission
Washington, DC 20549

Signature Continuation Page

Signature and Submission

The undersigned is the duly authorized representative of the issuer(s), identied in the field beside the individual's name below.

Issuer

Name of Signer

Signature

Title

Date

Issuer

Name of Signer

Signature

Title

Date

Issuer

Name of Signer

Signature

Title

Date

Issuer

Name of Signer

Title

Signature

Date

(Copy and use additional copies of this page as necessary.)
Form D 11

Summary

Angel capital exists and can be relatively easy to raise with a minimum of legal documents and effort. Venture capital is more expensive and much more protracted to acquire. Private placements can be accomplished by the company alone or with a placement agent and can provide significant amounts of capital.

Pitfalls

After reading this chapter, you will be able to:

- Identify a variety of potential legal difficulties and pitfalls encountered in raising capital.
- Identify those areas ripe for potential problems with the Securities and Exchange Commission, together with ways to avoid them.

Regulation 506 D: Areas of Opportunity and Uncertainty

Rule 506 of Reg D, as we have mentioned, represents the greatest opportunity for a company to raise capital easily. Regulation 506 permits the raising of an unlimited amount of capital, thus placing no dollar restrictions on the size of a raise. Additionally, a raise can be conducted by the company itself or placement agents and/or finders. However, as with all private placements, general solicitation or advertising is prohibited. General solicitation or advertising invalidates the exemption from registration with the Securities and Exchange Commission (SEC) and potentially creates legal and administrative problems that are best avoided.

Assuming for now that the company is conducting a raise by itself, how can the investors be identified, and how can the investment be sold to these prospective investors?

The private placement rules and regulations permit the sale of securities by an officer of the company, provided an existing relationship with that investor already exists. This creates the first opportunity and gray area for use and abuse of the private placement rules. Capital has been raised successfully by companies employing a salesperson who is an officer of the company. As an officer of the company, this salesperson is legally able to sell potential investors on the merits of an investment in the company.

How do we solicit those investors with whom we have no existing relationship without it being deemed a public or general solicitation? Since the officer has a finite number of contacts with whom relationships already exist, how does he or she expand beyond that initial circle of contacts?

Many medical companies have utilized a technique that can be adopted by other companies in other fields. The technique works like this: The medical company purchases a list of physicians who may be interested in or their practice may benefit by the medical company's product or service. This list could be in a state, multiple states, or the entire United States. Then the company sends a broadcast fax to the doctors inviting them to be part of a medical advisory board for the company. Such participation would involve the completion of three questionnaires per year and the attendance at one in-person meeting of the board. The compensation for such service would be 250 shares of the company's common stock per year. The faxed invitation requests physicians to fax back completed questionnaires along with their curriculum vitae and a time when it is convenient for the Vice President of Corporate Development to speak in more detail with the invited (and now interested) physicians.

During the initial conversation with interested physicians, the officer describes the company, the purpose of the medical advisory board, the products or services the company will be developing, why the physicians' participation can be helpful and utilized, *and* a description of the annual compensation. Inevitably, the discussion moves to a description of the company's capital raising and physicians' interest in becoming investors. Assuming a physician is interested, arrangements can be made to provide to him or her with the offering and disclosure materials and schedule another call for an in-depth sales session, because now a relationship exists.

The physician becomes a member of the advisory board and an investor. All these documents (invitation, completed questionnaire, and curriculum vitae) are contained in investor files and medical advisory board files.

Bingo—capital has been raised from an investor who did not have an existing relationship with the company and who was discovered through a solicitation for a different purpose.

Obviously, nonmedical companies can use this method by modifying the type of advisory board and the individuals solicited for membership. Companies must take great care to ensure that the board has substance and the questionnaires and meeting are conducted. It cannot just be a sham board to circumvent the nonsolicitation rules. You should know that the SEC has successfully sued at least one company that utilized this method of capital raising and successfully alleged fraud, among other things. It is truly one of the areas of opportunity and uncertainty in raising capital under Regulation 506 D. Excellent documentation and actual substance are required and still may not adequately protect the company and the individuals.

See Exhibits 4.1, 4.2, and 4.3 for an illustration of the invitation, the actual agreement, and one of the subsequent questionnaires.

EXHIBIT 4.1

Advisory Board Invitation

_____, INC.

Dr. _____, Co-Founder and chief scientist, of _____, Inc., formally requests your consideration for a compensated position on the _____, Inc. National Medical Panel. Dr. _____ was a former professor at _____ University for 23 years and a colleague of world-renowned _____ surgeon, Dr. _____.

_____, Inc has just announced the introduction of a *nonintrusive_____device*, developed, over the past 15 years by Dr. _____. _____ believes, based on trial data, that this device has the capability to **predict future pathological events**, specifically, but not limited to _____. The ability to accurately predict _____ could enable the potential of (1) saving many lives, (2) increasing the effectiveness of medical teams and (3) saving dollars both within the healthcare system and in malpractice costs.

We are seeking to enlist a limited number of physicians to participate in an advisory capacity to provide feedback, opinions, evaluations and the sharing of ideas to facilitate the company's growth,

FOR MORE INFORMATION ABOUT _____ NATIONAL _____ PANEL R.S.V.P. TOLL FREE BY CALLING (800) 000-0000, OR FAX (800) 000-0000

PLEASE VISIT OUR WEB SITE AT WWW._____.COM

NAME _____

ADDRESS _____

CITY/ST/ZIP _____

OFFICE TEL# _____ **BEST TIME TO CALL** _____

HOME TEL# _____ **BEST TIME TO CALL** _____

EXHIBIT 4.2

Advisory Board Agreement

_____, INC.

NATIONAL MEDICAL PANEL AGREEMENT

AGREEMENT is hereby entered into on «DATE_PACKAGE_SENT», between ___, hereinafter referred to as ''_____'', a Delaware corporation having its principal office at _____ and «FIRST» «LAST» «TITLE», hereinafter referred to as ''DOCTOR''.

1. **PURPOSE**.
   The purpose of this agreement is to acknowledge the undersigned DOCTOR'S participation on the National Medical Panel for _____.

2. **DUTIES/OBLIGATIONS**.
   Panel members' input will be used anonymously, as a group, for _____'S purpose only. All suggestions will be

   (*continued*)

(*continued*)

submitted to the company's Scientific Advisory Board and its Founders. _____ assumes any and all liability for the Panel's input. DOCTOR shall be obligated to perform or acknowledge the following as part of the Medical Panel of _____:

(A) Forward a copy of his/her Curriculum Vitae.

(B) Participate in two (2) of the annual teleconferences. Receive and respond to e-mails regarding _____'S new and existing technologies.

(C) Abide by a duty of CONFIDENTIALITY on behalf of _____, holding all proprietary information in trust and confidence, agreeing that it shall be used only in _____'S best interest and not for any other purpose, and further agreeing that it shall not be disclosed to any third party under any circumstances. Any and all information received by DOCTOR from _____ about new research, technology, company services, marketing, or business plans, shall be considered confidential and/or proprietary.

3. **COMPENSATION**.

(A) All expense paid accommodations at _____'S Annual Medical Panel Symposium weekend meeting (attendance optional).

(B) _____ shall issue DOCTOR the sum of (250) shares of _____'S stock per service year, for a period of two (2) years.

(C) DOCTOR will be eligible to receive a _____ Analyzer at a discounted purchase price once FDA clearance is received.

4. **TERMINATION**.

DOCTOR retains the right to terminate with _____ at any time. _____ has right of termination for cause. Upon termination by either party, DOCTOR shall retain any earned shares of Stock.

5. **ENTIRETY OF AGREEMENT**.

This two-page document contains the entire understanding of the parties. Any modification shall be in writing and executed by the parties hereto.

IN WITNESS WHEREOF, the parties named hereby set their hands and/or seals on the date first set forth above.

READ, APPROVED, AND ACCEPTED:

By: _____   By: _____

  MEDICAL PANEL DOCTOR   **_FOUNDER_**

                                            _____, Inc.

DOCTOR INFORMATION (*Please print clearly*)

Check below for stock certificate delivery location.

_____ **HOME:**   **Address:**   _____

                                              _____

                    Telephone: _____

                                              _____

_____ **OFFICE:**   **Address:**   _____

                                              _____

                    Telephone: _____

                                  Email: _____

NOTE: PLEASE MAIL A COMPLETED AGREEMENT AND "CV" TO:

Attn: Corporate Development

                        _____ **Inc.**

_____

_____

TEL 800-000-0000 FAX 800-000-0000

EXHIBIT 4.3

Quarterly Questionnaire

**NATIONAL MEDICAL PANEL AND
MEDICAL ADVISORY FORUM PARTICIPANTS
QUESTIONNAIRE
OCTOBER 16, _____**

Dear Members of the National Medical Panel:

We are pleased to provide you with our next questionnaire of 2008. We are delighted to seek your input as we prepare for FDA approval for our first product, The _____, in the fourth quarter of this year. The _____ is intended to display and analyze electrocardiographic information and to measure heart rate variability (HRV). These and other measurements are not intended for any specific clinical diagnosis. The clinical significance of HRV and other parameters must be determined by the physician.

This represents a major step in our commercialization efforts, and we are extremely excited about this and the products scheduled to follow, consisting of (a) the _____ for triaging trauma patients and (b) the _____ for risk stratifying patients at risk of Sudden Cardiac Death.

We are interested in your responses to the following questions. We recognize your busy schedules, but your responses have always been extremely important and valuable to us. Please fax your responses to (800) 000-0000.

As you may recall, we are planning on a business model that charges the physician for the analysis of the _____ file. Our original plans called for the files to be transmitted to an analysis center, where we would analyze the files and return a report to the physician. This business model is being implemented to better control the software and better know how many tests were being ordered by whom. Computer technology has evolved whereby we can provide you, the physician, in your office, the _____ analysis software as part of the digital EKG hardware. The _____ software will be thoroughly encrypted and controlled on a per-use basis by means of a key purchased by the physician with a certain number of uses included. We anticipate the reimbursement for the physician to be between $150 and $300 per test. Questions for which we would appreciate answers relating to this business model include those listed below.

Thank you again for your participation. Your time and effort is much appreciated.

PLEASE RETURN BY FAX TO 800-000-0000
Please print your answers clearly.

1. **On what types of patients would you anticipate performing the test and with what frequency? Check all that apply.**
   _____ MADIT II/SCD-HeFT
   _____ Heart disease who don't meet MADIT II/SCD-HeFT criteria for an ICD
   _____ Student athletes
   _____ Family history of sudden death
   _____ Elevated risk for heart disease (smoker, hypertensive, high lipids, etc.)
   _____ History of prior syncope
   _____ History of asymptomatic ventricular arrhythmias
   _____ Other: _____

2. **How would you market/make known the availability of this test?**
   To your patients: _____
   _____
   To your referring doctors: _____
   _____

   (continued)

(*continued*)

    To the medical community: _____

_____

    To the community at large: _____

_____

3. **What marketing help might be useful to you?**

    _____ Brochures

    _____ Assistance setting up dinners/talks with physicians

    _____ Assistance setting up community talks

    _____ Other:_____

4. **How many uses would you as a physician be willing to pur-chase and pay for in advance at:**

    $50 per test _____ $100 per test _____

5. **If there was no immediate insurance coverage available at the outset, do you believe your patients would be willing to pay $100 for the test out of pocket twice annually as a screen for _____?**

    Yes_____   No_____

    Comments _____

_____

_____

    PLEASE PRINT YOUR NAME CLEARLY: _____

    PHONE NUMBER: _____

Subscription Documents

We discussed subscription documents earlier; a sample set is included in Chapter 3 as Exhibit 3.1. Used in conjunction with a private placement memorandum (PPM), the subscription documents usually are included in the PPM as an appendix to that document. The subscription documents enable the company to ensure that it has completed its due diligence in determining whether the investor is accredited or not and clearly enables the investor to corroborate that he/she has received and reviewed the disclosure documents. This determination is critical, since theoretically, no more than 35 nonaccredited investors can be included in an exempt offering.

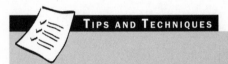

TIPS AND TECHNIQUES

It is truly best to have **NO** (as in zero) nonaccredited investors. Their disclosure requirements are different from those of accredited investors, and their presence always threatens the exemption.

Investor Count

As we have discussed, an offering exempt from registration under Regulation 506 D may have an unlimited number of accredited investors and no more than 35 nonaccredited investors. Although the regulations permit nonaccredited investors, their presence always presents complications that are not necessary. There are enough complications raising capital without making nonaccredited investors another one.

Additionally, although the rules permit an "unlimited" number of investors, more than 100 accredited investors invested in a private placement could cause the company to be impacted by the Investment Company Act and require registration.

Another cautionary point: A private company that has raised significant amounts of money through a series of well-conducted private placements *but* at the end of a fiscal year has more than 500 stock-holders and $10 million in total assets is required to file a Form 10 and become a 1934 Act reporting company. Obviously, the SEC and legal view is that even if the shares are not actively traded on a market, the number of investors is sufficient to warrant those investors the right to receive periodic reports. The easiest way to ensure that is to subject the company to the 1934 Act reporting requirements.

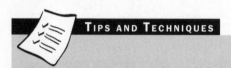

TIPS AND TECHNIQUES

There also is a technical requirement that a company keep count of who received the offering documents. That number is the real limitation on accredited and nonaccredited investors. In any event, because companies have been taken public with fewer than 100 investors, 400 investors in a private placement always will raise a red flag, should there ever be an inquiry. Monitor the investor count.

Risk Factors

Risk factors in a PPM or any other disclosure materials are designed to alert potential investors to the risks inherent in an investment in this particular company. They provide caution to investors and protection to the company, so they should be complete and address all the known and identified risks.

Having said that, most people, after reading the risk factors in most offering documents, would believe that only a complete fool would invest in the company. Consequently, most companies vigorously attempt to keep the risk factors disclosed to a minimum. *That is a woefully bad strategy.*

IN THE REAL WORLD

Risk factors ultimately protect the company if something should go wrong and an investor decides to litigate. Even though the litigation usually cannot be avoided, the presence of adequate risk factors goes a long way in defusing and disarming the litigant. Consequently, I view risk factors as extremely cheap insurance, and the company should ensure that they are complete and accurate. Realistically, investors read the risk factors (maybe) and do not necessarily base their investment decision on those risk factors. This is one area where it is best to overdisclose!

IN THE REAL WORLD

Companies that legitimately need capital to stay in business must raise that capital, whether it is construed as a continuous offering or not. I have never seen a case where the SEC worried about whether a company remained in business or whether the previous investors lost their investment as a consequence. In the real world, you have a fiduciary responsibility to keep your company viable and protect your existing investors—even if it means that you are continuously raising capital.

Offering Documents

Whether the raising of capital is being conducted through a private placement with a PPM or an institutional funding with a business plan, offering and disclosure documents will be utilized. Human nature being what it is, there is always a tendency to overaccentuate the positive and minimize the negative. In plain words, we are talking about sales puffery in an attempt to make investors believe that there is an urgent need to invest quickly in the next big thing.

 TIPS AND TECHNIQUES

Avoid the temptation! Besides potentially creating unnecessary legal liability, institutional investors will see right through sales puffery and refuse to invest for just that reason.

Form D

Under the Securities Act of 1933, any offer to sell securities must be either registered with the SEC or meet an exemption. Since we are discussing Rule 506 under Regulation D, one of the three rules providing exemptions from the registration requirements (the others are 504 and 505, as discussed in Chapter 3), registration is not required. Thus, these exemptions allow some companies to offer and sell their securities without having to register the securities with the SEC.

Although companies using these exemptions do not have to register their securities and the offerings and do not have to file reports with the SEC, they must file what is known as a Form D (see Exhibit 3.2 for an example) after they first sell their securities. Form D is a brief notice that includes the names and addresses of the company's executive officers and stock promoters but contains little other information about the company.

In February 2008, the SEC adopted amendments to Form D, requiring that electronic filing of Form D be phased in during the period September 15, 2008 to March 16, 2009. Although as amended, the electronic Form D requires much of the same information as the paper Form D, the amended Form D requires disclosure of the date of first sale in the offering. Previously, disclosure of the first date of sale was not required. The Office of Small Business Policy of the SEC has posted information on its Web page about the filing requirements for the new Form D, which must still to be filed within 15 days from the date of the first sale of the offering.

Companies that fail to file Form D (either intentionally or unintentionally) are not subject to sanction; however, Rule 507 disqualifies a company from using a Regulation D exemption in the future if the company has been enjoined by a court for violating Rule 503 by failing to file the information required by Form D. Consequently, companies have an incentive to make a Form D filing; they should do so to avoid the possibility that a court will enjoin the companies for violating Rule 503 and, as a result, disqualify them from using a Regulation D exemption in the future. The form is not complicated and with the new electronic filing requirements is not cumbersome. There is no excuse to trip over this violation.

Placement Agents and Finders

Often a company will not have the desire to raise capital by itself and will look to hire a firm or individuals to assist in the process. Such a decision does not relieve the company and its management of being involved in the process or preparing the disclosure materials. A third party may be able to identify prospective investors, but it is still the responsibility of the management team to sell those prospective investors on the company, its products or services, and the management team.

Placement Agents

The engagement of a placement agent is a formal step (similar but not as involved as engaging an underwriter, as is discussed in Chapter 5). A sample placement agent agreement is presented on www.wiley .com/go/capitalformation.

Placement agents are usually compensated by receiving a percentage of proceeds from the capital raise. For example, depending on the structure of the capital raise itself, the agent may be paid 10 and 10. This means that the agent will receive a cash commission equal to 10% of the proceeds of the raise plus a 10% equity commission equal to either 10% of the shares issued in the raise or a similar number of warrants to purchase shares at the price of the offering.

By way of example, let us assume the current raise was successfully completed and enabled the company to raise $6 million at $4.00

per share, resulting in the issuance of 1.5 million new shares of the company's common stock. With a 10 and 10, the placement agent would receive $600,000 cash (netting the company $5.4 million) and either 150,000 shares of common stock of the company or 150,000 warrants to purchase shares of the company's common stock for a period of five years at $4.00 per share.

TIPS AND TECHNIQUES

Legally, only a registered broker/dealer (B/D) can be paid a commission for the sale of securities. Hence, if the placement agent is not a registered broker/dealer, the law has been violated. This is why "finders" exist. Read on.

Finders

Many people and organizations assist companies in the raising of capital but are not registered B/Ds. They hold themselves out to be "finders." They are obviously so named because they find investors. They try to be compensated the same or in a similar fashion as placement agents. (See the Finder's Fee Agreement on www.wiley.com/go/capitalformation.) Remember, in order to receive a commission related to the sale of securities, the selling agent must be a registered B/D. Consequently, a finder is different from a placement agent in that the finder does not sell the securities; rather, the company meets with prospective investors and does the actual selling of the company, its products, management team, and prospects. A company can legally pay a finder a fee that resembles a commission; any legal problems may be the responsibility of the finder.

Placement agents (registered B/Ds) usually do an extensive job of selling the securities to their existing customers. That is why they are registered B/Ds. Rarely does the company have to meet with or answer questions to these investors. In contrast, finders do little selling; often, if not always, finders introduce the investment opportunity and leave the actual selling process to the company and management.

Romanian Raise

Unfortunately, there is a legitimate need for companies to raise capital. Because it is not an easy thing for many companies to do, the path is lined with unscrupulous people who prey on companies in search of capital and charge exorbitant fees to assist in capital raising, charge up-front fees without performance guarantees, and perform in an illegal manner.

One of these tactics is what I refer to as the Romanian Raise. Because of the ease of placing calls from outside the United States to the United States, and because of the fact that the SEC cannot touch individuals outside the United States, boiler rooms in Eastern European countries have appeared on the scene. These boiler rooms are busy centers of activity, often selling questionable goods by telephone. The term typically refers to a room where salespeople work using unfair, dishonest sales tactics, sometimes selling penny stock or committing outright stock fraud. The term carries a negative connotation and often is used to imply high-pressure sales tactics.

In the scheme, a company encountering difficulty in raising capital using conventional means is introduced to an individual who claims to be able to raise capital among his extensive European customer base. What this individual really may have is a series of boiler rooms in Romania and other countries that prey on U.S. companies. They also try to charge a "commission" that can range as high as 90%.

IN THE REAL WORLD

No matter how much difficulty you may be experiencing in raising capital, beware of the Romanian Raise and other scams. Unfortunately, there are many lowlifes out there. When you are desperate for capital, it is easy to get sucked in by one of them.

Summary

The world of private placements offers extensive opportunities to raise capital. It also has numerous pitfalls that can introduce legal problems that are best avoided. These pitfalls can be appropriately navigated with common sense and good, professional advisors.

CHAPTER 5

Public Markets: Are They Right for You?

After reading this chapter, you will be able to:

- Understand the perceived advantages of transforming your company from a private company to a public company.
- Understand the perceived negatives of becoming a public company.
- Make the appropriate decision for your situation.

What It Means to Become a Public Company

The siren song of the public markets has always been and will always continue to be a strong call to business sailors. Much like Ulysses, that siren song could easily be calling many a company to a disastrous event and painful result. In usual economic times, hundreds of companies are drawn to the public markets by the perception of significant and rewarding benefits. Often guided by experienced (and aggressive) management teams, many companies take their new capital and currency and parlay it into unprecedented growth. Bear in mind that this rapid growth also requires the assistance of excellent professional advisors.

But like all things, going public is not a panacea that cures all and ends all. The Cinderella stories of Google, Microsoft, and others can be counterbalanced by the horror stories of plunging share prices, shareholder litigation, management upheaval, and loss of control. Some of these companies would have failed anyway, but others could have avoided the disastrous results they experienced once in the public markets. Avoidance of disastrous results often can be achieved by ensuring that management truly understands the daunting rigors and dimensions of managing a public company. In addition, the risks of poor market timing and lack of adequate planning can also result in failure and disaster.

Becoming a successful public company takes planning, hard work, the right blend of talent, and, of course, luck.

 TIPS AND TECHNIQUES

Being public does not *always* ensure that your company will be able to raise capital easily and improve its financial condition. It is not unusual for companies to travel down the "road less traveled" through the public offering process, become public, and then face enormous difficulties in raising much-needed capital.

Benefits and Opportunities

The next list presents the nine most common (real or perceived) benefits of being a public company. Although the list is not all-inclusive, it represents the most significant reasons companies make the leap.

1. **Improved financial condition.** Depending on the route and method chosen to go public, the company may raise some capital in the process. As this money does not have to be repaid, it immediately improves a company's financial condition.

2. **Greater marketability.** Once a company is public, the investors (more specifically, the original owners) find themselves in a new and perceivedly more favorable position. Their ownership interests no longer lack marketability or liquidity, because the ownership interests that they now have usually can be sold in the market, providing certain legal restrictions are followed.

3. **Improved value.** The value of the company's stock may increase dramatically, starting with the initial shares offered. Companies whose shares are publicly traded often command higher prices than companies that are not publicly traded. Ostensibly, there are three reasons for this to be the case:

   a. Perceived marketability of the shares

   b. Perceived maturity/sophistication attributed to public companies

   c. The availability of more information about the company because of the required disclosure rules

4. **Personal portfolio diversification/estate planning.** Although they are not a driver in my mind, you cannot dismiss

the opportunities that becoming a public company presents for an entrepreneur with a significant (or entire) portion of his or her net worth tied up in the company. Becoming a public company provides diversification strategies and liquidity.

5. **Capital to sustain growth.** Both the proceeds from an initial public offering (if you choose to enter the public markets via that route) and the proceeds from subsequent offerings (see item 6) provide capital to the company. This is perhaps the most significant single benefit of becoming a public company. The proceeds can be used for a myriad of purposes, including working capital and debt repayment. The additional capital provides fuel to run a growth engine. A by-product of this was discussed in No. 3: higher valuation. Higher valuations usually result in higher trading multiples (price-earnings ratios), which can reduce dilution in capital raising and open up doors to raising other types of capital, as discussed in Chapter 2.

IN THE REAL WORLD

As we will see when we discuss the mechanics of going public, there are no absolute assurances that a deal will get done. If it does not get done, the company has stumbled badly, incurred significant expenses, and not raised any capital or become a public entity. That is why I always consider the execution risk inherent in both the manner in which a company goes public and the need for the capital it is raising.

6. Improved opportunities for future financing. By going public, a company theoretically improves its net worth and builds a larger equity base as well as an investor following. This improved capital position should lower the cost of both debt and equity capital in the future. It also should enable the company to, with relative ease, raise additional capital for future growth, because the perception exists that it is easier for an established company to raise capital in the public markets than it is for a private company to do so.

IN THE REAL WORLD

Willie Sutton robbed banks because that is where the money is. Companies go public because that is where the capital is, and they need to access that capital. Given today's uncertain capital markets, there is no assurance that just because a company has become public, it can raise additional capital.

7. Pathway to mergers and acquisitions. Mergers and acquisitions are always part of a company's long-range growth and strategic plans. Unfortunately, private companies often lack the financial connections and resources to accomplish an aggressive merger and acquisition strategy. Obviously, a merger may provide a product diversification solution and completion of product lines, additional executive talent and depth, economies of scale, and entry into otherwise closed markets. The going-public process provides a company with two additions to its financial resources that private companies do not possess: potentially more cash, through subsequent financings/offerings, and the use of the company's own stock as currency, since it now has an established value in the marketplace. The use of your company's stock as a currency has many perceived advantages from both a business and tax perspective that may enable a company to accelerate its merger strategy.

8. **Enhanced corporate image and increased employee participation.** Being a public company with shares that are actively traded can bring recognition and credibility to the company, thus enhancing its corporate image and competitive position. By being able to capture the attention of the financial community and related press, the company can obtain free publicity, which further boosts its corporate image and creates even higher demand for the stock. This has a beneficial cycle of driving demand, thus increasing the price of the stock, thus further increasing demand. Additionally, once the company becomes an established public company, it can offer employees meaningful stock option programs and restricted stock award programs, driving employee loyalty and making recruitment easier.

9. **Listing on a stock exchange.** A goal of any public company should be to have its shares listed on a stock exchange. This enhances the company's image and facilitates many things that are beneficial to the company. Listed companies are more closely watched by the financial press. Meaningful restrictions preclude many institutional investors from investing in a company not traded on an exchange. There are a variety of

exchanges currently available from which to choose; many of them did not even exist five years ago.

The last place that any public company would want to be traded is on the Pink Sheets or on the Bulletin Board. The Pink Sheets is an electronic quotation system operated by Pink OTC Markets that displays quotes from broker-dealers for many over-the-counter (OTC) securities. These securities tend to be inactively traded stocks, including penny stocks and those with a narrow geographic interest. To be quoted in the Pink Sheets, companies do not need to fulfill any requirements (e.g., filing financial statements with the SEC). The OTC Bulletin Board or OTCBB is an electronic quotation system in the United States that displays real-time quotes, last-sale prices, and volume information for many over-the-counter (OTC) equity securities that are not listed on the NASDAQ stock exchange or a national securities exchange. Companies quoted on the OTCBB must be fully reporting (i.e., current with all required SEC filings) but have no market capitalization, minimum share price, corporate governance, or other requirements to be quoted. Companies that have been "de-listed" from stock exchanges for falling below minimum capitalization, minimum share price, or other requirements often end up being quoted on the OTCBB. However, this is where many companies may have to start their public experience. A major part of the company's strategy should be to take those steps that will enable the movement of the company's listing to an exchange.

Drawbacks

Just as there are opportunities and benefits to being a public company, there are also drawbacks. Some of these can be mitigated by good planning and good professional advisors. The next list presents nine drawbacks.

1. **Loss of control.** Depending on the number of shares sold to the public (and the company's capitalization at that point in time), the company founder will, in all likelihood, lose control of the company. If this is an absolute point of contention for you, consider going public very carefully.

TIPS AND TECHNIQUES

Other ways to maintain control may include the use of a dual class of stock in which voting control is retained by the founder by having a second class of common stock that he or she owns with all the voting control; however, this is often perceived for what it really is and viewed negatively by the investing public.

As a practical matter, loss of control should not be of primary importance. Once the first dollar is taken from other investors, management's fiduciary responsibility is to run the company for the benefit of *all* the stockholders. This important point is often overlooked by founders with insatiable egos, such as Bernie Ebbers, Richard Scrushy, and others.

2. **Sharing your success.** As I have said throughout this book, investors share the risks of your business (up to a point)—but they will also share your success. That fact gives rise to planning

considerations for the public event. If financing can be obtained, other than equity, to drive rapid short-term growth and profitability, postpone the going-public decision. With the additional growth and profitability, the company will be more valuable and you will incur less dilution.

3. **Loss of privacy.** Of all the changes that occur when a company goes public, the most difficult to deal with is the loss of privacy. The Securities and Exchange Commission (SEC) requires mindboggling disclosures in the public domain; it is really like living in a fishbowl. Although these disclosures need not include every detail of the company's operations, information that could significantly affect investors' decisions must be disclosed.

   Because of the fishbowl environment, where transparency is required and representative of good corporate conduct, related party transactions, perquisites for executives, and other such benefits often are discontinued prior to or during the transition to becoming a public company.

4. **Limiting management's freedom to act.** By virtue of becoming a public company, management surrenders a certain degree of the freedom it enjoyed as a private company. (As I have said many times, however, once that first outside investment dollar is received, even in a private company, management suddenly answers to a different master.) Management of a public company must obtain board of director approval on major issues and also stockholders' approval on certain issues. It no longer has the ability to make unilateral decisions without considering the ramifications of those decisions on all the stakeholders.

IN THE REAL WORLD

I still maintain that if management always has the investors in mind, whether it is one investor or many, from the day that the first investment dollar is taken, the limitation on management's ability to act will not present a real problem.

5. **Periodic reporting.** As a public company, the company is subject to the periodic reporting requirements of the SEC. This includes not only the filing of quarterly and annual reports but reports announcing major company events as well as share purchases and sales by company insiders. These requirements may necessitate that the company hire additional accounting staff, implement improved accounting systems, and make more extensive use of advisors such as attorneys and accountants. (Some of these costs are also summarized in item 6.)

6. **Initial and ongoing expenses.** Going public will be a costly endeavor and will require a significant and extensive management team commitment of both time and energy. Depending on the method by which the company actually transitions to a public company, out-of-pocket costs can range from several hundred thousand dollars to millions of dollars. And this is just company time and accounting, legal, and printing fees. Once the company is public, there are the continuing costs of filings, stockholder meetings, stockholder reports, and proxies.

In addition, there are the ongoing costs and trouble of complying with Sarbanes-Oxley and both the internal control reporting by management and the external audit of that report. These costs can range into the millions of dollars annually and are why many companies have ended their plans to become public or decided to pursue this idea outside of the United States.

7. **Shareholder expectations.** Investors will always be expecting greater things relating to company performance and stock price. Managing these expectations is one of the greatest challenges of a management team. It is difficult to deal with shareholder expectations, thus creating the short-term benefit versus the long-term strategy dilemma. Despite the best intentions of a strategic plan to deliver long-term value, management gets evaluated with a report card every 90 days. Shareholders are more interested in their stock price today and what you have done for them lately. This perspective can frustrate many management teams. They have to continually remind themselves that the good execution of a good strategic plan to deliver long-term value is always the best management strategy.

TIPS AND TECHNIQUES

Management should have one official spokesperson for the company who interacts with the public and ensures the uniformity of message. This is especially important if shareholders have unrealistic views regarding current stock performance.

8. Restrictions on selling existing shareholder's shares. Controlling or major stockholders of a public company (which includes the senior management and directors, sometimes referred to as Section 16 reporting persons) are not free to sell their shares at will. The SEC has restrictions on when and how many shares insiders may sell. Management must be aware of these restrictions along with the restrictions on trading with what would be perceived as insider knowledge.

IN THE REAL WORLD

Management, working with counsel, can identify the people who are legally regarded as insiders and Section 16 reporting persons and also publish company policies and procedures to ensure that appropriate laws are followed, that officers and directors make timely filings of certain transactions, and that sufficient blackout rules exist to avoid trading with perceived inside information.

9. Fiduciary responsibilities. As the owner of a private company, the money you invested and risked was your own. Once you receive money from investors, the money you risk is theirs and decisions that you make have to be for the benefit of all stockholders. *You become accountable to them!* Too many times, I have seen chief executives of public companies view the company as still theirs and lead it and themselves to a very destructive ending.

Decision to Go Public

The decision to go public is never an easy one. However, this decision does require a great deal of thought by management and the board of directors. The factors that will weigh into the overall decision to go or not go include timing and readiness of the company and the market.

Is This the Right Time?

As in with most things in life, the timing of a company's decision to go public is extremely critical. Go public too soon, and the company will be punished in the market. Go public too late and miss a market upswing, and the company will be punished in the market.

If the decision to go public is driven by the need to obtain capital, consider whether that capital can be obtained from nonpublic sources. If so, maybe the decision to go public can be postponed, and the raised capital can be used to drive profitability and growth. Then the company's value at the public transition will be increased, resulting in decreased dilution to existing shareholders.

Is a well-developed strategic operating plan in place? If not, or if such a plan is not executed well, the performance of the stock in the public market will be adversely affected (i.e., go down), leaving investors with a bad taste in their mouths for the company and its prospects. Then it will be difficult (or impossible) to raise capital in the future as it is rare for impaired credibility to be repaired.

The most significant risk (execution risk) in a classic going-public transaction is that the transaction does not close, leaving the company with significant expenses that must be paid and no new capital with which to pay them. (See the process described in Chapter 6.) The reason for such an event may be bad market events or poor financial performance by the company, causing the underwriters to abandon the deal, or the underwriters many not have been able to attract enough attention to sell the deal, even at a reduced price. *This is a terrible situation—there is nothing else that can be said about it.*

TIPS AND TECHNIQUES

There is almost no way to fully prevent the situation where a going public transaction does not close, but it is always best to ask yourself: Am I putting myself in a situation where if Japan invades North Korea and the markets freeze up, I can still survive with this transaction incomplete? If the answer is no, it is best to build several contingency plans into the overall plan. As you will see, in going public (no matter which method you use), there exist numerous and always-present execution risks over which the company has no control but around which it must be prepared to navigate.

Is the Company Ready?

This may be the most difficult question that must be answered and involves a variety of factors:

- **Size (is the company big enough?).** There have always been varying criteria as to whether a company was the right size to enter the public markets. This "size" factor also enabled the investing public and the underwriters to be more comfortable that the companies were seasoned and had experienced management. Then came the dot-com boom, and companies were rushed to the public markets with inexperienced management, a business plan written on the back of a cocktail napkin, and no hopes of ever achieving profitability. Combine those fiascoes with the frozen financial markets of 2008–2009, and size becomes even more important in determining suitability to be a public company. The days of a company with less than $100 million in revenue and no profits successfully completing a public offering are over or relatively rare, at least. The driving force for these smaller companies may be an innovative new product and a superior management team (see the next bullet point).

- **Management (does management have the right experience?).** The time for management to analyze its capability to manage a public company is when it is still private and before any assessment is irreversible. Furthermore, the absence of creditable public company management may prevent the company from attracting the attention and/or support of underwriters and other finance professionals critical for it to succeed. The old saying "Don't bet on the horse—bet on the jockey!" is critical here. A superior management team can take an average product or situation and make it successful. A mediocre management team can take a great product and manage it to mediocrity. Additionally, the management team of a public company has significantly different responsibilities. It must deal with growth as well as all the external third parties, such as credit analysts, stockholders, financial analysts, and the like, looking in. It is commonplace for several key management positions to be revamped just prior to becoming a public company.

- **Growth (is there sustainable growth in the future?).** Investors look for both a record of consistently high growth and the potential for that growth to be sustained in the future. The growth rate often translates into a multiple by which the stock is valued. The higher the sustainable growth rate, the higher the multiple. This, of course, can lead to significant appreciation in the company's stock price and a much lower cost of capital for the company in the future.

- **Information systems (can the company provide timely and reliable information?).** A public company has to provide timely and reliable information to its investors and the public. If the systems are not capable of doing that, they need to be modified to do so.

- **Use of proceeds (do the proceeds provide the right amount of capital and for the right purposes?).** The size of an offering should not be dictated by how much the company can raise, but rather what the right amount is for the purposes intended. The intended purposes ultimately should be to provide more growth and higher future earnings, or the dilution related to the increased number of shares cannot be justified.

Is the Market Ready?

Markets constantly vary with an unending and unpredictable ebb and flow. And they do this quickly. If fact, I believe that the markets are admittedly emotional, and the moods of investors change from bullish to bearish and back again, to the consternation of everyone, including the experts. Investor acceptance of new companies is undoubtedly cyclical but not predictable. There is always a window of opportunity, and that window can close quickly. As you will see in Chapter 6, there lies significant execution risk inherent in any transition from a private to public company. Japan can invade North Korea; the Fed could go bankrupt; and any other piece of market-breaking news could occur, causing your transaction to fail—for reasons totally beyond your control. The market could have been ready when you initiated the going-public process but have changed during the process.

Advance Planning

Let us assume that you have evaluated all the facts and decided that the company and the markets are ready. You make the decision to go public in some fashion. One of the most critical steps is the planning. The earlier the steps in the process can be adequately planned for and dealt with, the better everyone and everything will be.

Advance planning needs to begin as early as possible in the process. This can mean anywhere from six months to three years in advance of the actual event. By paying attention to the early planning considerations, the cost and burden of the going-public event can be reduced and the company will have a much stronger image and generate long-term investor interest. Planning in this manner will end up paying dividends in the form of a stronger and more stable aftermarket, something every public company desires.

The first area that should be addressed comes under the heading of corporate housekeeping. (If you have been following the earlier chapters in this book, this stage may require less work than if the company and its management have not paid much attention to the following items.) Corporate housecleaning takes place from the time the decision to move forward is made and may not end until documents are filed with the SEC. Under corporate housekeeping, you should ask these questions:

- Does the company's capital structure need changing? Changing the corporate structure at this late date may involve significant tax implications and generally is done to simplify the capital structure in contemplation of functioning as a public company. Changes may involve reducing the classes of stock outstanding or retiring debt through a stock exchange.

- Do the company's articles of incorporation need to be modified to provide for an increase in the number of authorized shares? Additional authorized shares may be needed. It is better to issue them while the company is still private; otherwise, the issuance will require a stockholder vote.

- Should the stock be split (or reverse split) before the company goes public? Stock splits usually are done to improve the company's marketability and may be recommended by the company's advisors. The target stock price usually is between $10 and $20 per share; the number of shares is adjusted based on the company's projected valuation to arrive at that figure.

TIPS AND TECHNIQUES

While a stock split is a mechanical adjustment and does not change the underlying economics of ownership, try to explain that to stockholders who have just been the recipient of a reverse split and now hold far fewer shares than they originally did. Their economic ownership (percentage of total value) has not changed, but their perception of holding fewer shares is a nightmare to overcome.

- Should a group of affiliated companies be combined? A public company generally is organized as a single entity, perhaps with subsidiaries. Affiliated but stand-alone companies are a negative, and the public wants to see this structure united under the parent.

- Are the company's stock records adequate and accurate? Proper records are a must for a public company and may require cleanup in advance of the going-public transaction.

- Are the company's transactions or arrangements with owners and management appropriate? Public markets have different standards. Often situations that exist in private companies must be modified as part of the going-public process to a more acceptable form or structure. Usually this modification can be accomplished with a legal audit of such items as:

  - Employment contracts
  - Stock option plans
  - Debt and lease arrangements

- Shareholder or management loans

- Rights of first refusal

- Charter and bylaws

- Major supply contracts

- Have all major contracts and employment agreements been put in writing? Do they need to be amended?

- Does management possess sufficient depth and experience for a public company, especially in the new Sarbanes-Oxley litigious environment?

It is also never too soon to begin cultivating relationships with professional advisors who can help the company and its management succeed. Professional advisors include:

- **Investment bankers.** Start courting the bankers early in the company's history so that they can develop a familiarity with the company. In Chapter 6, we describe the selection process, which is an art in and of itself.

- **Board of directors.** In a private company, the board is less important. As the company prepares to be a public entity, however, board composition is another measure of the competence and professionalism of the company and its readiness to operate in the public fishbowl. Directors should be selected who have specific skill sets, including:

  - Industry knowledge

  - Financial expertise (in fact, the audit committee has to have an individual designated as a financial expert to meet current listing requirements)

- Capital contacts to help the company raise future capital more easily

- Good business sense

The board should be viewed as a means to help guide the company to success, although the actual responsibility for day-to-day management rests with the management team.

- **Insurance advisors.** One of the criteria to attract board members is the presence of adequate and well-placed D&O (directors and officers) insurance. The absence of such insurance will make it more difficult, if not impossible, to attract qualified board members. To ensure the insurance is a good program, the company will need good insurance agents, not just order takers.

- **Compensation experts.** One of the drivers of attracting quality management is the presence of adequate and well-planned compensation strategies that involve the utilization of compensation experts.

The last part of advance planning revolves around the development (and communication) of a sound business plan. A sound business plan is an invaluable management tool that can be used in a variety of ways. At a minimum, business plans need to be well written and are used to:

- Set the goals and objectives for the company's performance. It is here that strategic planning really begins. The business plan should be used as a tool to set the direction of the company over a three-year period. It serves as a road map to identify the action steps and processes to guide the company. Often entrepreneurs in this stage complain that daily execution leaves little room for planning.

IN THE REAL WORLD

While managerial personnel often feel the pressure of time limitations, you must reflect on the question: What do I spend most of my time doing? If you are an upper-level manager, you should be spending the majority of your working hours in the areas of planning and setting policy. In a survey of Fortune 500 chief executives conducted years ago, these executives responded that they allocated the largest segment of their time to long-range planning and setting policy. Still, many wished that they had even more time for long-range planning.

- Develop and document milestones along the business's path to success. Often entrepreneurs cannot see the forest for the trees. A business plan can provide the entire management team with an objective basis for determining whether the business is on track.

- Provide the basis for internal and external communication. The company's story must be told and retold to both insiders and external sources, such as investors, stockholders, lenders, and analysts. As a public company, the most important part of the story is the future, not the past. The past serves to enable others to determine whether your future story is creditable. If you have not been able to achieve your plans to date, what can make anyone think you will do so in the future? The business plan serves as both the history and the future that enable third parties to evaluate how realistic the business plan is.

- Summarize the future financial information, which consists of financial projections for the next several (three) years. That enables the reader of the business plan to see where you are headed.

It is important to develop the business plan and the related forecasts, but those forecasts will not be shared with the investing public. They really serve as an internal road map.

Summary

After having finished this chapter, you should now be aware of:

- What it means to be a public company
- The benefits of being a public company
- The drawbacks and disadvantages of being a public company
- Some of the major decisions/questions that you must make/answer with your management team to determine whether the time is right to make that historic leap (sometimes known as "One small step for a man, one giant leap for mankind").

You have considered the facts and have decided to proceed. How do you accomplish the transition from private company to public company? We examine the processes in Chapter 6.

Entering the Public Markets Conventionally

After reading this chapter, you will be able to:

- Understand one of the most common ways in which a transition can occur from being a private company to a public company.
- Understand the enormous amount of work and time that is involved in that process.

Formal Process: Underwriting

The most direct (and often the best) method of going public is through an underwriting. This is the pathway that is the traditional initial public offering (IPO). It is exhaustive and expensive but often can provide the best results for a seasoned company. In an underwritten offering, the investment bankers (underwriters) agree to purchase shares of stock from the company at a price to be determined. The company goes through a process of registration with the Securities and Exchange Commission (SEC), and once the registration is filed, the company goes on a road show to create interest in the company and the stock. At the end of the road show, when the registration statement is deemed effective, the offering is priced. If the price is acceptable to the company, the deal gets priced (done). The following day, the company's stock starts trading and the excitement starts. Three days later, the company receives the proceeds from the underwriter of the initial offering. That is a very brief discussion of the process. Now let us look at the details of the process and identify all the minefields and how to avoid them.

Who Gets Involved?

The ultimate responsibility for going public falls on the shoulders of the company (and quite probably the person reading this book). Ultimately, however, the success of an offering depends on a concentrated team effort. The team includes:

- Company executives
- Auditors
- Attorneys
- Underwriters

- Investor/public relations firm
- The financial printer (last but not least)

You also have another team member over which you have no control: the SEC. Let us examine each team member's role and contribution.

Company Executives

Company executives obviously play a pivotal role in the entire process once the decision has been made to proceed. That decision does not end their involvement; it really only intensifies it. The principal involvement will fall on the chief executive officer and the financial team, but a large number of executives from across all disciplines will play an important role and have serious time-consuming involvement. They will be spending a considerable amount of time meeting with attorneys, underwriters, financial press, and others during the process and especially during the due diligence conducted by the underwriters.

IN THE REAL WORLD

The amount of time that company executives will devote to this process cannot be overemphasized. Due diligence meetings, drafting sessions, and road shows all require intensive and concentrated time commitment. Jokes are often made as to who is running the company while the company goes public since it is obvious that no one is left back in the office. This is a truism. The company needs a strong management team so that the daily operations can be delegated to others during this extended and painful process.

Executives will meet with auditors, attorneys, and underwriters to plan the entire process and timetable. This initial meeting (often called the all-hands organization meeting) can involve 16 or more people and take the better part of a day; it includes the allocation of responsibilities and deadlines. This meeting is critical because of the large amount of legal, financial, and operational information that must be accumulated and included in the registration statement (which is discussed later in this chapter).

 TIPS AND TECHNIQUES

The key to any successful undertaking is planning. Careful and thorough planning during the organizational meeting may make the difference between a successful process and a failed process. Due dates have to be established *and met.* The entire process is dependent on each piece getting completed when scheduled. Detailed planning increases the chance of success.

Auditors

Auditors play a significant role in this complex process. If the company does not already have an auditor and audited financial statements, it is starting the going-public process from behind the proverbial 8–ball. These financial statements will become the backbone of the financial disclosure material included in the process. The auditors will also play a key role in responding to SEC questions during the process, and they will have to provide comfort letters to underwriters on a variety of information contained in the offering documents and registration statement. Their comfort is a part of the due diligence performed by the underwriters, which is why it is so important; without their being satisfied by their due diligence efforts, the offering will be impossible to complete.

Having an experienced auditor is of critical importance, especially one who is qualified to do business with the SEC. It is not unusual for underwriters to request that auditors provide negative assurance regarding the accuracy of information (i.e, "comfort") that is beyond the purview of the financial system. If these requests are made, the underwriters have to be told "No!" Auditors need to be able to focus on the information they are comfortable in providing—which is generally financial information.

Attorneys

Attorneys play a critical and extensive role in helping execute the public offering. Their primary responsibility is to assist you in complying with all the applicable federal and state securities laws and regulations. Because of the highly complex nature of securities law, it is critically important to select a firm with broad experience in securities law.

If your law firm (which has been serving the company well over time) does not have the expertise to deal with securities laws, it is not necessary to terminate that relationship. It is not uncommon for a public company to have a law firm that handles its general corporate matters and another firm that strictly handles securities matters. That may be the most desirable way to proceed, depending on the company's relationship with its law firm(s).

As part of their responsibilities, the attorneys will have to review all your existing contractual obligations and ascertain whether amendments to the articles of incorporation are necessary. They will perform the laborious task of drafting the registration statement (which includes the offering documents or prospectus) and coordinating all correspondence with the SEC. You will rely heavily on their involvement, work, and counsel. Be advised that it is not an inexpensive endeavor.

Underwriters

Underwriters play the central role in actually selling your offering and completing the going-public process. (Later in this chapter, we discuss how to select an underwriter.) The managing underwriter has the primary responsibility for determining the initial price of the shares to be sold. This firm performs the function of coordinating the overall offering process and keeping the "order books" as the offering proceeds. This is why the managing underwriter is often referred to as the "book runner" and manages the process with the other co-managers. Some underwriting firms are just part of the selling syndicate. They have the distribution channels, contacts, and experience to reach a much broader group of investors, lend more credibility to the offering, and target investors for whom your company may have a specific appeal. Underwriters also have a primary responsibility for maintaining a strong aftermarket for your securities. (An underwriting firm's ability in this area is considered during the selection process.)

IN THE REAL WORLD

Unfortunately, there are a multitude of investment banker jokes, all characterizing them as high-priced prostitutes. However, I have been able to develop relationships with several bankers who are serious and professional and whose reputation is above reproach. That has been accomplished over a 40-year career dealing with the Street. They are out there—you just have to find them. They will serve your company the best.

Public Relations/Investor Relations Firm

The public relations/investor relations (PR/IR) firm will play a critical role in the aftermarket. Because of the quiet period imposed by the SEC prior to the offering, this firm may not be a major participant in the going-public process.

Having a public company that is a well-kept secret (and one whose stock trades by appointment only) will not benefit the company. That is where the PR/IR firm comes into play. It is this firm's job to help the company get its story out to the financial investing public, consisting of both individual retail investors and institutional funds that take large positions in public companies.

The PR/IR firm needs to be part of the process so it understands the company's story from day one and can hit the ground running as soon as the quiet period ends.

The best way to select an PR/IR firm (and there may be one for investor relations and a separate one for public relations, since they cater to different audiences) is by reputation, which comes from recommendations. You should ask for recommendations from your investment bankers, your lawyers, and other public companies with whom you may have a relationship.

Financial Printer

The selection of a financial printer is a seemingly a mundane issue. Rest assured, it is not. An experienced (customer service–driven) printer contributes to the timeliness and efficiency of the registration process as well as the periodic filings necessary once the company becomes public. Significant time demands are placed on the printer in the final stages of the registration process; revised drafts may be required on a same-day basis, and the prospectus is printed the night before the registration statement becomes effective.

There are big financial printer firms (such as Bowne and RR Donnelly) and smaller, less expensive firms (such as Vintage Filings). Consider this decision carefully, and base it on the recommendations of others. The printing bill can be one of the single largest costs of going public. This is another place to exercise due care.

I believe that the choice of a financial printer should be driven by relationships. Over 16 years and four public companies, I have used three different printers but only one customer service representative. I follow him wherever the printing business may take him because he gives me service and makes sure the job gets done to my satisfaction and to my time requirements.

SEC

As you will see later in this chapter, the final step in the process before you become a public company is to receive clearance from the SEC. The SEC is not responsible for evaluating or regulating the quality of securities offered to the public. Rather, the SEC attempts to protect the public interest by ensuring that adequate information is provided to prospective and current investors to allow them to properly evaluate their investment decisions and the quality of your securities.

There are two principal acts by which securities law is administered:

1. The 1933 Act (also known as the Truth in Securities Act) has two primary requirements:

   a. It requires most companies to register public offerings of securities with the SEC before they are sold to the public.

   b. It contains provisions that impose civil and criminal liabilities on persons preparing registration statements that, when effective, contain a material misstatement or omission. This act is of extreme importance to executives. We discussed exemptions from the 1933 Act in Chapter 3 when we talked about private placements. We also emphasized that exemption from registration does not exempt you from the antifraud provisions of the 1933 Act in making false disclosures.

2. The 1934 Act also has two purposes:

a. To prevent unfair practices in securities markets

b. To provide for regular periodic reporting

Underwriting the Offering

As we described briefly at the beginning of this chapter, the underwriting process is involved and can take as long as nine months, depending on the SEC. There have been instances where a company was in the registration process for over two years. That is why I always talk about the execution risk inherent in an offering of this nature.

Selecting Underwriters

Selecting the managing underwriter (and the rest of the co-managers) is a key step toward a successful IPO. Reputation of the firm may be a key factor in selecting an underwriter for a small firm, as are many other factors. One of the first steps is for a company to look in the mirror and do an evaluation of itself as it is today and of its future plans. Where will the company be geographically (that may influence the selection of a regional underwriter as opposed to one with a national scope)? Is the industry very specialized, and are there underwriters who focus on that industry? Is the company sufficiently developed to attract a specific underwriter's interest? You may have an interest in engaging a specific firm, but that firm may have absolutely no interest in your company. Selection is always a two-way street. Do not forget: Underwriters get paid only if the offering is a success. They will not want to expend their time, energy, and money unless they are confident that sufficient interest exists in your company.

When you begin to approach candidates, make sure you have that well-developed business plan we have discussed throughout this book. Otherwise, you will not attract serious interest. The presentation of the business plan and company story (usually in a PowerPoint slide show format) also indicates to prospective underwriters how well company executives can communicate the story and gives an early indication of how they might perform on a road show.

After you have been through this abbreviated process, you should develop a list of potential firms to meet with and pitch the deal. The criteria for which firms should be put on the list include:

- **Reputation.** Prospective investors consider the reputation of your managing underwriter, which sometimes can overshadow the merits of the deal itself. If the managing underwriter is well respected, he or she will be able to form a strong syndicate that will increase the probability of success for the offering and for support in the aftermarket. Underwriters earn this reputation by providing top-quality service to their clients.

- **Experience.** The underwriting firm should have direct experience in underwriting IPOs as well as in the type of security you intend to offer. Also, experience in your specific industry is critical when it comes down to pricing the offering.

- **Syndication and distribution capability.** Depending on the size of the offering, does the underwriting firm have the capability to deliver? A broad distribution will provide your stock a larger market, and will also avoid having the ownership concentrated in just a few customers. The underwriters should have a blend of both retail and institutional clients to provide you both types of ownership.

- **Aftermarket support.** This is a critical element of any successful offering. It does the company absolutely no good to have a successful offering at $10.00 per share and then watch the price wither because there is no aftermarket support from both a pricing and volume standpoint.

- **Research capability.** While research has always been theoretically separated from investment banking (by the proverbial Chinese Wall) so that one department doesn't influence the other department, there is an even greater Chinese Wall today as a result of the frauds of the early 2000s and the recent financial crisis. Now research efforts truly are separated from investment banking efforts. Does the underwriting firm have the capability to provide written research on your company at the appropriate time? Such research coverage will broaden the interest in your stock and help the aftermarket activity, as well as provide additional credibility for the company.

- **Continuing financial advisory services.** The underwriting firm should have the resources to provide the company with ongoing investment banking services, advice on proposed mergers and acquisitions, and a full range of advisory services.

- **Cost.** The cost of an IPO can be substantial; however, this should not be a primary driver of the underwriter selection. Fees charged by underwriters are usually standard and fixed.

Depending on how many firms are on your initial list, you and your team should obviously narrow the selection. Some of the narrowing may have been done for you by virtue of firms telling you that they are not interested because you do not meet their specifications. Do not be offended—it is a two-way street. However, the next step is to come up with a short list of approximately six firms to be invited to make in-person presentations.

Beauty Contest

The final step is what I refer to as the beauty contest. The final group of underwriting firms should be invited to make formal presentations to the company's board of directors, who make the final selection. Having such a beauty contest enables potential underwriters to present their credentials with the actual representatives from the underwriting firm who will be servicing the company. Board members can ask relevant questions and obtain a feeling about how well each firm will represent the company's interests. The final selection becomes a decision of the board of directors, which is appropriate, considering the importance of the decision to the company.

Beauty contests can be very surprising. It has been my experience that the favorites often stumble and dark horses emerge as favorites during them. One company that I took public was headquartered in Florida. The six finalists were to come to Los Angeles, where the board meeting was being conducted. One firm had managed to leverage its way into the process on the Friday before the Monday board meeting, based on its relationship with one venture capital firm backing the company—clearly this firm was a very dark horse. One firm paged me on Sunday night and advised me that it was bowing out of the process because its flight had been canceled and there was no way that its team could arrive in time. I told the caller to make the presentation to the board by telephone and fax me the presentation. What was the outcome? The last-minute firm was selected as the lead underwriter because of the quality of its presentation, its team, and its knowledge of the industry. The firm that was not there in person was selected as one of the two co-managers because of the quality of its presentation and team—despite the fact the team was not even in the room. (I have a relationship with the winning banker to this day, despite his travels through numerous other firms.) This is a perfect example of not counting your chickens before they are hatched. Never take anything for granted, and always have the beauty contest.

Working with Underwriters

Once the selection has been made, you will be working very closely with the underwriter for a long and intense period of time and, it is hoped, well into the future.

The first formal contract with the underwriter is a letter of intent. (Go to www.wiley.com/go/capitalformation for an example letter of intent.) The actual contractual arrangement between the company and the underwriter is contained in the underwriting agreement, but that is not signed until the day of pricing. It is a lengthy document that is reviewed by the company's counsel and the underwriter's counsel. There is no legal obligation to complete the offering until that agreement is signed, which is generally why it is signed the day of pricing.

The letter of intent (which is generally signed by the underwriter and the company) details the agreed-on underwriter's commission, range of offering price (maybe), and other negotiated terms of the offering. It is not a binding obligation for the offering to be completed, but its existence may obligate the company to pay certain expenses if the offering plans are terminated.

There are generally two types of offerings: a firm commitment and best efforts.

Under a firm commitment underwriting agreement, the underwriter agrees to purchase all the shares in the offering and then resell them to the public. All shares not resold to the public are still paid for by the underwriter and held for its own account. Hence, the term "firm commitment." This form of agreement provides the company with the most assurance of raising the required funds and is the form generally used.

Also included with a firm commitment is an overallotment option (sometimes referred to as a green shoe). This option generally allows the underwriter to purchase up to 15% additional shares at the agreed-on price for a period of 30 days. It allows the underwriter to

IN THE REAL WORLD

The reference to firm commitment and best efforts is confusing. A firm commitment underwriting agreement is the best but still does not provides a guaranty that funds will be raised. Since the agreement generally is not signed until the day of pricing, the underwriter does not really commit until it is assured of completion. Consequently, it assumes no risk in such a proposition. However, an underwriter would not propose a firm commitment underwriting unless it had a high degree of confidence in completing the transaction.

have more shares if the offering is very successful (and also provides more capital to the company).

Under a best efforts underwriting, the underwriter agrees to use its best efforts to sell up to $XX of securities. There is no assurance that they will raise the desired amount of capital, hence the term "best efforts."

Viewed another way, a firm commitment is really all or nothing; a best effort may enable the company to raise some capital, but usually a minimum amount must be raised before escrow can be broken and funds released to the company.

Pricing is another variable that cannot be guaranteed. Pricing is not finalized until just before the registration becomes effective, because the pricing has to be reactive to market conditions, which include how well the offering was received by the market. Although a range is estimated for the offering, it is never finalized until the order book is filled. Initially, the range is estimated based on comparables with other companies in the same business and industry and on price-earnings ratios. Rest assured, pricing an offering is an art, not a science; often emotions have to be removed from the experience.

For example, if a company is trying to sell 3 million shares at an estimated range of between $10.00 to $12.00 per share, the underwriter will attempt to fill its book with 15 million shares of orders. This causes the pricing to become firm. Because every purchaser will be cut back, it ensures that there will be an active aftermarket. If the order book is even stronger, the underwriter may raise the price and/ or increase the shares in the offering, subject to the company's agreement. The pricing of the deal is a very fluid situation, which can go the other way as well. Orders may be weak, forcing a reduction in the price and/or a reduction in the number of shares ultimately being sold. In one case, the company may receive more capital than expected (or needed), and in the other, the company may receive less, creating other problems.

 TIPS AND TECHNIQUES

It is not uncommon for emotions to run high and explode at the pricing meeting. Executives have been known to shout expletives at the bankers over a $0.50 issue in pricing. Remember four things:

❶ You elected to go through this process after a careful and thorough analysis.

❷ Besides wanting to be public, your company needs the money.

❸ It was usually anticipated (until the problems of 2007 to 2009) that the initial trading following a pricing would result in at least a 15% uptick in the trading price from the offering price.

❹ Investors who made money on the IPO will remember that and be there the next time the company needs money with open checkbooks. *Do not lose sight of this fact!*

The underwriting commission (or discount) is generally the largest single expense of the offering; however, printing and accounting and legal bills are not inconsequential. The range of standard commissions charged is approximately 6% to 10%. Factors influencing this discount rate include whether it is a firm commitment and the anticipated marketability of the shares. Occasionally the underwriter will request additional compensation in the form of warrants. This is more common with smaller deals and smaller underwriters. It is not usually the case with more established underwriters. If warrants are included, make sure the number and exercise price are agreed to in advance and in writing.

The way the underwriting commission is shared has not always been straightforward. In fact, it more resembles rocket science. Exhibit 6.1 is a chart demonstrating the distribution of the gross spread (underwriting commission) on one deal from my past. If this is not convoluted, nothing is!

Underwriters often request reimbursement of their out-of-pocket expenses. This is not uncommon and does make the going-public process even more expensive, because the typical expenses for which reimbursement is sought are legal expenses. Underwriters'

EXHIBIT 6.1

Chart of Distribution of Gross Spread in a Typical Transaction

BREAKDOWN OF GROSS SPREAD

Gross Spread

Management Fee
(20% of Spread)
Paid to banking departments
of managing underwriters

- Equal
- Unequal

Selling Concession
(60% of Spread)
Sales of commission paid to stock
brokers who sell ** the stock

Underwriting Concession
(20% of Spread)
Pays expenses of syndicate*
Net, if any, remitted of underwriters in
proportion of shares underwritten**

Managing Underwriters
(Approx. 40% of all shares)

Syndicate Members
(Approx. 60% of all shares)

Retail / Free Retention
(Approx. 40% of all shares)

Managing Underwriters
(Approx. 30% of all shares)

Syndicate Members
(Approx. 10% of all shares)

Institutional Pot
(Approx. 60% of all shares)
Shares sold by managing underwriters to U.S. and foreign
institutions

- "Friendly"
- "Competitive"
- Hybrid

* Roadshow, Travel and Entertainment, Legal, Stock Stabilization vary.
**Shares sold generally substantially from shares underwritten

counsels are usually larger firms, thereby increasing the overall expense.

In a public offering (which is what we are talking about here), the underwriter's commission is usually standard. In a private placement, as discussed earlier, the placement agent's fees generally can run 10-10-3, which translates to a 10% cash commission, 10% of the shares sold issued as shares or warrants, and a 3% unaccountable expense allowance (which usually works out to be additional commission).

Another standard request in dealing with underwriters is a right of first refusal on future financings. Although this request may seem innocuous, it can adversely affect the company's ability to conduct a future financing. The reason is that a different underwriter may not be interested in taking the company on as a client if it knows its role can be usurped by an existing obligation to another underwriter.

If a right of first refusal cannot be avoided, you should consider negotiating a time limit after which that right expires *or* a provision that the right expires any time it is available but not exercised.

Registration Process

The registration process begins, as far as the SEC is concerned, when you have reached a preliminary understanding with an underwriter on the proposed public offering. This is important, as once the process begins, the company is in a quiet period and is subject to SEC regulations on what may or may not be done to promote the company.

The registration process, therefore, technically begins with the organization meeting. This is the all-hands meeting discussed earlier.

From the conclusion of that meeting onward, the company is in registration and has to be especially mindful of what it does; there are strict prohibitions on its ability to promote itself during the registration period. This prohibition is to avoid the practice of priming the pump and jumping the market in anticipation of an offering.

From a timing perspective, the process from this meeting to closing can be as short as several months to as long as years. This fact underscores the need for intensive planning and cooperation among the company, accountants/auditors, lawyers, underwriters, and printer.

The primary focus, in terms of effort, will be in the preparation of the registration statement for filing with the SEC. Registration statements are legal documents comprised of two parts. Part I consists of the prospectus (or offering circular) that is widely distributed to underwriters and potential investors as the selling document. Part II contains additional information that is required by and provided to the SEC. The entire registration statement (like all filings with the SEC) becomes part of the public record and is available for inspection.

The rules have been liberalized over recent years to make it easier to raise capital, but the registration statement that most IPOs will use is Form S-1. The SEC's intent and modus operandi has been to streamline the disclosure rules for already seasoned public companies to access capital markets rapidly. However, since IPOs typically involve companies that have never been subject to public scrutiny, the entire process is much more involved.

Typical information requirements of a Form S-1 include (a copy of an S-1 is included on www.wiley.com/go/capitalformation):

Part I—Information Required in Prospectus

Item 1. Forepart of the Registration Statement and Outside Front Cover Page of Prospectus

Item 2. Inside Front and Outside Back Cover Pages of Prospectus

Item 3. Summary Information, Risk Factors, and Ratio of Earnings to Fixed Charges

Item 4. Use of Proceeds

Item 5. Determination of Offering Price

Item 6. Dilution

Item 7. Selling Security Holders

Item 8. Plan of Distribution

Item 9. Description of Securities to Be Registered

Item 10. Interests of Named Experts and Counsel

Item 11. Information with Respect to the Registrant

Item 11A. Material Changes

Item 12. Incorporation of Certain Information by Reference

Item 12A. Disclosure of Commission Position on Indemnification for Securities Act Liabilities

Part II—Information Not Required in Prospectus

Item 13. Other Expenses of Issuance and Distribution

Item 14. Indemnification of Directors and Officers

Item 15. Recent Sales of Unregistered Securities

Item 16. Exhibits and Financial Statement Schedules

Item 17. Undertakings

Due to the legal nature of this document, attorneys are heavily involved with its preparation. There are also several important SEC rules and registration that govern what is included. These rules are Regulation S-X, which governs the form and content of financial statements, and Regulation S-K, which governs disclosures not related to the financial statements.

As you can see, the SEC requirements are highly technical and change frequently. Consequently, most companies rely on their attorneys to prepare most of the document. The company is heavily involved, because usually there are regular drafting sessions where the entire team of accountants, attorneys, and underwriters meet to review the document in process and make changes to fit the company's story.

IN THE REAL WORLD

It has been my experience that weekly drafting sessions occur until the registration statement is sufficiently drafted so the next stage can commence. Imagine weekly, all-day meetings with 16 people in a conference room reviewing the text of the registration statement and suggesting changes to clarify, emphasize, and otherwise change the story. It represents a heavy expenditure of time and money but is truly necessary.

As the process unfolds, two conflicting purposes become painfully apparent regarding the prospectus part of the registration statement.

1. The prospectus (because it is distributed to every potential investor/purchaser) is used as a selling document by the underwriters in forming the syndicate. Therefore, everyone will be posturing to make this part of the document as glowing and upbeat as possible.

2. The prospectus is used as a disclosure document, which serves as protection against any liability under the 1933 Act for misleading and omitted financial information on the part of the company, its executives, and the underwriters. Consequently, everyone is interested in ensuring the document has complete and *candid* disclosure, which may not be that flowery.

Balancing these conflicting views is accomplished through reliance on the attorneys and the underwriters. Rest assured that while the final document may not paint as flowery a picture as desired, the underwriters and potential investors are accustomed to this type of required disclosure. As I mentioned previously, if a potential investor read all the risk factors in any offering document or prospectus, there would be no investment made.

Due Diligence

"Due diligence" is a term heard throughout the registration process. This is the process by which the underwriter and its counsel conduct a reasonable investigation that will support the belief that the statements made in the registration statement are true and do not omit any information necessary to make them not misleading.

Under the 1933 Act, a company is absolutely liable, regardless of due diligence, for any material misstatements or omissions in the registration statement. Consequently, as part of the due diligence process (and because the documents have to be filed as exhibits to the registration statement), every document and contract and agreement will be read and compared to its description in the registration statement. Site visits might be conducted by a whole tour group consisting of company representatives, attorneys, and investment bankers. This stage is also time consuming and involves significant expense.

IN THE REAL WORLD

Be prepared for this part of the process. In one IPO with which I was involved that included 25 acquisitions, a whole week was devoted to a coast-to-coast tour of facilities. I was the tour guide with 11 people in tow.

As part of its due diligence, the underwriter typically requires that auditors provide the "comfort letter" mentioned earlier. A comfort letter is lengthy and involves the accountants performing agreed-upon procedures to various unaudited information in the registration statement so that they can give negative assurance regarding its accuracy (i.e., "nothing came to their attention that would lead them to believe the information was inaccurate"). While this is part of the overall due diligence, it is not delivered until the end of the process (i.e., as of the effective date and then again at the closing.) During the early stages, the letter is drafted and shared with the underwriter for comment and agreement. During the drafting stage of the registration statement, the underwriter identifies items for which it will seek comfort, some of which will not be given by the accountants.

Filing and the SEC

Once the registration statement is completed, it is filed with the SEC. The SEC then has 30 days in which to review the registration statement and provide comments to be addressed in a revision. This is where some of the execution risk occurs. The SEC generally takes 30 to 45 days to provide a comment letter. Depending on the nature and extent of comments, the review process could take months before the registration statement can be deemed and declared effective, resulting in the actual sale of the securities. The company and counsel have no control over this process.

IN THE REAL WORLD

The preparation of the registration statement can take months, depending on how complex the company is, how well it has prepared with audits and documentation, and how fast the attorneys can draft. One company I took public that made 25 acquisitions in its first year of operations started the drafting process in April (i.e., organization meeting and entering the quiet period) and filed its first draft of the registration statement in mid-September.

Also, the review by the SEC may take several amendments. In one situation with which I was involved, the first comment letter (received after 45 days) had more than 70 comments. By the time we were able to address the comments and file the amendment, our financial statements in the registration statement went stale. They had to be updated, and then the underwriter insisted that the nine-month stub period be audited. The second comment letter we received had more than 30 comments. The last comment letter we received had 4 comments. We filed the registration statement initially on September 16 and finally went effective on February 4 of the following year, just 11 days before the nine-month stub audited amounts went stale, which would have required the annual December 31 financial statements to be audited before we could have completed the offering—at least a 45- to 60-day delay!

When the comment letter is received, attorneys, accountants, and company personnel should take a day to digest the comments. Some will be mundane, some will be archaic, some will be ludicrous, some will indicate a clear lack of understanding of the company or the business, and some will be significant. The one-day cooling-off period is necessary to let the emotions run and be prepared to respond rationally. (Go to www.wiley.com/go/capitalformation for a sample comment letter and responses.)

The next step is to gather the attorneys, accountants, and company personnel together and go through the letter comment by comment, discussing the meaning of each one and the best way to respond, and assigning responsibilities. Some responses will best be drafted by the company, some best by the attorneys, and some best by the accountants. The attorneys will also be charged with the responsibility of modifying the registration statement to consider the comments. Assign deadlines by which comments must be back, or the process will drag on forever.

Once the process is complete and the attorneys are confident that no outstanding issues could result in what is called a recirculation, the preliminary prospectus is ready to be printed, and the road show is scheduled. The preliminary prospectus is also referred to as a red herring because of the red print down the left-hand side, indicating that it is preliminary and subject to completion. The price ranges on the cover are blank and are not filled in until pricing is agreed to and the pricing amendment is filed.

A recirculation issue is a material item of disclosure in the registration statement (and also in the preliminary prospectus that is distributed to prospective investors) with which the SEC has a serious disagreement. This can be disclosure or accounting issues. If the road show is conducted and the SEC determines that a material item has to be revised, it will require that the registration statement be amended and the prospectuses reprinted and recirculated to everyone who received an earlier prospectus. This time-consuming issue may cause investors to walk away from the deal.

TIPS AND TECHNIQUES

Because of tight time frames, it is not uncommon for preliminary prospectuses to be printed before discussions with the SEC are totally complete. However, if any outstanding issues could be considered "recirc" issues, the company is taking a huge risk. The attorneys usually can advise whether an outstanding issue is significant enough to be a recirc issue. If any are, my advice is to wait until they are resolved to the satisfaction of the SEC before printing the preliminary prospectus and conducting the road show. Basically, if there is a recirc issue after or during the road show, the deal is dead (DOA), and a lot of time, expense, and energy will have been flushed down a drain.

Completing the Offering

The underwriter schedules a road show that lasts approximately two weeks. It is the marketing for the deal as allowed by the SEC. Company representatives can discuss and present only what is contained in the prospectus. Nothing that has not been disclosed in the document can be discussed with prospective investors.

A typical road show starts in Europe (which serves as a good rehearsal stage), then moves to California and starts working its way east to conclude in Boston and New York. Typically, it lasts two full weeks with a day in each city and meetings that start at breakfast and last until evening when the plane leaves for the next city. (Take carry-on luggage only, please.)

During the road show, the syndicate is forming and orders are being taken for the offering. The managing underwriter (who is running the book) accumulates all the orders and, based on the reaction in the market, decides on the appropriate pricing for the deal on the last day in conjunction with the co-managers. Then the company is advised of the pricing. If the company accepts the pricing and agrees to it, the underwriting agreement (now binding) is signed. (See an example underwriting agreement on www.wiley.com/go/capital formation.) The company's stock starts trading the next day, to the delight of everyone.

The company and the attorneys have to prepare an amendment to the registration statement reflecting the pricing, changing all the uses of proceeds to reflect actual amounts, and file the pricing amendment and print the completed prospectus, which has to be delivered to all purchasers.

Three days after pricing, the deal closes, and the company receives the net proceeds after the accountants deliver an updated comfort letter for the three-day period since pricing (often referred to as the bring-down letter, so named because it brings the original comfort letter current to closing).

Then a huge closing dinner is scheduled to celebrate a lot of hard work and a successful process of raising capital, as well as a milestone event in the company's history.

The closing dinner is viewed as a celebratory event at which much fun is had. Generally, company executives roast the bankers, lawyers, and accountants and present gag gifts and a goofy PowerPoint slide show. The bankers roast everyone. It is wise to keep a little notebook through the entire process to keep track of all the embarrassing and funny incidents that took place so they can be "memorialized" at the closing dinner.

Expenses

Now that the exuberance has died down and the company's coffers are full, it must pay the expenses of the offering. At closing, the underwriter's commission (and any direct expenses agreed to) is deducted from the proceeds received by the company. Now the company has to pay:

- Its attorneys
- Underwriter's attorneys
- Accountants
- Printer
- Its own expenses for the road show

These are not small bills. I have had accounting and legal bills run in excess of $1 million, plus a printing bill of $500,000. The size of the expenses is directly related to how complex the registration statement and the company were to describe, the efficiency of the audits, and the number of revisions to printed documents and amendments to the registration statement.

The expense of going public (as I have mentioned earlier) is not small. Consequently, the company must have an excellent reason for doing so. Capital needs are one. Because of the expenses, the amount of capital raised should not be less than $25 million. A strong desire to be public is another that has to be justified by the reasons for the desire. Going public clearly is not for the faint of heart.

Summary

Now you have reviewed the important steps in the most common ways of becoming a public company, which involves the underwriting process and the assistance of company executives, auditors, attorneys, underwriters, a financial printer, and others, as well as a significant investment in time and money.

Now that you understand the processes of going public the conventional way (as well as how expensive it is), we examine some lower-cost alternatives in Chapter 7.

The Public Markets– Other Issues

After reading this chapter, you will be able to:

- Understand several alternative ways in which a transition can occur from being a private company to a public company.
- Compare these alternative methods to the traditional initial public offering.
- Select the best alternative for your company based on all the facts.
- Learn some tried and true tips on operating a public company.

Reverse Merger (Shell Game)

One of the alternatives to a traditional initial public offering (IPO) that has been employed for decades is the reverse merger. To understand the attraction of a reverse merger, you have to understand the concept of shell companies. Shell companies are critical to your ability to complete a reverse merger.

A shell corporation (or shell company) is a company that has no significant assets or operations. In and of itself, this is not illegal. Most shell companies are created in one of two ways.

1. The existing public company ceases its operations by virtue of (1) the sale/acquisition of its assets or (2) a bankruptcy filing, which concludes with the company having no assets other than its corporate shell (hence the name shell company). Despite its having no assets, it is still capable of trading on an exchange or on the Over-the-Counter ("OTC") Bulletin Board or pink sheets. It is this characteristic that gives it value.

2. A shell corporation can be formed by its promoters filing a Form 10 under the 1934 Act. A Form 10 is similar to a registration statement with respect to the information about the company that it contains. Because the filing is made on a Form 10 and under the 1934 Act, the company becomes a public reporting company that is required to file periodic reports with the Securities and Exchange Commission (SEC), but the stock has no place to trade, and the underlying shares of stock are not registered and cannot trade. It is merely a "reporting" company.

The first kind of shell is much more valuable, as it already is trading and shares are being purchased and sold. However, this kind of shell also brings with it skeletons in the closet. The going price for a trading shell can be $1 million in cash and a 10% carried interest. A nontrading shell is usually much cheaper, since it does not offer the advantage of having a trading history, but has the expenses of being a reporting company that still has to establish its shares for trading.

A Form 10 is a registration statement filed under the 1934 Act. Established companies (not just shells) can go public by filing a Form 10. In fact, depending on the company, it may be required to file a Form 10. For example, if a company has raised money through a series of private placements and, at the end of a fiscal year, has 500 stockholders and $10 million in total assets, it is required to file a Form 10, because it really has become a public company by virtue of its having so many shareholders. Although the investors cannot just trade the stock, the SEC wants them to be fully informed by requiring the filing of periodic reports.

Conversely, a company with established operations and fewer than 500 stockholders can file a Form 10 and become a public reporting company. However, doing this offers few advantages.

The information required on a Form 10 includes (see also the sample Form 10 on www.wiley.com/go/capitalformation):

Item 1. Business

Item 2. Financial Information

Item 3. Properties

Item 4. Security Ownership of Beneficial Owners and Management

Item 5. Directors and Executive Officers

Item 6. Executive Compensation

Item 7. Certain Relationships and Related Transactions

Item 8. Legal Proceedings

Item 9. Market Price of and Dividends on the Registrant's Common Equity and Related Stockholder Matters

Item 10. Recent Sales of Unregistered Securities

Item 11. Description of Registrant's Securities to Be Registered

Item 12. Indemnification of Officers and Directors

Item 13. Financial Statements and Supplementary Data

Item 14. Changes in and Disagreements with Accountants on Accounting and Financial Disclosure

Item 15. Financial Statements and Exhibits

From a practical standpoint, there is no immediate benefit for a company to go public through simply the filing of a Form 10. Going public in this way:

- Raises no capital
- Does not enable the company to trade any shares until it files a 1933 Act registration statement, which, as we have seen, takes time and money
- Subjects the company to required periodic reporting and increased expenses

Since there probably is not a good reason to going public via a Form 10 filing, let us examine the reverse merger route more closely.

Transaction Process

A reverse merger is the acquisition of a public company by a private company to bypass the lengthy, complex, and expensive process of going public through a traditional IPO as described in Chapter 6. The transaction usually requires reorganization of the capitalization of the acquiring company, and it is, in fact, accounted for as a recapitalization. In such a transaction, the shareholders of the private company (usually a very limited number) acquire control of the public shell company and then merge it with the private company. The private company shareholders receive a substantial majority of the shares of the public company and control of its board of directors. Because of the usual limited number of shareholders in the private company, this type of transaction can be completed in a number of weeks.

Consider this scenario: ABC is a public shell corporation with 1,000 stockholders and 25 million shares outstanding that is the remnants of a manufacturing company that sold off all its assets. It has limited trading and is controlled by one of its officers. DEF is a private biotechnology company that has 15 shareholders and desires to go public through a reverse merger with ABC. Prior to the merger, ABC does a 1:25 reverse stock split, leaving it with 1 million shares outstanding, and immediately issues 10 million shares to DEF shareholders in exchange for all of DEF's shares in DEF. The DEF shareholders will own 10/11 of ABC (approximately 90%), and the ABC shareholders are left with approximately 10% of ABC. While, legally, ABC acquired DEF, the shareholders of DEF really acquired ABC—hence the term "reverse merger."

Benefits

There are a number of benefits of having a public company status.

- The company may be able to command a higher price for a later offering of its securities.

- Going public through a reverse merger allows a privately held company to become publicly held at a lesser cost.

- Presumably, the change in status through a reverse merger can result in less stock dilution than through a traditional IPO.

- A reverse merger simplifies the process of going public and separates it from the act of raising capital. While raising capital is combined with going public in a traditional IPO, these two functions can be separated in a reverse merger transaction. A company can go public without raising additional capital.

- The company will be less susceptible to market conditions. Traditional IPOs have substantial execution risk, because the deal relies on market conditions, conditions over which senior management has little control. As we have already discussed, if the market is off, the underwriter may pull the offering. The market does not need to plunge dramatically for the offering to get pulled. If a company in registration is in an industry that is generating unfavorable headlines and falling out of investment favor, investors may shy away from the deal. In a reverse merger, since the deal rests solely between those controlling the public and private companies, market conditions have little bearing on the situation.

- A reverse merger may represent a more productive use of time by management. The process for a traditional IPO can last as long as a year or more. When a company transitions from an entrepreneurial venture to a public company fit for outside ownership, strategic managers can spend their time in beneficial or detrimental ways. Time spent in meetings and drafting sessions related to an IPO can have a disastrous effect on the growth upon which the offering is predicated and may even nullify such growth. In addition, during the many months it takes to put an IPO together, market conditions can deteriorate, making the completion of an IPO unfavorable. By contrast, a reverse merger can be completed in as few as 30 days.

- There are greater financing options, such as:
  - The issuance of additional stock in a secondary offering
  - An exercise of warrants, in which stockholders have the right to purchase additional shares in a company at predetermined prices; when many shareholders with warrants exercise their option to purchase additional shares, the company receives an infusion of capital
  - The increased likelihood of other investors to invest in a company via a private offering of stock when a mechanism to sell their stock is in place, should the company be successful
  - Increased liquidity of company stock
  - Higher company valuation due to a higher share price
  - Greater access to capital markets
  - Ability to acquire other companies through stock transactions (i.e., different currency)
  - Ability to use stock incentive plans to attract and retain employees

Taint

Reverse mergers always come with some history and some shareholders. Sometimes this history can be bad and manifest itself in the form of sloppy records, pending lawsuits, and other unforeseen liabilities. Additionally, these shells sometimes may come with angry or deceitful shareholders who are anxious to dump their stock at the first chance they get.

Additionally, in the old days of shell transactions, unscrupulous promoters were (and probably still are) common. The completion of a reverse merger did little to inform the public of the private company's operations and financial status, despite the fact that the private company was really the going-forward entity.

The SEC resolved this problem in 2005 by adopting rules relating to filings by reporting shell companies. These rules were intended to protect investors by deterring fraud and abuse in the public securities markets involving shell companies. These rules were promulgated to provide greater transparency to investors in legitimate shell companies.

Under the new rules, the SEC defines a "shell company" as a registrant with no or nominal operations and either no or nominal assets consisting solely or primarily of cash. Furthermore, the rules require three things:

1. When reporting an event that causes it to cease being a shell company, a shell company must file a Form 8-K with the SEC containing the same type of information that it would be required to file to register a class of securities under the 1934 Act. (This filing document sometimes is referred to as a Super 8-K.). It basically contains the same information as a registration statement and *must be filed within four days* following the consummation of the merger. (See the Super 8-K on www.wiley.com/go/capitalformation.)

2. A check box was added to the cover pages of 10-Qs and 10-Ks for a registrant to identify itself as a shell company.

3. A shell company was prohibited from using a Form S-8. (A Form S-8 is an abbreviated form of registration statement commonly used to register the underlying shares of employee benefit plans. Unscrupulous promoters used to use Form S-8 to register securities [with a minimum of information] that would be issued to individuals as compensation for their assistance or role in a transaction, thus giving them freely trading stock that could be immediately sold for cash).

TIPS AND TECHNIQUES

It is extremely important to be ready for the reverse merger transaction to close so that the Super 8-K can be filed punctually. This preparation involves having the necessary audited information available and the document prepared well in advance by the attorneys. A newly public entity does not want to be late with its first filing—it really sets a bad tone.

Pump and Dump

As we discuss in the next section, part of the due diligence needs to be focused on the shell shareholders and promoters. If they are looking for quick liquidity and a big gain, they could be planning a pump and dump.

A pump-and-dump scheme is when individuals spread news and instigate buying in a company's stock that results in a steep and dramatic rise in the company's stock price. After the stock price goes up sufficiently, these promoters sell their shares at a price that is not realistic, resulting in a windfall profit for them, followed by a sharp fall in the company's stock price, leaving everyone else holding their shares of stock (which they may have paid a higher price for), thus putting these investors in the proverbial "trick sack."

Naturally, pump and dumps are illegal, but they still happen. Companies, especially those participating in a reverse merger transaction, have to be especially careful.

Taking Appropriate Precautions

Just because a company is a shell company does not mean that it does not have any problems. In fact, it may have more than its share of problems. The private company contemplating going public through a reverse merger transaction needs to do its share of due diligence as in any acquisition transaction and must be even more focused on several different areas:

- Does the public shell have any lurking or hidden liabilities that can come out of the woodwork after the acquisition and create potential problems for the merged entity? These problems could be tax related, litigation related, or just simply unrecorded liabilities.

- Who owns the shares, and how many shareholders are there? Is it expected that they will want to dump and run postmerger, or can the downward pressure on the stock price be minimized with the application of a few basic precautionary steps, such as lockup agreements?

- Are there any other skeletons in the closet that need to be considered or otherwise planned for? Are there any skeletons lurking in the shell company that are so onerous that the transaction should not even be completed with this shell company and another shell company should be sought as the merger partner?

One way the acquiring or surviving company can safeguard against the dump after the takeover is consummated is by requiring a lockup on the shares owned by the group from which it is purchasing the public shell. Other shareholders that have held stock as investors in the company being acquired pose no threat in a dump scenario because the number of shares they hold is not significant, and, unfortunately for them, the number of shares they own is likely to be reduced by the reverse stock split that often occurs as part of a reverse takeover.

Possibly the biggest caveat is that most chief executive officers (CEOs) are naïve and inexperienced in the world of publicly traded companies, unless they have previous experience as an officer or director of a public company. (See the section later in this chapter entitled "Operating a Public Company.")

A major disadvantage of going public via a reverse merger is that such legitimate transactions introduce liquidity to a previously private stock only if there is bona fide public interest in the company. This means that interest has to be generated by promotion and by attracting the interest of the investing public and analysts.

Making the Shares Trade

Once the merger is completed, the next objective is to have the shares actually trade in an orderly fashion. As discussed earlier, a reverse merger probably will be completed with a shell company that is publicly reporting but may not be trading anywhere meaningful.

In order to initiate trading and the use of a symbol to identify the company, it is necessary to utilize a sponsoring broker/dealer (B/D) who will act as the initial market maker (i.e, the entity buying and selling the shares—thus making a market) and who files a Form 211 (see Exhibit 7.1).

EXHIBIT 7.1

Form 211

FINra
Financial Industry Regulatory Authority

FORM 211

General Instructions

Complete this form to initiate or resume quotations in the OTC Bulletin Board®, the Pink Quote or any other comparable quotation medium. By completing this form, your firm is representing that it has satisfied all applicable requirements of Securities and Exchange Commission (SEC) Rule 15c2-11 and the filing and information requirements of NASD Rule 6640. It is not necessary to file this application if a member qualifies for an exception or exemption provided by paragraphs (f)(1)-(5) or (h) of Rule 15c2-11.

Send the completed form, a photocopy of the completed form and two copies of the required Issuer Information to FINRA, OTC Compliance Unit, 9509 Key West Avenue, Rockville, MD 20850-3329. If you have any questions, call the OTC Compliance Unit at (240) 386-5100.

Check the applicable quotation medium(s):

☐ OTC Bulletin Board

☐ Pink Quote

☐ Other (name of quotation medium)

Part 1 – Issuer and Security Information

Provide the information requested below:

1. Exact name of Issuer and predecessor (if any) _____

2. Address of principal executive offices _____

    _____

3. Telephone number of principal executive offices _____

4. Type of security (check one) ☐ Domestic Security   ☐ ADR   ☐ Foreign Security   ☐ DPP

5. State of incorporation _____ Country of incorporation _____

6. Complete title and class of security to be quoted _____

7. Symbol of security (if assigned) _____ CUSIP (if assigned) _____

8. Par or stated value of security _____

9. Total securities outstanding at the end of the Issuer's most recent fiscal year _____

    _____

10. Name and address of transfer agent _____

    _____

11. List any restrictions on the transfer of the security _____

    _____

12. Price of initial quotation entry _____ Bid _____ Ask _____

    ☐ No price at this time _____

If you are requesting to enter a bid and/or ask price, you must also provide a clear statement of the following information:

The basis upon which the priced entry was determined: _____

The factors considered in making that determination: _____

Part 2 – Required Issuer Information

Check the applicable box (select only one) that corresponds to the category of Issuer information accompanying this application. To determine the applicable category, carefully review paragraphs (a)(1)-(5) of Rule 15c2-11 under the Securities Exchange Act of 1934 (1934 Act) and paragraph (g), which defines "reasonably current" information for purposes of paragraph (a)(5).

Provide two copies of all required information (except for EDGAR documents) along with this completed form.

RECENT OFFERINGS

☐ **(a)(1)** Provide the prospectus that became effective less than 90 calendar days prior to filing this Form 211, as specified by Section 10(a) of the Securities Act of 1933 (1933 Act).

SEC Effective Date: _____   Date Security(ies) Issued: _____

☐ **(a)(2)** Provide the offering circular that became effective less than 40 calendar days prior to filing this Form 211, as provided for under Regulation A under the 1933 Act.

SEC Effective Date: _____   Date Security(ies) Issued: _____

☐ **(a)(3) REPORTING COMPANIES LISTS:**

The Issuer's most recent annual report filed pursuant to Section 13 or 15(d) of the 1934 Act or the annual statement referred to in Section 12(g)(2)(G)(i) of the 1934 Act. Quarterly and other current reports filed after the Issuer's most recent annual report or statement. List below each report or statement and applicable amendments filed by the Issuer through EDGAR that your firm has in its possession that meets the requirements of this section.

Name of Report or Statement	Report or Statement Date	EDGAR Filed Date

☐ **(a)(4) FOREIGN PRIVATE ISSUERS**

Provide the following information regarding the Issuer's reliance upon Rule 12g3-2(b) of the 1934 Act.

The foreign exchange(s) on which the subject class of securities is listed that, either singly or together with the trading of the same class of the Issuer's securities in another foreign jurisdiction, constitutes the primary trading market for those securities.

_____

The location of the Internet Web site or electronic information delivery system that the member firm would provide upon request to any person to direct them to the information that the Issuer published electronically pursuant to Rule 12g3-2(b).

_____

☐ **(a)(5) NON-REPORTING AND ALL OTHER COMPANIES**

The applicant must make the Issuer information filed in conjunction with section (a)(5) of this form available upon request to any person expressing an interest in a proposed transaction with the subject security filed. Provide the Issuer's most recent balance sheet, profit and loss and retained earnings statements, equivalent financial information for the two prior fiscal years for the Issuer or any predecessor company, and the documents that support the information provided in this form.

a. Describe the Issuer's business.

b. Describe the products or services offered by the Issuer.

c. Describe the Issuer's facilities.

d. List the name(s) of the current Chief Executive Officer(s) and members of the Board of Directors
of the Issuer.

e. Is the firm that is submitting this form, or any person associated with it, affiliated directly or indirectly with the Issuer?

☐ Yes ☐ No If yes, what is the affiliation?

f. Is the quotation being published or submitted on behalf of any other broker-dealer?

☐ Yes ☐ No If yes, what is the name of the broker or dealer?

g. Is the quotation being published or submitted directly or indirectly on behalf of the Issuer or any director, officer or any person who is directly or indirectly the beneficial owner of more than 10%
of the outstanding units or shares of any equity security of the Issuer?

☐ Yes ☐ No If yes, what is the name of the person, and what is the basis for any exemption under the federal securities laws for any sales of such securities on behalf of this person?

Part 3 – Supplemental Information

Please review paragraphs (b)(1)-(3) of Rule 15c2-11 and provide the information requested below.

(b)(1) Describe the circumstances surrounding the submission of this application. Include the identity of any person(s) for whom the quotation is being submitted and any information provided to your firm by such person(s).

_____

_____

_____

_____

(b)(2) Has the Issuer or its predecessor (if any) been subject to a trading suspension order issued by the SEC during the past 12 months? If a trading suspension order has been issued, provide two copies of the order or of the SEC's public release announcing the trading suspension order.

Check the appropriate box: ☐ Trading suspension order or release enclosed. ☐ Not applicable.

_____

_____

_____

_____

(b)(3) Provide any material information, including adverse information regarding the Issuer, that your firm is aware of or has in its possession. (Do not list information already provided in Part 2.) If your firm does not possess such information, state "None" below.

Identify any applicable information by name and date.

_____

_____

_____

_____

Part 4 – (Complete for OTC Bulletin Board quotation requests only)

Fiscal Year End Date (MM/DD)
_____

Date of Incorporation (MM/DD/YYYY)
_____

Standard Industrial Classification (SIC) Code
_____

(a) **Complete if the Issuer files periodic reports through the SEC's EDGAR system.**

   • Provide the 10-digit Central Index Key (CIK) number. (The CIK is a unique identifier assigned by the SEC to all companies and people who file disclosure documents through EDGAR with the SEC.)

_____

(b) **Complete if the Issuer does not file periodic reports through the SEC's EDGAR system.**

   • Name of regulatory authority where the Issuer files periodic financial reports:

_____

   • Telephone number of the regulatory authority:
_____

   • The Issuer's filing cycle. (Check one)

   ☐ Quarterly

   ☐ Semi-Annually

   ☐ Annually

   ☐ Other (Describe the filing cycle)
_____

   • List the required reports filed by the Issuer for the current fiscal year.

Name of Report or Statement	Report or Statement Date	EDGAR Filed Date

Part 5 – Certification

The undersigned must have a reasonable basis for believing that the information accompanying this form is accurate in all material respects and that the sources of the information are reliable.

By signing this document, I acknowledge and certify that my firm has a reasonable basis for believing that the information accompanying this form (including required EDGAR filed documents not provided) is accurate in all material respects and that the sources of the information are reliable ("affirmative review obligation") as required by Rule 15c2-11 under the 1934 Act and NASD Rule 6640. I understand and acknowledge that this affirmative review obligation applies to all subsequent submissions made in connection with this Form 211 application. Further, I certify that I have examined this form and, to the best of my knowledge and belief, it is true, correct, and complete. I understand and acknowledge that copies of this form, accompanying documents, and subsequent submissions made in connection with this Form 211 application may be provided to the Securities and Exchange Commission, or other regulatory agencies, Pink OTC Markets Inc., and to the public upon request through the Pink OTC Markets Inc.

Name, title and signature of firm employee to contact regarding information contained in this Form 211 application.

Name	Title
Signature	Date
Phone	Fax

Name, title, and signature of the registered principal of the firm responsible for this Form 211 application, and all subsequent submissions made in connection with this application.

Name	Title
Signature	Date
Firm Name	

(Firm must be a Pink OTC Markets Inc. subscriber if application is for the Pink Quote.)

Address		
City	State	Zip
Firm CRD#	Market Participant Identifier	

Investor protection. Market Integrity.

1735 K Street, NW
Washington, DC 20006-1506
www.finra.org
© 2008. FINRA. All rights reserved.
09_0040.1-00/09

The basic concept behind Rule 15c2-11 was to provide fully reporting public companies with an easy way to have their securities quoted on the National Association of Securities Dealers' Over-the-Counter Bulletin Board (NASD OTCBB). A company intending to obtain a quotation for its securities only has to file some simple disclosures through Form 15-c-211, commonly known as Form 211, with NASD. Once approved, the company will be able to trade its stock on the OTCBB. The B/D cannot accept any compensation for sponsoring the company and earns its livelihood as the exclusive market maker for the first 30 days of trading. This provides the B/D with a unique position and also ensures that spreads (the difference between the bid and the asked price) will be wide, enabling the B/D to generate a profit on the spread.

TIPS AND TECHNIQUES

It is extremely important to interview the sponsoring broker/dealer in much the same manner as you perform due diligence on the shell company. You have to have a good feeling that the sponsoring B/D will treat the company well and ethically.

Although there are no stringent financial requirements to be listed on the OTCBB, the NASD ensures that the company's affairs are in order and that there are at least 40 to 50 shareholders and sufficient float before approving Form 15-c-211. The entire process takes about three to six months. Once NASD approves Form 15-c-211, the company can have its securities quoted on the NASD OTCBB.

Operating a Public Company

Now that you have successfully gone public, the challenge does not end there. Responsibilities of being a public company can become onerous and tedious. If you have been operating your company (as I have recommended earlier) as a public company, the tasks have become a normal daily part of your routine. If not, there will be regular surprises along the way.

Periodic Reporting

The first task is the requirement for periodic reporting. Unlike private companies, public companies are required to file regular and timely reports with the SEC. The importance of compliance with the periodic reporting requirements cannot be overemphasized. Periodic reports represent a primary form of communication with your shareholders and the financial community in general. Reports that are poorly prepared, incomplete, or late may adversely affect your investors and the company's public relations. They also may lead to SEC sanctions, generate ill will toward the company by the SEC staff, and adversely affect future financing efforts by precluding the use of simplified registration forms.

The first of these periodic reports is a 10-Q, which is a quarterly report. This summarized report contains unaudited quarterly financial statements and management's discussion and analysis of financial condition and results of operations. In addition, certain specified events (e.g., legal proceedings, changes in terms of securities, certain defaults, and matters submitted to a vote of the shareholders) need to be disclosed in the 10-Q. The 10-Q needs to be filed between 30 to 45 days following the end of each of the first three calendar quarters. The exact timing will be determined based on the company's size and status.

The 10-K is the primary report used annually to update much of the information contained in the registration statement or the Super 8-K. Much of the information in the Form 10-K is also required in various other SEC filings or in the annual report to shareholders prescribed by the SEC's proxy requirements. Instead of including in the current Form 10-K information that already has been submitted in previous SEC filings or in an annual report to shareholders, a company often incorporates by reference to the previously filed document or annual report to shareholders. For example, a company may include as an exhibit to the Form 10-K a copy of the annual report containing the audited financial statements to shareholders in lieu of reproducing the same financial statements in the 10-K.

This is commonly referred to as a "wraparound," because the 10-K wraps around the glossy annual report to shareholders, which contains much of the information required in the Form 10-K. The opposite kind of wrap is where the annual report is wrapped around the 10-K with a glossy cover and shareholder letter, thereby avoiding the expense of a glossy annual report.

Reports on Form 8-K are required to be filed after specified significant events, including change of control (as discussed with the reverse merger), significant acquisition or disposition of assets, bankruptcy, change in independent auditors, resignation of a director, or any other event considered of material importance to shareholders. This form is intended to ensure that there is a filing for events of which shareholders and potential investors should be aware immediately.

The events requiring disclosure, generally within four days of their occurrence, are summarized in Exhibit 7.2.

EXHIBIT 7.2

Events Requiring Disclosure

Business and Operations

- Entry into, amendment of, or termination of a material definitive agreement (oral or written) not made in the ordinary course of business, including all agreements between the company and officers or directors
- Bankruptcy or receivership of the company

Financial Information

- Completion of the acquisition or disposition of a significant amount of the company's assets
- Public announcement, release or update of disclosing material, nonpublic information regarding the company's results of operations or financial condition for a completed period
- Occurrence, acceleration, or increase of either a direct financial obligation that is material to the company or a direct or contingent material financial obligation arising from an off–balance sheet arrangement
- Commitment to an exit or disposal plan, disposal of a long-lived asset, or certain terminations of employees, in each case under which material charges to the company will be incurred
- Conclusion that a material charge for impairment to an asset is required under generally accepted accounting principles

Securities and Trading Markets

- Certain notices of delisting or failure to satisfy a listing rule on the national securities exchange or association that maintains the company's listing; transfer of listing
- Unregistered sale of securities
- Material modifications to shareholder rights, either through modification of instruments defining shareholder rights or by issuance or modification of another class of securities

Accountants and Financial Statements

- Resignation, dismissal of, or change in the company's independent accountant
- Conclusion by the company, or advisement by its accountants, of the unreliability of previously issued financial statements, audit reports, or interim reviews due to error

Corporate Governance and Management

- Change in control of the company
- Departure or appointment of principal officers or directors
- Amendment to articles or bylaws of the company
- Change in fiscal year of the company
- Temporary suspension of trading under the company's employee benefit plans

- Certain amendments to or waivers of code of ethics provisions

Regulation FD

- Disclosure of certain material nonpublic information (NOT four days—simultaneous if intentional, promptly if not intentional)

Other Events

- Any event the company deems important to shareholders (NOT four days—since voluntary, no deadline)

Timely Reporting

It is extremely important for a public company to file all periodic reports punctually with the SEC. Failure to do so could have significant implications for the company, including the inability to use abbreviated registration forms in future capital raises.

If a company finds itself in a position of having to file a 10-K or 10-Q later than its required due date, it is imperative that a Form 12b-25 (see Exhibit 7.3) be filed with the SEC no later than one day after the original due date for the filing, together with the reasons for the failure to make a timely filing.

As contained in the SEC rules, with respect to any report or portion of any report that is not filed punctually because the registrant is unable to do so without unreasonable effort or expense, such report shall be deemed to be filed on the prescribed due date for such report if:

EXHIBIT 7.3

<table>
<tr><td></td><td>OMB APPROVAL</td></tr>
</table>

OMB APPROVAL
OMB Number: 3235-0058
Expires: June 30, 2009
Estimated average burden
hours per response 2.50

UNITED STATES
SECURITIES AND EXCHANGE COMMISSION
Washington, D.C. 20549

SEC FILE NUMBER

CUSIP NUMBER

FORM 12b-25

NOTIFICATION OF LATE FILING

(Check one): ☐ Form 10-K ☐ Form 20-F ☐ Form 11-K ☐ Form 10-Q ☐ Form 10-D ☐ Form N-SAR
☐ Form N-CSR
For Period Ended: _____
☐ Transition Report on Form 10-K
☐ Transition Report on Form 20-F
☐ Transition Report on Form 11-K
☐ Transition Report on Form 10-Q
☐ Transition Report on Form N-SAR
For the Transition Period Ended: _____

Read Instruction (on back page) Before Preparing Form. Please Print or Type.
Nothing in this form shall be construed to imply that the Commission has verified any information contained herein.

If the notification relates to a portion of the filing checked above, identify the Item(s) to which the notification relates:

PART I — REGISTRANT INFORMATION

Full Name of Registrant

Former Name if Applicable

Address of Principal Executive Office *(Street and Number)*

City, State and Zip Code

PART II — RULES 12b-25(b) AND (c)

If the subject report could not be filed without unreasonable effort or expense and the registrant seeks relief pursuant to Rule 12b-25(b), the following should be completed. (Check box if appropriate)

(a) The reason described in reasonable detail in Part III of this form could not be eliminated without unreasonable effort or expense

☐ (b) The subject annual report, semi-annual report, transition report on Form 10-K, Form 20-F, Form 11-K, Form N-SAR or Form N-CSR, or portion thereof, will be filed on or before the fifteenth calendar day following the prescribed due date; or the subject quarterly report or transition report on Form 10-Qorsubject distribution reporton Form 10-D, or portion thereof, will be filed on or before the fifth calendar day following the prescribed due date; and

(c) The accountant's statement or other exhibit required by Rule 12b-25(c) has been attached if applicable.

PART III — NARRATIVE

State below in reasonable detail why Forms 10-K, 20-F, 11-K, 10-Q,10-D, N-SAR, N-CSR, or the transition report or portion thereof, could not be filed within the prescribed time period.

SEC 1344 (04-09)   **Persons who are to respond to the collection of information contained in this form are not required to respond unless the form displays a currently valid OMB control number.**

(Attach extra Sheets if Needed)

PART IV — OTHER INFORMATION

(1) Name and telephone number of person to contact in regard to this notification

(Name)	(Area Code)	(Telephone Number)

(2) Have all other periodic reports required under Section 13 or 15(d) of the Securities Exchange Act of 1934 or Section 30 of the Investment Company Act of 1940 during the preceding 12 months or for such shorter period that the registrant was required to file such report(s) been filed ? If answer is no, identify report(s).　　　Yes ☐　No ☐

(3) Is it anticipated that any significant change in results of operations from the corresponding period for the last fiscal year will be reflected by the earnings statements to be included in the subject report or portion thereof ?

　　　　　　　　　　　　　　　　　　　　　　　　　　　　　　　　Yes ☐　No ☐

If so, attach an explanation of the anticipated change, both narratively and quantitatively, and, if appropriate, state the reasons why a reasonable estimate of the results cannot be made.

_____

(Name of Registrant as Specified in Charter)

has caused this notification to be signed on its behalf by the undersigned hereunto duly authorized.

Date _____　　By _____

INSTRUCTION: The form may be signed by an executive officer of the registrant or by any other duly authorized representative. The name and title of the person signing the form shall be typed or printed beneath the signature. If the statement is signed on behalf of the registrant by an authorized representative (other than an executive officer), evidence of the representative's authority to sign on behalf of the registrant shall be filed with the form.

ATTENTION

Intentional misstatements or omissions of fact constitute Federal Criminal Violations (See 18 U.S.C. 1001).

GENERAL INSTRUCTIONS

1. This form is required by Rule 12b-25 (17 CFR 240.12b-25) of the General Rules and Regulations under the Securities Exchange Act of 1934.

2. One signed original and four conformed copies of this form and amendments thereto must be completed and filed with the Securities and Exchange Commission, Washington, D.C. 20549, in accordance with Rule 0-3 of the General Rules and Regulations under the Act. The information contained in or filed with the form will be made a matter of public record in the Commission files.

3. A manually signed copy of the form and amendments thereto shall be filed with each national securities exchange on which any class of securities of the registrant is registered.

4. Amendments to the notifications must also be filed on Form 12b-25 but need not restate information that has been correctly furnished. The form shall be clearly identified as an amended notification.

5. *Electronic Filers:* This form shall not be used by electronic filers unable to timely file a report solely due to electronic difficulties. Filers unable to submit reports within the time period prescribed due to difficulties in electronic filing should comply with either Rule 201 or Rule 202 of Regulation S-T (§232.201 or §232.202 of this chapter) or apply for an adjustment in filing date pursuant to Rule 13(b) of Regulation S-T (§232.13(b) of this chapter).

6. Interactive data submissions. This form shall not be used by electronic filers with respect to the submission or posting of an Interactive Data File (§232.11 of this chapter). Electronic filers unable to submit or post an Interactive Data File within the time period prescribed should comply with either Rule 201 or 202 of Regulation S-T (§232.201 and §232.202 of this chapter).

2

1. The company files the Form 12b-25 and furnishes the explanation for the company's inability to file the report in a timely manner without unreasonable effort or expense

2. The registrant represents in the Form 12b-25 that:

   A. The reason(s) causing the inability to file timely could not be eliminated by the registrant without unreasonable effort or expense; and

   B. The subject annual report will be filed no later than the fifteenth calendar day following the prescribed due date; or the subject quarterly report will be filed no later than the fifth calendar day following the prescribed due date; and

   C. The report/portion thereof is actually filed within the period specified.

IN THE REAL WORLD

The risks of having a delinquent filing impact the company in the future are so severe that my recommendation is to never use this provision. In my opinion, it is far better to file on time and later amend than to file late in the first place, unless by filing on time, the necessary amendment involves items of a material nature.

Public and Investor Relations

As an officer or director of a public company, you suddenly have acquired what may be described as a mixed blessing. You now have shareholders who rely on the analysts or the financial press and will critically evaluate your management's performance. These shareholders will also measure your progress against their expectations and your competitors. This has far-reaching implications for the way you conduct the business. Your new measure or report card is the company's share price, which from the shareholders' perspective is the critical measure. Many executives are not used to this fishbowl management style.

Furthermore, having a public company that is a well-kept secret (and one whose stock trades by appointment only) will not benefit the company. That is where the public relations/investor relations firms come into play. It is the job of this firm to help the company get its story out to the financial investing public, which consists of both individual retail investors and institutional funds that take large positions in public companies. A part of your management time will be devoted to road shows, meeting with prospective investors, and getting the company story out there.

Shareholder Meetings

A public company is required to have an annual shareholder meeting. Many companies view such meetings with trepidation because of investor gadflies, who attend larger company meetings and pester management with questions and proposals. Smaller and newly public companies should treat these annual meetings as great opportunities to showcase the company and its achievements and should use the meetings as a great investor relations tool. A presentation should be made that resounds well with the stockholders; it can be the regular investor relations presentation. The importance of the meetings as a promotional opportunity should not be minimized.

Short-Term Profit versus Long-Term Growth

As a public company, you are faced with the immediate dichotomy and dilemma of (1) trying to maximize profits and short-term earnings growth or (2) investing for the long term, knowing that those decisions will bring the greatest return to the stockholders. The pressure is intensified, since there is always a 90-day report card when quarterly earnings are announced and you have some shareholders who are impatient, faulty in their thinking, and shortsighted. They would prefer the pump-and-dump scenario, which would allow them to maximize their short-term profit and exit through the sale of their shares. Bowing to the pressure created by such shareholders is not wise, though it is always tempting.

While some argue that the financial markets are shortsighted, they are probably not, but they definitely do not want to see anything but steady and sustainable revenue and earnings growth. This fact dovetails into another part of the investor relations program: to ensure that the company's strategy and milestones are communicated clearly and often to Wall Street and Main Street.

 IN THE REAL WORLD

Prior to Sarbanes-Oxley, financial managers were motivated to maintain reserves that could be reversed into income. This was often (and probably still is) referred to as having "pennies in the bank" to ensure that earnings targets were never missed. The penalty for missing an earnings target was far more severe to the company's stock price than the reward for beating the Street's estimate. In one company I managed, I kept a jar of pennies in my desk so that every quarter (as expected) when the vice chairman would come in and ask for that extra penny of earnings, I would reach into my desk drawer and give him one with the admonition: "That is going to be the only penny you are getting from me." Sarbanes-Oxley has made managing earnings much more onerous, but again, we have to be realistic. Decisions may be made that will save a penny as opposed to the nickel it might bring three years down the road. Managers have to be realistic in what they do, as well as comply with the law.

Compliance with the Law

Now that the company is public, in addition to the periodic reporting requirements, there are other legal compliance matters that must be strictly followed. They include:

- **Proxy Solicitation.** Because a public company has shareholders across the country (and overseas), and few actually attend the shareholder meeting, management must solicit the authority to vote their stock (i.e., solicit their proxies) at the annual shareholder meeting. Proxies usually account for the majority of the votes cast at a meeting. The SEC requires that before proxies can be solicited, a proxy statement with required disclosures must be furnished to shareholders. The content of the proxy statement is specified in the SEC regulations and varies depending on the types of matters that require shareholder approval that year.

- **Shareholders with 5% Ownership Shareholders.** Shareholders who accumulate a 5% ownership interest in the company suddenly have to disclose that stake with a 13D filing, which becomes public information. Holders of 5% or more in private companies do not have to make a similar disclosure. It obviously requires a sensitivity and an adjustment to ensure that the filings are made.

- **Insider Trading and "Short-Swing Profits."** A major adjustment occurs regarding insider trading because all officers and directors are required to report their holdings on specified Forms 3, 4, and 5 (see Exhibits 7.4, 7.5, and 7.6). A Form 4 is required to be filed with the SEC within two days of a change in ownership, whether that comes from purchases, sales, grants, or the issuance of options. The company must also disclose in its annual report how many forms were filed delinquently; this is (at least to me) a very embarrassing disclosure. Additionally, in order to prevent the use of insider information, these officers and directors are subject to the "short-swing profits" provisions of the 1934 Act. The provisions apply to any profits realized by insiders on the purchase and sale or sale and purchase of any of the company's securities within a six-month period, *whether these transactions were based on insider information or not.* The 1934 Act also prohibits insiders from selling shares that they do not own (i.e., short sales) or selling shares they do own but do not deliver in a timely manner (i.e., short sales against the box).

- **Restricted Stock—Rule 144.** Another adjustment people must make is that if they are issued stock of a public company or acquire shares in a private placement, those shares are restricted

EXHIBIT 7.4

FORM 3

UNITED STATES SECURITIES AND EXCHANGE COMMISSION
Washington, D.C. 20549

INITIAL STATEMENT OF BENEFICIAL OWNERSHIP OF SECURITIES

Filed pursuant to Section 16(a) of the Securities Exchange Act of 1934, Section 17(a) of the Public Utility Holding Company Act of 1935 or Section 30(h) of the Investment Company Act of 1940

1. Name and Address of Reporting Person	2. Date of Event Requiring Statement (Month/Day/Year)	3. Issuer Name and Ticker or Trading Symbol	
(Last) (First) (Middle)	06/25/2008	4. Relationship of Reporting Person(s) to Issuer (Check all applicable)	5. If Amendment, Date of Original Filed (Month/Day/Year)
(Street)		Director 10% Owner Officer (give title below) Other (specify below)	6. Individual or Joint/Group Filing (Check Applicable Line) Form filed by One Reporting Person Form filed by More than One Reporting Person
(City) (State) (Zip)			

Table I - Non-Derivative Securities Beneficially Owned

1. Title of Security (Instr. 4)	2. Amount of Securities Beneficially Owned (Instr. 4)	3. Ownership Form: Direct (D) or Indirect (I) (Instr. 5)	4. Nature of Indirect Beneficial Ownership (Instr. 5)
Common Stock	0	O	

Table II - Derivative Securities Beneficially Owned
(e.g., puts, calls, warrants, options, convertible securities)

1. Title of Derivative Security (Instr. 4)	2. Date Exercisable and Expiration Date (Month/Day/Year)		3. Title and Amount of Securities Underlying Derivative Security (Instr. 4)		4. Conversion or Exercise Price of Derivative Security	5. Ownership Form: Direct (D) or Indirect (I) (Instr. 5)	6. Nature of Indirect Beneficial Ownership (Instr. 5)
	Date Exercisable	Expiration Date	Title	Amount or Number of Shares			

Explanation of Responses:

Reminder: Report on a separate line for each class of securities beneficially owned directly or indirectly.

* If the form is filed by more than one reporting person, **see** Instruction 5 (b)(v).

** Intentional misstatements or omissions of facts constitute Federal Criminal Violations See 18 U.S.C. 1001 and 15 U.S.C. 78ff(a).

Note: File three copies of this Form, one of which must be manually signed. If space is insufficient, see Instruction 6 for procedure.

Persons who respond to the collection of Information contained in this form are not required to respond unless the form displays a currently valid OMB Number.

/s/
_____   _____
** Signature of Reporting Person   Date

{FT498400;1}

EXHIBIT 7.5

FORM 4

UNITED STATES SECURITIES AND EXCHANGE COMMISSION
Washington, D.C. 20549

STATEMENT OF CHANGES IN BENEFICIAL OWNERSHIP

Filed pursuant to Section 16(a) of the Securities Exchange Act of 1934, Section 17(a) of the Public Utility Holding Company Act of 1935 or Section 30(h) of the Investment Company Act of 1940

OMB APPROVAL	
OMB Number:	3235-0287
Expires:	February 29, 2008
Estimated average burden hours per response	0.5

☐ Check this box if no longer subject to Section 16. Form 4 or Form 5 obligations may continue. See Instruction 1(b).

1. Name and Address of Reporting Person*	2. Issuer Name and Ticker or Trading Symbol	5. Relationship of Reporting Person(s) to Issuer (Check all applicable)
(Last) (First) (Middle)	3. Date of Earliest Transaction (Month/Day/Year)	Director 10% Owner
		Officer (give title below) Other (specify below)
(Street)	4. If Amendment, Date of Original Filed (Month/Day/Year)	6. Individual or Joint/Group Filing (Check Applicable Line)
(City) (State) (Zip)		Form filed by One Reporting Person
		Form filed by More than One Reporting Person

Table I - Non-Derivative Securities Acquired, Disposed of, or Beneficially Owned

1. Title of Security (Instr. 3)	2. Transaction Date (Month/Day/Year)	2A. Deemed Execution Date, If any (Month/Day/Year)	3. Transaction Code (Instr. 8)		4. Securities Acquired (A) or Disposed Of (D) (Instr. 3, 4 and 5)			5. Amount of Securities Beneficially Owned Following Reported Transaction(s) (Instr. 3 and 4)	6. Ownership Form: Direct (D) or Indirect (I) (Instr. 4)	7. Nature of Indirect Beneficial Ownership (Instr. 4)
			Code	V	Amount	(A) or (D)	Price			

{F1499483;1}

Table II - Derivative Securities Acquired, Disposed of, or Beneficially Owned
(e.g., puts, calls, warrants, options, convertible securities)

1. Title of Derivative Security (Instr. 3)	2. Conversion or Exercise Price of Derivative Security	3. Transaction Date (Month/Day/Year)	3A. Deemed Execution Date, if any (Month/Day/Year)	4. Transaction Code (Instr. 8)		5. Number of Derivative Securities Acquired (A) or Disposed of (D) (Instr. 3, 4 and 5)			6. Date Exercisable and Expiration Date (Month/Day/Year)		7. Title and Amount of Securities Underlying Derivative Security (Instr. 3 and 4)		8. Price of Derivative Security (Instr. 5)	9. Number of derivative Securities Beneficially Owned Following Reported Transaction(s) (Instr. 4)	10. Ownership Form: Direct (D) or Indirect (I) (Instr. 4)	11. Nature of Indirect Beneficial Ownership (Instr. 4)
				Code	V	(A)	(D)	Date Exercisable	Expiration Date	Title	Amount or Number of Shares				

Explanation of Responses:

/s/ _____   ___ / ___ / ___
** Signature of Reporting Person   Date

Reminder: Report on a separate line for each class of securities beneficially owned directly or indirectly.

* If the form is filed by more than one reporting person, *see* Instruction 4 (b)(v).

** Intentional misstatements or omissions of facts constitute Federal Criminal Violations *See* 18 U.S.C. 1001 and 15 U.S.C. 78ff(a).

Note: File three copies of this Form, one of which must be manually signed. If space is insufficient, *see* Instruction 6 for procedure.

Persons who respond to the collection of information contained in this form are not required to respond unless the form displays a currently valid OMB Number.

{FT498483;1}

EXHIBIT 7.6

FORM 5

☐ Check box if no longer subject to Section 16. Form 4 or Form 5 obligations may continue. *See Instruction 10b.*
☐ Form 3 Holdings Reported
☐ Form 4 Transactions Reported

UNITED STATES SECURITIES AND EXCHANGE COMMISSION
Washington, D.C. 20549

ANNUAL STATEMENT OF CHANGES IN BENEFICIAL OWNERSHIP OF SECURITIES

Filed pursuant to Section 16(a) of the Securities Exchange Act of 1934, Section 17(a) of the Public Utility Holding Company Act of 1935 or Section 30(h) of the Investment Company Act of 1940

OMB APPROVAL
OMB Number: 3235-0362
Expires: February 28, 2011
Estimated average burden
hours per response........ 1.0

1. Name and Address of Reporting Person*	2. Issuer Name **and** Ticker or Trading Symbol	5. Relationship of Reporting Person(s) to Issuer (Check all applicable)

(Last)   (First)   (Middle)

(Street)

(City)   (State)   (Zip)

2. Issuer Name **and** Ticker or Trading Symbol

3. Statement for Issuer's Fiscal Year Ended (Month/Day/Year)

4. If Amendment, Date Original Filed (Month/Day/Year)

5. Relationship of Reporting Person(s) to Issuer (Check all applicable)

___ Director   ___ 10% Owner
___ Officer (give   ___ Other (specify
title   below)
below)

6. Individual or Joint/Group Reporting (check applicable line)
___ Form Filed by One Reporting Person
___ Form Filed by More than One Reporting Person

Table I — Non-Derivative Securities Acquired, Disposed of, or Beneficially Owned

1. Title of Security (Instr. 3)	2. Transaction Date (Month/Day/Year)	2A. Deemed Execution Date, if any (Month/Day/Year)	3. Transaction Code (Instr. 8)		4. Securities Acquired (A) or Disposed of (D) (Instr. 3, 4 and 5)			5. Amount of Securities Beneficially Owned at end of Issuer's Fiscal Year (Instr. 3 and 4)	6. Ownership Form: Direct (D) or Indirect (I) (Instr. 4)	7. Nature of Indirect Beneficial Ownership (Instr. 4)
			Code	V	Amount	(A) or (D)	Price			

Reminder: Report on a separate line for each class of securities beneficially owned directly or indirectly.
* If the form is filed by more than one reporting person, see instruction 4(b)(v).

(Over)   SEC2270 (1-05)

Table II — Derivative Securities Acquired, Disposed of, or Beneficially Owned
(e.g., puts, calls, warrants, options, convertible securities)

1. Title of Derivative Security (Instr. 3)	2. Conversion or Exercise Price of Derivative Security	3. Transaction Date (Month/Day/Year)	3A. Deemed Execution Date, if any (Month/Day/Year)	4. Transaction Code (Instr. 8)	5. Number of Derivative Securities Acquired (A) or Disposed of (D) (Instr. 3, 4, and 5)	6. Date Exercisable and Expiration Date (Month/Day/Year)	7. Title and Amount of Underlying Securities (Instr. 3 and 4)	8. Price of Derivative Security (Instr. 5)	9. Number of Derivative Securities Beneficially Owned at End of Issuer's Fiscal Year (Instr. 4)	10. Ownership Form of Derivative Securities: Direct (D) or Indirect (I) (Instr. 4)	11. Nature of Indirect Beneficial Ownership (Instr. 4)
					(A) · (D)	Date Exercisable · Expiration Date	Title · Amount or Number of Shares				

Explanation of Responses:

** Intentional misstatements or omissions of facts constitute Federal Criminal Violations.
See 18 U.S.C. 1001 and 15 U.S.C. 78ff(a).

Note: File three copies of this Form, one of which must be manually signed.
If space provided is insufficient, *see* Instruction 6 for procedure.

Potential persons who are to respond to the collection of information contained in this form are not required to respond unless the form displays a currently valid OMB number.

_____
** Signature of Reporting Person

_____
Date

Page 2

252

TIPS AND TECHNIQUES

The best way to ensure compliance with the law is for the company to develop strict policies and blackout windows when insiders cannot trade the stock. These windows usually occur around the release of earnings and other sensitive information. It is critical to keep in mind that it is unlawful for anyone (officers, directors, or employees—or anyone who has inside information) to trade securities on the basis of this inside information. This also applies to people who may have been tipped off (''tippees'').The SEC is taking this very seriously. Recently high-profile CEOs have been sent to jail for insider trading and, in one case, not even for transactions involving their own company's stock (Martha Stewart). This matter should be taken very seriously.

and subject to holding periods. That is because generally the shares were sold or issued under exemptions from registration, as discussed in Chapter 3. Before they can be sold in the market, 144 shares (for other than controlling shareholders) are subject to a six-month holding period.

Summary

After having finished this chapter, you should understand:

- Some alternative methods to a traditional IPO to take a company public

- The ramifications of operating a public company that are different from a private company
- The compliance issues to which public companies are subject
- Some of the nuances of public company management dealing with expectations and the public at large

The transition to a public company is not easy, inexpensive, or for the faint of heart. However, if done properly, it can have its share of rewards.

CHAPTER 8

Exit Strategies

After reading this chapter, you will be able to:

- Understand the alternative exit strategies that exist for your company.
- Select the best alternative for your company based on all the facts.

What Is an Exit Strategy?

An exit strategy is literally a means of escaping the current situation. It typically relates to an unfavorable situation. From one perspective, an organization or an individual without an exit strategy may literally be in a quagmire. At its worst, an exit strategy will enable the organization or the individual to save face. At best, an exit strategy will peg a withdrawal to the achievement of an objective worth more than the cost of any continued involvement.

Historically, the term "exit strategy" was used in internal Pentagon critiques of the Vietnam War. It remained relatively obscure to the general public until the Battle of Mogadishu, Somalia in 1993, when the U.S. military involvement in that United Nations' peacekeeping operation cost the lives of U.S. troops without a clear objective. Republican critics of President Bill Clinton derided him for having no exit strategy, although he had inherited an active military operation from his predecessor, President George H. W. Bush. The criticism was revived later against the U.S. involvement in the Yugoslav wars, including peacekeeping operations in Bosnia and Kosovo and the Kosovo war against Serbia. The term has been adopted by critics of the current U.S. involvement in Afghanistan and Iraq. President George W. Bush has been said to have no exit strategy to remove troops from Iraq, and critics worried about the number of soldiers and Iraqi civilians who would suffer injury or death as a result. As of this writing, President Barack Obama has not yet publicly announced an exit strategy for the troops in Afghanistan.

Moving this term into the business arena, no business plan written does not conclude with an "Exit Strategy" section. Thus, in entrepreneurship and strategic management, an exit strategy, exit plan, or strategic withdrawal is a way to terminate either one's ownership of a company or the operation of some part of the company. Entrepreneurs and investors devise ways of recouping the capital they have invested in a company. The most common strategy is simply to sell their equity position to someone else.

Now that we understand the history of an exit strategy, where and how is it really used?

Business plans today usually identify an exit strategy as taking the company public or a strategic sale of the company.

We have just devoted a significant amount of time and space to the various ways of taking a company public. Based on all the work that is required to accomplish that objective and the securities laws that come into play, it is highly unlikely that a founding entrepreneur can realistically exit from his or her "baby" as either one of the selling shareholders in an initial public offering (IPO) or after the stock is trading through the direct sale of shares into the public market. (Although there are vehicles to accomplish the sale of shares as an officer or director of a public company, these 10(b)-5 selling plans, as they are called, are not easy to implement successfully.)

 TIPS AND TECHNIQUES

Although IPOs often are listed in business plans as a potential exit strategies, it is highly unlikely that this exit strategy is realistic. As I like to say, "Going public is not the final destination; it is only the beginning of the journey." All too often, entrepreneurs take their companies public and, because of adverse circumstances, watch the value of their stock holdings plummet without any real ability to legally sell their shares on the way down. Hardly a successful "exit."

If faced with a significant ownership as an executive officer or director of a public company, be prepared to lock in the value of a portion of your ownership through the creative use of legally available techniques, such as collars. In a collar, the shares are not actually sold, but in exchange for receiving a significant portion of any gains resulting from further upward movement in the price of the stock, a third party is willing to assume the risk of any losses resulting from any downward movement in the price of the stock. (Collars are highly complex transactions but do afford entrepreneurs some significant protection against watching the value of their holdings evaporate into thin air.)

Thus, a more realistic exit strategy is to work toward the outright sale of the company, whether the company is private or public. Interestingly enough, I believe that going public is just the beginning of the journey, because generally, the act of going public is accomplished to raise capital or utilize a company's own stock as currency in acquiring other companies for growth. Because public markets and private acquirers are interested in a continuing growth story, the strategic decisions are very similar—hence the journey.

A fundamental part of any successful exit is, therefore, continued growth in both revenue and profitability. Many entrepreneurs believe they can accomplish this as they always have—by the seat of their pants. Not so, especially in today's complex and challenging environment. Thus, the first place to start moving toward an exit is the development of the company's strategic plan.

Before we discuss the art of strategic planning and how it is critical and necessary to sustain the business, I would like to examine some more basic questions. These questions should help you determine whether you are in a position to sustain your business through the strategic planning process. While a yes to all of these questions will by no means indicate that your business is exempt from all the daily frustrations of increasing costs, tight money, and personnel problems, it does mean that you have a significantly better chance of executing any strategic plan.

Role of Management

The first question is: In your role as president or other management personnel, are you confident you understand exactly what the functions of management are? This may be a simple question, but you would be surprised how anything but an unqualified yes results in unproductive efforts at profitability, cash flow, and survival, the fundamentals of sustaining any business.

I am sure that you have heard various definitions of management, such as "getting things done through other people" or "the coordination of human effort." Regardless of your familiarity with this term, the fact remains that the effectiveness with which a particular endeavor is managed has come to be recognized in most instances as the single most important ingredient to the long-range success of that endeavor.

This management process includes decision making, the application of selected managerial techniques and procedures, and the motivation of both individuals and groups to accomplish identified objectives.

Before an individual can adopt a particular style of management, he or she must consider what the real role of management is. Two conceptual extremes should be discussed: the market theory, which views the role of management as consisting of reactive decisions based on events as they occur, and the planning and control theory, which views the managerial role as being comprised of decisions that are forward looking and that are based on assessments of future expected developments. Most managers base their actions on the latter concept, the planning and control theory. This concept rests on the belief that the primary success factor in an enterprise is the competence of management to plan and control the activities of the company.

Entrepreneur versus Executive

A little later we discuss certain management techniques of which all managers should possess an awareness. First, however, let us discuss the responsibilities of management with respect to those variables over which there is some control. In planning for and controlling those variables that significantly affect the success of the company, whether it is small or large, management must continually:

- Plan
- Organize
- Staff
- Direct
- Control

Graphically, these five responsibilities or functions can be depicted as shown in Exhibit 8.1. Most companies that possess good management are those that have adopted management styles which respond to the need for imaginative use of these five basic management functions.

Managerial Functions

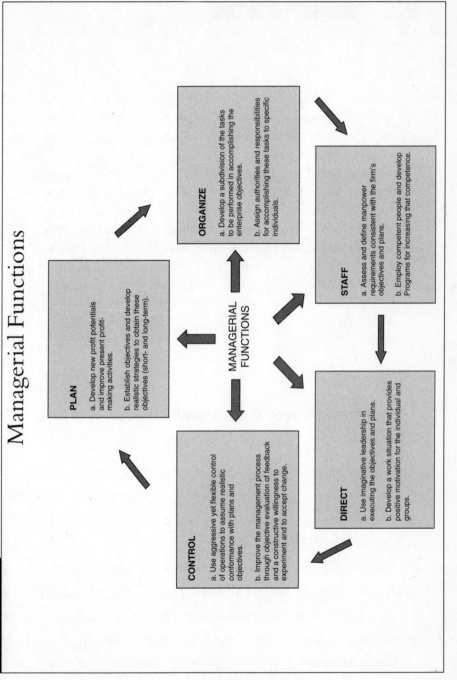

MANAGERIAL FUNCTIONS

PLAN

a. Develop new profit potentials and improve present profit-making activities.

b. Establish objectives and develop realistic strategies to obtain these objectives (short- and long-term).

ORGANIZE

a. Develop a subdivision of the tasks to be performed in accomplishing the enterprise objectives.

b. Assign authorities and responsibilities for accomplishing these tasks to specific individuals.

STAFF

a. Assess and define manpower requirements consistent with the firm's objectives and plans.

b. Employ competent people and develop Programs for increasing that competence.

DIRECT

a. Use imaginative leadership in executing the objectives and plans.

b. Develop a work situation that provides positive motivation for the individual and groups.

CONTROL

a. Use aggressive yet flexible control of operations to assume realistic conformance with plans and objectives.

b. Improve the management process through objective evaluation of feedback and a constructive willingness to experiment and to accept change.

Entrepreneurship involves the creative thinking and risk-taking mentality to start a business. The first major milestone an entrepreneur's company reaches is $1 million of revenue. Ninety percent of all start-up companies never achieve this goal. The next cut point is $10 million in revenues. Ninety percent of all entrepreneurs cannot move beyond this level, because they lack the managerial skills necessary to do so or because they lack the self-confidence to surround themselves with smart people who possess these skills. Typical entrepreneurs surround themselves with people against which they can shine. The smartest chief executive officers (CEOs) are those who surround themselves with people who are smarter than they are, which lets them accomplish their vision.

Determination of Goals and Direction of the Company

The second question is: Am I doing all I should to keep my organization on target, not only by determining goals for profits, but also by guiding the members of the organization toward agreement on and achievement of these goals?

Successfully managed companies usually follow a hierarchy of goals in arriving at strategic and profit plans. This planning process should be viewed as a continuing task, not as a seasonal endeavor to be suffered through only at the beginning of each fiscal year. As shown in Exhibit 8.2, you proceed from a written expression of the

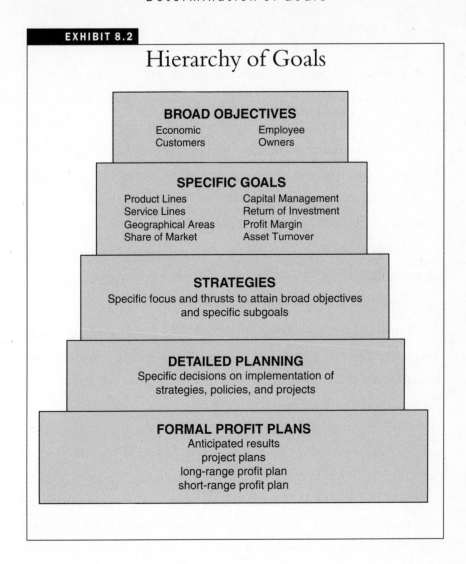

EXHIBIT 8.2

Hierarchy of Goals

BROAD OBJECTIVES
Economic   Employee
Customers   Owners

SPECIFIC GOALS
Product Lines   Capital Management
Service Lines   Return of Investment
Geographical Areas   Profit Margin
Share of Market   Asset Turnover

STRATEGIES
Specific focus and thrusts to attain broad objectives
and specific subgoals

DETAILED PLANNING
Specific decisions on implementation of
strategies, policies, and projects

FORMAL PROFIT PLANS
Anticipated results
project plans
long-range profit plan
short-range profit plan

broad long-range objectives of the firm down to the formulation of formal profit plans.

It is imperative that certain aspects of the profit planning and control process be formalized. In this manner:

- Planning and control are logical and consistent endeavors.

- The environment in which individuals work will be assured of having a reasonable degree of consistency and stability.

- Objectives and goals must be reduced to writing in order to avoid the misinterpretation of essential goals, objectives, and procedures by the diverse group of managers and employees existing in almost any company.

- To achieve mutual understanding, formalization of certain goals, policies, and procedures is essential.

- Formalization requires the establishment of realistic deadlines for both decision making and planning.

You should, however, be sensitive to the fact that there exists a very real hazard in overformalizing the management process. In any situation, inflexible administration will hurt a company's ability to respond quickly to changing circumstances.

While managerial personnel often feel the pressure of time limitations, you must reflect on the question: What do I spend most of my time doing? If you are an upper-level manager, you should be spending the majority of your working hours in the areas of planning and policy setting. Most Fortune 500 chief executives have repeatedly indicated in interviews that they allocated the largest segment of their time to long-range planning and policy setting. Still, many of these CEOs still wished that they had even more time for long-range planning and human resource management.

Exhibit 8.3 illustrates in a rough sense the proportion of time different individuals should spend in either planning or controlling the activities of any organization. It might be interesting for you to

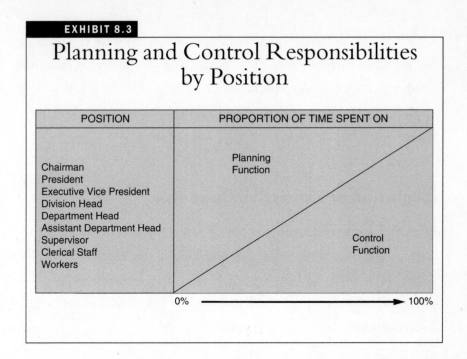

EXHIBIT 8.3

Planning and Control Responsibilities by Position

POSITION	PROPORTION OF TIME SPENT ON
Chairman President Executive Vice President Division Head Department Head Assistant Department Head Supervisor Clerical Staff Workers	Planning Function Control Function

0% ——————————————————→ 100%

keep a diary of your activities during a particular week and compare them to the proportions shown in the chart. You can easily see how much planning effort is required to sustain a profitable organization. All of you know how easy it is to put off the more loosely defined job of planning in favor of directing daily activities. Upper-level management must, however, avoid this temptation if it is to serve its proper role: directing the company toward profitability while ensuring long-term survival. Put another way, this means sustaining and growing your business!

One fact that management must be constantly aware of is that the motivation of human resources is central to effective management. Management must understand that employee participation in the establishment of company goals, plans, and policies with which they will be directly involved is recognized as one of the more effective approaches to motivation at all organizational levels. Proper planning and control provides a method for resolving any problems encountered with respect to agreement on goals, since effective participation by all levels of management is required in the development of these goals, related policies, and their implementation.

Evolution of Executive Concerns

Now that we have examined some concepts of management, let us start to look at strategic planning and how it can blend successfully with these concepts of management. But first, let us focus on how one great corporate leader summarizes the key fundamental belief. This leader said:

> I firmly believe that any organization in order to survive and achieve success must have a sound set of beliefs on which it premises all its policies and actions.
>
> Next, I believe that the most important single factor in corporate success is faithful adherence to those beliefs.
>
> And, finally, I believe if an organization is to meet the challenge of a changing world, it must be prepared to change everything about itself except those beliefs as it moves through corporate life.

This leader, of course, was Thomas Watson, Jr., the chairman of IBM. As you look at IBM today, isn't this what the company is continuing to do in order to retain its competitive edge and sustain its business?

The real evolution of executive concern can be seen pictorially in the next series of charts. To summarize, initially, as can be seen in Exhibit 8.4, the focus is on operations; efficiency is a concern,

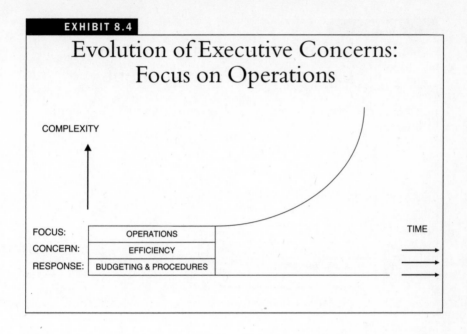

EXHIBIT 8.4

Evolution of Executive Concerns: Focus on Operations

COMPLEXITY

TIME

FOCUS:	OPERATIONS
CONCERN:	EFFICIENCY
RESPONSE:	BUDGETING & PROCEDURES

and the logical response is budgeting and procedures (profit planning and control).

As the complexity increases in the organization, the time required by the executive team will increase. In Exhibit 8.5, we can observe an additional focus of executive concern: the resources of the business; the concern is risk, and response is long-range planning. This part of the process together can be considered operational management, as it governs the day-to-day operations of the business.

The entity encounters unprecedented competitive intensity because of:

- Global economy

- Scarce resources

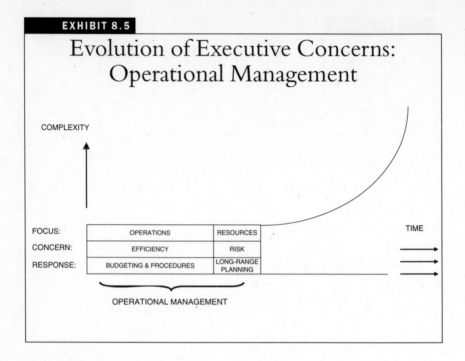

EXHIBIT 8.5

Evolution of Executive Concerns: Operational Management

COMPLEXITY

FOCUS:	OPERATIONS	RESOURCES
CONCERN:	EFFICIENCY	RISK
RESPONSE:	BUDGETING & PROCEDURES	LONG-RANGE PLANNING

OPERATIONAL MANAGEMENT

TIME

- Expensive money

- Availability of information

- Maturing managerial technology

- Leveling of people's ability

- Deregulation

- Reduced growth

We can see in Exhibit 8.6 that the focus shifts to the competition; the concern is position, and the response is strategy. The aim of the strategy is to achieve positions of sustained advantage that result in higher and more secure returns than comparable investments. Unfortunately, if the strategy is not implemented and the position is not achieved, then, logically, performance does not result.

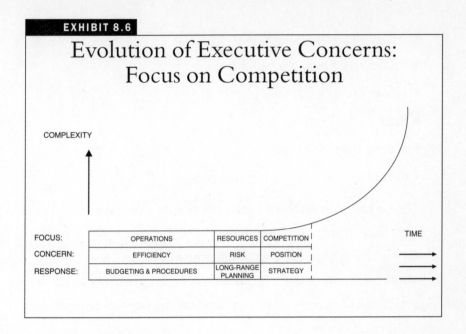

EXHIBIT 8.6

Evolution of Executive Concerns: Focus on Competition

FOCUS:	OPERATIONS		RESOURCES	COMPETITION
CONCERN:	EFFICIENCY		RISK	POSITION
RESPONSE:	BUDGETING & PROCEDURES		LONG-RANGE PLANNING	STRATEGY

In the United States, we have seen various ideas implemented in the pursuit of performance, including:

- Back to basics
- Quality circles
- Productivity through people
- Consensus
- Theory Z
- Corporate culture

All of these ideas have led us to *In Search of Excellence* (the Thomas J. Peters and Robert H. Waterman classic), which gave us other ideas, such as:

- Bias for action
- Close to the customer

- Autonomy and entrepreneurship
- Productivity through people
- Hands on, value driven
- Stick to the knitting
- Simple form, lean staff
- Simultaneous loose-tight properties

These concepts furthered the evolution of executive concerns to Exhibit 8.7, which added the focus on performance and a concern about execution with the logical response of excellence.

However, one of the ominous facts about growth and decay is that the current success of an organization does not necessarily constitute grounds for optimism.

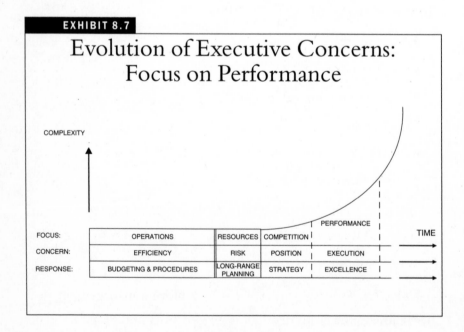

EXHIBIT 8.7

Evolution of Executive Concerns: Focus on Performance

FOCUS:	OPERATIONS	RESOURCES	COMPETITION			TIME
CONCERN:	EFFICIENCY	RISK	POSITION	EXECUTION		
RESPONSE:	BUDGETING & PROCEDURES	LONG-RANGE PLANNING	STRATEGY	EXCELLENCE		

IN THE REAL WORLD

Many companies have achieved dramatic growth, which they interpreted as success. One CEO of a company where I worked was fond of saying "If you grow the top line by 30% per year, some of it has to trickle down to the bottom line." Unfortunately, he would not listen to opposing views, and the company grew from $245 million in revenues to just under $1 billion in two years. He also drove it into bankruptcy years after I left in frustration. Growth hides many warts that suddenly become apparent when the growth slows; then it is too late to react to the absence of the growth and the need to focus on profitability and cash flow.

Change has been accelerated as a result of speed of communications, increased pressure of competition, and number of sources available. Consequently, survival under conditions of intense competition and accelerating change depends on the ability of the organization to adapt to, and take advantage of, the environment better than others do. Exhibit 8.8 illustrates the added focus on change as a result of this acceleration of change; the concern is renewal of the organization, and the logical response is innovation.

Thus, if you were to look at the entire spectrum of executive concerns, you can see that the combination of focus on competition, performance, and change becomes the organization's grand strategy, as depicted in Exhibit 8.9.

The aim of a grand strategy is to achieve a management technique that results in stronger strategic positions, higher quality

EXHIBIT 8.8

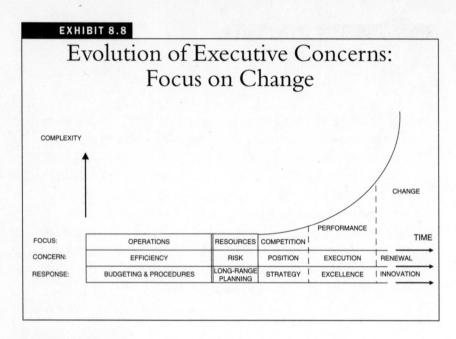

Evolution of Executive Concerns:
Focus on Change

EXHIBIT 8.9

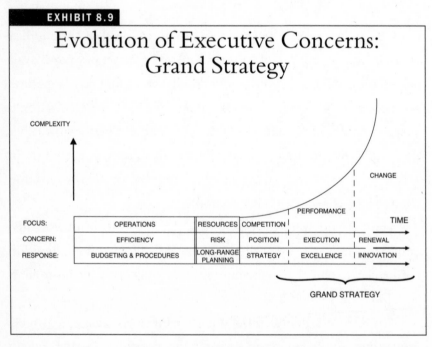

Evolution of Executive Concerns:
Grand Strategy

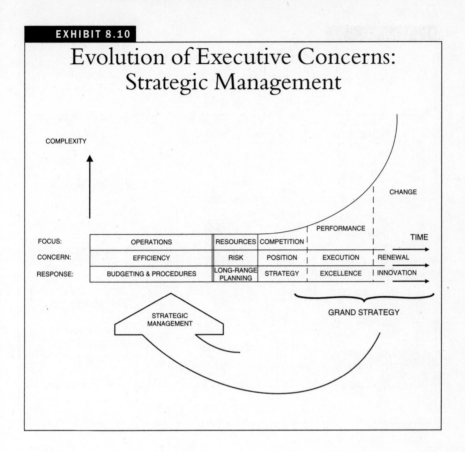

EXHIBIT 8.10

Evolution of Executive Concerns: Strategic Management

FOCUS:	OPERATIONS	RESOURCES	COMPETITION		
CONCERN:	EFFICIENCY	RISK	POSITION	EXECUTION	RENEWAL
RESPONSE:	BUDGETING & PROCEDURES	LONG-RANGE PLANNING	STRATEGY	EXCELLENCE	INNOVATION

STRATEGIC MANAGEMENT

GRAND STRATEGY

execution, and more effective renewal than competing organizations. Of utmost importance is the relationship of grand strategy to operating management, which gives rise to strategic management. Strategic management is operational management driven by grand strategy—not the other way around (see Exhibit 8.10).

Strategic management results in:

- Strategy for position versus competition
- Excellence for execution to get performance
- Innovation for renewal to cope with change

EXHIBIT 8.11

Focus Concept of Strategic Management

FOCUS FRAMEWORK	STRATEGIC MANAGEMENT IS....	EXECUTIVE CONCERNS
MISSION		FOCUSING CHANGE
GOALS	GRAND STRATEGY	
		ACHIEVING PERFORMANCE
OBJECTIVES		
		PREEMPTING COMPETITION
	driving.....	
STRATEGIES		RESOURCE ALLOCATION
ACTION PLANS		
	OPERATIONAL MANAGEMENT	OPERATIONAL IMPLEMENTATION

All this occurs in order to determine how best to manage the operations and how best to allocate the critical resources. See Exhibit 8.11 for a summary.

Development of the Strategic Plan

Now that we have identified the concept of strategic management, let us turn our attention to the actual development of strategy and the strategic plan. The most productive way to develop a strategic plan that encompasses the bold steps inherent in strategic management is in a logical and focused manner.

Management must first build a foundation of shared values, primary purposes, and goals. Attention is then directed to the formulation of quantified objectives and innovative strategies, which are used to develop action plans to implement agreed-upon directions.

The first such element is the vision of the corporation, which is the central concept for the future development of the organization. It is embodied in the mission of the organization, which pulls together (1) values, or the shared beliefs of the members of the organization, (2) vision, or the central strategic excellence position to be sought, and (3) other purposes that may be related to the organization's stakeholders, such as stockholders, employees, suppliers, community, public, and customers. This mission provides strategic integration of every element of the business through a common focus. The shared purposes provide focus by driving strategy, and the shared values provide control by guiding execution. This can best be seen by comparing Exhibits 8.12 and 8.13.

Once the mission is developed, it has to be fulfilled. Strategy rests on the concept that achieving positions of superiority relative to forces in the external marketplace or environment allows the organization to fulfill its purposes. However, the best strategy, unimplemented, and the strongest position, unachieved, can yield only disappointment. Grand strategy provides that missing link between concept and implementation. An organization's grand strategy is its blueprint for building, exploiting, and renewing the positions from which superior performance results. As a starting point, the strategic excellence position (SEP) represents the distinctive capabilities that,

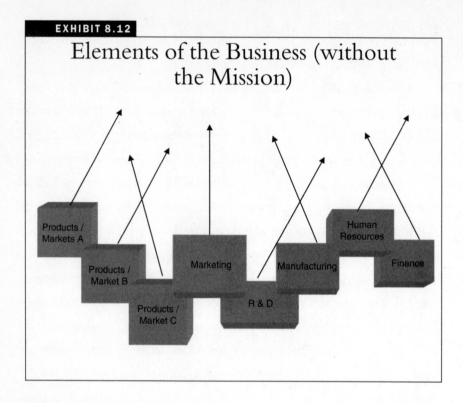

EXHIBIT 8.12

Elements of the Business (without the Mission)

Products / Markets A

Products / Market B

Products / Market C

Marketing

R & D

Manufacturing

Human Resources

Finance

in effect, differentiate the organization in the marketplace in a strategically significant manner. Competitive success follows from focusing every element of the organization on a strategic vision. Implementing that vision requires the development of superior competence, or the ability to excel, in a set of distinctive capabilities that have special value to a particular part of the marketplace. However, it should be noted that excellence by itself is not enough. Excellence in areas of strategic significance (i.e., that determine the outcome of competition in the marketplace) is what is needed.

Exhibit 8.14 presents some examples of SEPs. We can readily relate these SEPs to our perceptions of what makes companies both different and successful.

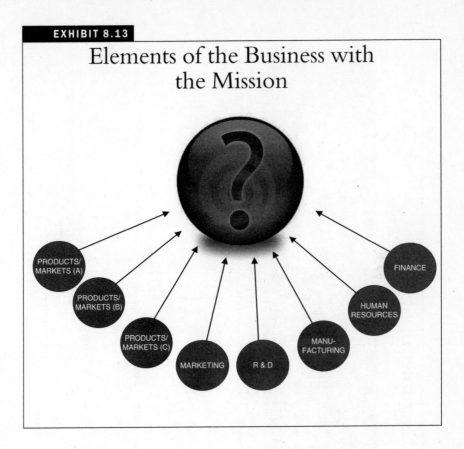

The next step is to develop a set of goals that relate to the mission by defining a desired set of values. The goals should, in essence, represent a distinctive set of capabilities or supporting SEPs that are required to achieve the central concept. Again, this relates to the hierarchy of goals discussed earlier and can pertain to specific areas, such as product lines, service lines, share of market, human resources, and return on investment. They are stated in somewhat lofty terms, as idealistic aspirations, and may not be totally attainable, but they drive the organization in a unified way toward the mission. For example, Scandinavian Airlines

EXHIBIT 8.14

Examples of SEPs

| RAW MATERIALS & COMPONENTS | PRODUCT R&D | PROCESS R&D | MANU- FACTURING | DISTRIBUTION | MARKETING | RETAILING | SERVICE | FINANCE AND ADMINIS- TRATION |

| Toyota | 3M | Dow Chemical | Emerson | Frito-Lay | Procter & Gamble | Benetton | IBM | General Electric |

| Supplier Control | Product Innovation | Low-Cost Processes | Productivity | Distributor Service | Scale | Demand Responsiveness | Customer Service | Strategic Planning |

System (SAS) may state that its vision (or mission) is to be the businessman's airline. As one of its goals, it may desire to run more planes on time than the competition. This is a lofty goal driven by the vision and may not be totally attainable. As another part of this set of goals, there could be one related to providing the best possible service to customers. Again, the goal is something that may not be totally measurable or attainable, but it is consistent with the central vision.

Objectives, however, are specific, measurable, and quantifiable. As shown in Exhibit 8.15, the stated objective of SAS is to reduce average delayed departure at Stockholm Airport by 10 minutes by January 1, 2011.

EXHIBIT 8.15

Scandinavian Airlines System Strategy

Scandinavian Airlines System

VISION   To be the businessman's airline

GOAL   Running planes more on time than
                    competition

OBJECTIVE   Reduce average delayed departure at
                    Stockholm Airport by 10 minutes by 1/1/11

STRATEGY   Buy more deicing equipment

ACTION   Airport operations manager will assess how
PLAN   many machines needed, solicit bids from 3
                    suppliers, and prepare associated staff hiring/
                    training plans by 6/1/10 for management
                    approval

Because the objectives are both specific and measurable, the company can revise them periodically and cope with change and renewal without having to completely redo the strategic plan.

Although it may seem logical to complete the objectives at this point, sometimes it is necessary to develop the strategies prior to completing the measurement part of the objective.

Strategies are the business-, function-, and culture-focused directions and resource commitments to achieve the objectives. They are supported by detailed action plans that specify who, how, and when the action steps will be completed. This gives the CEO the ability to monitor progress and ensure that the plan is being implemented. As we have said earlier, a strategy that is not implemented is of no use to the organization.

Exhibit 8.16 is an example of a strategic plan for a small company that is, of course, supported by detailed action plans. The difficult work is during the foundation phase, when the values, vision, stakeholder analysis, and strategic excellence position are all identified. In a well-orchestrated strategic planning process, the objectives and strategies fall into place logically.

Why Is Strategic Planning Important?

The development of a strategic plan for any company is a significant undertaking and is definitely the first step in sustaining and growing the business. It has to proceed through a logical series of steps embodying the grand strategy. These five steps include:

1. Development of the vision/mission, which is the central concept for the organization's future development. It encompasses

The Focus Framework

GOALS

OBJECTIVES

STRATEGIES

MISSION
To be the world leader in developing, manufacturing, and selling instruments for laser surgery.

PROJECT LEADERSHIP
Be recognized as having the most innovative and highest-performance products.

NEW PRODUCTS
Introduce devices for use in at least three new major branches of surgery within three years.

- Double the funding level for our three existing Product Introduction teams.
- Establish three new teams during the next twelve months.

EXISTING PRODUCTS
Reduce the user costs of existing devices by 20% per year over each of the next five years, while improving performance characteristics.

- Commit $250K to develop a long-term productivity improvement program.
- Establish joint research projects with teaching hospitals and major university laser technology departments.

GROWTH
Expand the use of surgical laser technology to become part of the surgeon's standard repertoire while maintaining our market share.

GROWTH
- Have one of our devices installed in 80% of U.S. teaching hospitals and at least 200 foreign teaching hospitals by 1990.
- Expand the use of the technology to at least five new major surgical applications within the next four years.

- Undertake demonstration educational programs covering target markets in the U.S. and abroad
- Develop innovative financing schemes for initial placements
- Complete substitution of own sales force for agencies by 1987.
- Develop and implement a marketing program including advertising, speakers, and technical articles
- Selectively fund high-profile use of our devices.

PROFITABILITY
Earn a return on investment sufficient to attract financial resources to fund our growth and produce leadership.

NEW PRODUCTS
Introduce devices for use in at least three new major branches of surgery within three years.

- Actively seek external research financing and investigate R&D partnership.
- Raise debt/equity ratio limit to ??

the shared beliefs of members of the organization; other purposes related to the organization's stakeholders (including owners, employees, customers, suppliers, the community etc.); and, of strategic importance, the central strategic excellence position to be sought.

2. Identification of the goals, which represent the distinctive capabilities toward which the organization will strive.

3. Specification of the objectives by which progress and success will be measured.

4. Identification of the specific strategies, whether they are functional, business, and/or cultural, to achieve the objectives.

5. Development of the specific action plans by which the strategies will be implemented and progress monitored by the CEO.

This process is healthy. It enables the company to feel good about itself and its beliefs, especially as it adheres to those beliefs while changing everything about itself except those beliefs as it moves through corporate life to success. As shown in Exhibit 8.17, strategic planning is truly the first step to sustaining and growing any business.

Real Exit

Now that we have determined that to get to an exit, we have to strategically plan *and execute flawlessly*—what is the real exit? Despite whatever else may be written, the real exit is an acquisition/sale of the company. There are usually two kinds of buyers: strategic and financial.

EXHIBIT 8.17

Grand Strategy

- **MISSION**
    - **VALUES . . .**   Shared beliefs of members of the
      organization
    - **VISION . . .**   Central strategic excellence position
      to be sought
    - **OTHER
      PURPOSES . . .**   Related to shareholders, employees,
      suppliers, the public

- **GOALS**
    - Goals related to developing the desired set of values
    - Distinctive set of capabilities: the supporting SEPs
      required to achieve the central concept
    - Other purposes related goals

- **OBJECTIVES**
    - Product priorities
    - Market priorities
    - Other (growth, return on investment)

- **STRATEGIES**
    - Business-, Function-, and Culture-focused directions, and
      resource commitments to achieve the objectives

- **ACTION PLANS**
    - Who?
    - What?
    - When?

Financial buyers are typically private equity funds. They make an acquisition because they believe they can buy the business for $X and sell the business for $3X. The return that they generate through a higher sales price is achieved by making financial enhancements to the business, which increases revenues and profitability, which results in a much higher selling price.

Because financial buyers usually provide a certain part of the purchase price in equity but borrow the remainder, there is little flexibility in how much they can (or are willing to) pay for a business. Additionally, they typically also make postacquisition management decisions that may increase profitability and cash flow for the short term so they can flip the company, even though these decisions would not make long-term sense.

Strategic buyers, however, are capable of paying more. They are already operating a business/company in the specific space and can achieve synergies and cost reductions that will provide an immediate increase in profitability and a much greater stimulus to growth.

 IN THE REAL WORLD

Do not think that strategic buyers will be less interested in increasing profitability and cash flow. They just may do it differently. Expect them possibly to take even greater drastic actions to change the company's structure, culture, and manpower.

Now that a decision has been made to sell that business, how does that work, and what strains does it put on the company?

Process

If you thought the due diligence process for an initial public offering was rigorous, wait until you see the acquisition due diligence. It will make a digital examination by a physician look welcome.

A senior member of the purchaser's management—probably the person who will manage the company after the acquisition—will lead the due diligence team. The team will also include appropriate additional staff and external legal counsel and accounting advisors. Important members of the acquiring due diligence team will have specific expertise in your company's business; they will be up to date on tax laws covering mergers and acquisitions and will be experienced in accounting for both your industry and business combinations. To be even more effective, the due diligence team members will also be experienced in making inquiries in sensitive situations and will understand the concerns of the acquirer, which may not necessarily be the same concerns as yours.

The due diligence team will be focused on answering these questions to their satisfaction:

- Will the transaction be profitable to the investor?
- Will the acquisition be friendly or hostile?
- Is the acquirer willing to engage in a hostile takeover?
- Do any government regulations restrict or prohibit the acquisition?
- How can the company be managed effectively?

These questions are obviously designed to ascertain whether the acquirer is even interested in pursuing the deal. If the decision is to move forward because those questions were answered satisfactorily, comparatively easy questions remain. However, the ease of these questions relates to how things will be managed going forward and disclosures that have to be made. They may have a traumatic impact on the company—both psychologically and operationally. Those questions are:

- What is the company's financial position based on its historical financial statements?

- What disclosures were not made?

- What investment returns and cash flow can be expected from the company?

- How should the acquisition be structured?

- What are the tax considerations?

- What financing arrangements are available for the acquisition and at what cost?

- How will the purchase price be allocated among the company's assets?

- What external reporting requirements will have to be met by the acquirer?

- Who will supervise postacquisition management and administration?

These questions are largely to ensure that the acquirer knows everything about your company before the acquisition takes place. Answers to these questions are often deal breakers; if acquirers do not like the answers, they can call off the transaction.

The overall goal of the due diligence program for the acquirer is to obtain specific information relevant to the company and identify potentially serious problems or deal breakers as quickly as possible. These deal breakers typically are lawsuits, tax exposures, or tax consequences arising from the transaction; matters relating to relations among labor, unions, and management; or other potential contingencies previously undisclosed in the financial statements and other public documents. Additionally, a comprehensive due diligence program will:

- Provide the acquirer with independent assurance that the company's financial statements and other public disclosures are complete and accurate

- Assess the reasonableness of any forecasts for the company and its future operations

- Help structure the transaction and arrive at a fair purchase price primarily for the acquirer and in a manner that will provide the acquirer the best results

- Assist in determining the fair value of assets for allocation of purchase price, including determining whether unrecorded liabilities exist and the appropriate accounting for them

- Assess the reasonableness of the restrictive covenants set forth in any financing agreements the company may have and whether the acquisition will present any covenant problems for the acquirer

- Provide information on external reporting requirements, especially Securities and Exchange Commission (SEC) regulations

- Advise on management and administrative decisions after the acquisition is completed

TIPS AND TECHNIQUES

Many acquisition teams fail to focus on developing the integration plan during due diligence (which is the best time to develop it). Such a plan will identify how the company's operations *and people* will be folded into the acquirer. It will provide you with a road map of how the acquirer intends to deal with your company and its people. The acquirer may not share the plan with you, but it should. And you should ask to see the plan.

Historical Financial Statements

Your company's historical financial statements have presented the company's financial position, results of operations, and cash flows in accordance with generally accepted accounting principles. Many small companies prepare financial statements for internal use only, or tax-basis financial statements. Thus, not everything that is of interest to a potential acquirer is disclosed in the financial statements. Although required disclosures have increased significantly over the past years, companies differ in degree of compliance and judgment on what disclosures are adequate. Acquirers seeking control of a company will always want more information than what is provided in the historical financial statements, regardless of the basis on which they have been prepared.

More important to an acquirer than what is recorded is what has *not* been recorded or disclosed. Thus, an acquirer will be focused on discovering these types of items in performing the due diligence.

Quality of Earnings

Generally accepted accounting principles offer the financial statement preparer a variety of accounting alternatives that determine how assets and liabilities are recorded and how revenue is recognized. This choice of accounting principles influences the quality of earnings—that is, management's choice of accounting practices and the existence of certain nonrecurring or unusual transactions included in the financial statements. For example, such analysis assesses the impact of the choice of depreciation and amortization methods and lives, the choice of functional currency for foreign operations, and revenue and expense recognition practices.

Understanding your company's quality of earnings provides the acquirer a better perspective on the actual earnings trend as well as your company's real worth. It also will help in forecasting future results, which will be the basis for determining the purchase price to be paid for the company (and thus your exit value).

A by-product of this analysis is that the acquirer obtains information to help determine whether your accounting methods are compatible with its own. Such information is useful in considering how best to conform the acquirer's and target's accounting policies.

Meeting with the Auditors

The due diligence team will want to meet with your independent auditors to review their work papers.

IN THE REAL WORLD

The company's credibility goes down significantly if the financial statements have not been audited. That is why I always recommend treating the company as a "public" company, whether it is or not, and having the financial statements audited.

The purpose of this review is to identify items the auditors considered but did not require the company to disclose in the financial statements. Such items may be immaterial for a fair presentation of financial position, but they may have implications for a potential acquirer. Generally, these items relate to contingencies or unusual transactions that were (or were not) recorded in the current year.

The quality and reputation of the independent auditor may also influence the extent to which certain due diligence procedures are necessary, as would the existence of an internal audit function. The absence of independent auditors will definitely increase the amount of work the acquirer performs in the due diligence process.

Forecasts and Projections

As part of the negotiations, the company may have prepared forecasts of results of operations and cash flows for the next several years. (I always recommend that this be done as part of the normal operating process anyway). The due diligence team will review the appropriateness of the assumptions used in the forecasts and verify their reasonableness.

TIPS AND TECHNIQUES

Do not forget that the forecasts will heavily involve assumptions and influence the ultimate purchase price (and exit value). You will be aggressive in your assumptions, but the due diligence team will be anything but. That conservative approach to forecast assumptions by the acquirer can have dramatic implications on that exit value.

Additionally, many acquirers will want to make their own forecasts using their own assumptions, including how they intend to finance the acquisition. (Many accounting firms have developed financial models that, given a set of assumptions, prepare projected balance sheets, income statements, and statements of cash flows.) These models also can be used to analyze the acquirer's proposed return on investment and provide information on the postacquisition consolidated entity. It also may detect a "hidden" deal breaker (i.e., significant negative cash flow or related concerns).

The due diligence team will then review your company's forecast and compare it to the company's earlier long-range plans, if they exist. The team will also examine earlier plans to see whether previous objectives were achieved. This is a real test of your company's credibility and whether your plans in the past were realistic or pie in the sky.

Structuring the Deal

The acquirer's financial and legal advisors usually are involved primarily with structuring the terms of the acquisition, because there are a great many elements to consider in structuring a deal. Given a marketplace swamped with acquisition opportunities, transactions must be put together carefully so acquired values, reported earnings, and cash flows are maximized, and desired rates of returns are achieved. Furthermore, more emphasis is now placed on taking advantage of your company's tax situation or its unique synergy with an acquirer's existing operation. Highly leveraged buyout transactions—deals that use your company's cash flow to fund the debt incurred—are common, as are bust-up business combinations—deals in which many of the your businesses may be sold to fund the acquisition.

Allocating Purchase Price

One of the more complex accounting matters addressed during the due diligence process relates to allocating the purchase price to the assets acquired (your company's assets).

The purchase price allocation process will provide the acquirer an educational overview of the acquisition and the relevant accounting and tax rules. Additionally, it will include these tasks:

- Selection of personnel to perform the allocation, including their outside professionals (independent auditors, attorneys, valuation consultants, and investment bankers) and assignment of individual responsibilities

- Identification of any external reporting requirements (and due dates) and establishment of a project timetable

- Analysis of the business acquired, including a determination of which components will be held and which divested, if any

- Determination of how the acquired assets and liabilities will be valued, whether there are identifiable intangible assets, and what documentation standards should be established

- Determination of whether appraisals of some or all of the assets of the acquired company should be performed (additionally, actuaries may be helpful to evaluate the status of health and benefit plans)

- Review of the acquired company's liabilities to ascertain whether additional amounts should be provided for underaccruals or contingencies

- Review of the relevant tax issues and evaluation of certain tax elections that may be taken by the acquiring company

- Review of the acquired company's accounting policies to identify any differences compared with the acquiring company's policies

- Final review, evaluation, and consolidation

The procedures may not be completed in this order; typically, several tasks will be performed simultaneously. It is essential, though, that all elements of the process be coordinated to ensure that significant areas are properly addressed on a timely basis. This process primarily benefits the acquirer, although, depending on the allocations, there may be adverse consequences to you as the seller, primarily from a tax standpoint.

Financial Covenants

No matter how an acquisition is structured, most business combinations today involve issuing or assuming debt or preferred stock. The due diligence team will pay close attention to the covenants drafted into the financing agreements. These covenants often do not receive enough attention because borrowers are more interested in the availability of funds, the timing of the loan, and the terms of the loan. Thus, covenants—often boilerplates not specifically tailored to the transaction at hand—are overlooked amid standard representations, warranties, and other events of default. Frequently, the covenants were developed early in the negotiations and never updated to reflect changes as negotiations progressed.

The due diligence team will determine how the covenants were developed. The lender will be questioned if the covenants are unclear or too complex to calculate and monitor. The due diligence team will offer alternatives if there is an easier measurement criterion. Definitions, stated or implied, will be reviewed carefully by the accountants in light of purchase price allocation decisions and resulting financial statement classifications. The impact of adopting new accounting standards also will be considered.

The due diligence team should assess the cushion that the financial covenants allow. Do they significantly restrict the postacquisition entity from operating normally with respect to short-term financing, leasing, capital expenditures, or routine operations? Is a default likely if actual results deviate only slightly from plan? If the answer is yes, negotiations with the lenders should be reopened.

Debt Repayment Schedule

The due diligence team will also carefully review the planned debt repayment schedule. Especially in highly leveraged transactions, the acquirer will have to be comfortable that the timetable for repayment can be made from your company's cash flows. To determine whether principal and interest payments can be met, the repayment schedule should be compared to the latest postacquisition forecast—not necessarily the same forecast used to attract the buyer to your company or the forecast that the acquirer first presented to the lender.

Reporting Requirements

Acquirers that are public companies have to have people on the due diligence team that will ensure the acquisition will comply with various SEC reporting requirements. That is why routine audits of your company are so important, because serious consequences may result if audits have to be performed exclusively to meet SEC reporting requirements.

Publicly held companies are required to comply with Form 8-K rules. These mandate that a current report (on Form 8-K) be filed with the SEC within 15 days after the acquisition. Audited financial statements of the acquired business must accompany the report or be submitted under cover of Form 8 within 60 days thereafter. Up to three years of income statements and statements of cash flows and two year-end balance sheets may have to be presented, which is why I routinely emphasize the audit idea.

Quarterly and annual financial statement acquisition footnotes must be prepared, including the pro forma revenue and net income disclosures required by accounting principles. More extensive pro forma disclosures may have to be presented if the acquisition is occurring in connection with a public debt or stock offering. For leveraged transactions, debt disclosures must be amended. Furthermore, various tax elections and returns may have to be filed.

When a purchase transaction is final, consolidation-elimination entries will be established to expedite the closing process. The accountants also must prepare intangible asset amortization schedules. In addition, it may be desirable, if not always required, to push down to the accounts of your company the excess of the purchase price paid over the book value.

When common stock equivalents or other convertible securities are issued as part of the consideration to you as the seller, revised earnings per share calculations may have to be made in the acquirer's financial statements.

Management and Administration

Members of the due diligence team often are the only acquirer representatives to have significant contact with your company personnel below the senior executive level. Therefore, it is not unusual for the acquirer to ask the due diligence team for advice on your human resources. The due diligence team should obtain your organization chart and make tactful inquiries about reporting lines and job responsibilities.

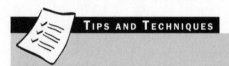

TIPS AND TECHNIQUES

This is where you have to be prepared for gut-wrenching decisions that could severely affect your company's culture and personnel. While you as the seller may not have much say in protecting people, be prepared for the worst, especially if the acquirer is a strategic buyer that could eliminate most of your personnel and achieve synergies. The best way to protect your personnel in such a case is to negotiate good severance packages.

Acquirers often have members of the due diligence team review the target's salary structure and existing employee benefit plans. Thought should be given to how your benefit plans, if any, can be converted equitably to those of the acquirer. These decisions may have tax implications.

A comprehensive due diligence review also should include an assessment of your financial control systems. This includes your company's internal audit function (if one exists) and the planning and budgeting function. Acquirers expect additional assurance from the due diligence team on whether these systems are reliable and can generate accurate financial information. System weaknesses should be identified quickly, and practical suggestions for improvement should be developed as part of the due diligence process. Do not forget that your controls will be wrapped into the management certification the acquirer will be making under Sarbanes-Oxley Section 404, and that will be important for the acquirer.

Transaction (Closing)

Now that you have gone through all the necessary pain of the due diligence and have agreed on price, structure, and postacquisition management, the transaction has to take place and close. Given normal circumstances, there may be a hold-back for contingencies, unrecorded liabilities, and so on. This is perfectly normal and acceptable. Once you get to the closing table and sign mountains of documents, the consideration, if cash, will be wired to your bank account; if it is in some other form, it will be issued. *The exit is complete.* Go celebrate. You have accomplished the life cycle of a company: formation, funding, operations, and exit.

Summary

After having finished this chapter, you should understand:

- The real exit strategies that exist for your business
- The exit strategy most likely to be implemented

- The implications of executing that strategy, both in terms of accomplishing it and the process involved, as well as its impact on your company

The accomplishment of a successful exit strategy is the dream of every entrepreneur. It is a shame that very few of them get to achieve it.

CHAPTER 9

Success in the Real World

After reading this chapter, you will be able to:

- Reflect on the various ways to form a business enterprise
- Reflect on the various types of capital and methods to raise it
- Reflect on the going-public decision and exit strategies
- Confidently select the best alternatives for your idea or company based on all the facts

Formation Process

In this book, we have reviewed the various forms by which a business venture can be organized, including:

- Proprietorships

- Partnerships

- Limited partnerships

- Limited liability companies

- Corporations

Each of these types of entities has numerous advantages and disadvantages. Some are suitable for a family enterprise and some are not.

If you are serious about starting a business that you believe can be successfully grown and nurtured with the right kind of capital (and hence are reading this book), the forms of structure that offer tax advantages in addition to protection from liability may not be the most appropriate. The selection of structure is based on the long-term view with the endgame in sight.

Despite all the sexiness of limited partnerships and limited liability companies and the tax advantages they may offer, I do not think they are the most ideal structure by which to form a business enterprise. Significant tax advantages are realized only if the enterprise is losing money and those losses can be used to offset otherwise taxable income on the tax returns of the founder and the other investors/owners. Unfortunately, if the long-term intent is to lose money, there is no real compelling reason to worry about the long-term view. The only reason for such a view is if this is a specific enterprise formed for a specific purpose, such as the ownership of a real estate venture. In this case, the tax losses so generated can be deducted, and the endgame is the sale of that property at an ultimate profit after the property has been operated for a period of years.

Consequently, I recommend that the structure of a business for growth should be a corporation from the very outset. A corporation is a well-known and accepted form of business, and investors understand what they are getting in such an enterprise.

The best advice with which to operate in the real world is under the "KISS" principle: *Keep it simple, Stupid.* When pitching a business for investment or sale, simplicity is the concept that wins in the long run.

Set your sights on the best target.

Capital Raising

Upon formation, the corporation has a variety of alternatives of debt and equity available with which to finance the business plan. As mentioned, they consist primarily of:

- Straight debt
- Convertible debt

- Mezzanine debt
- Common stock
- Preferred stock
- Convertible preferred stock
- Mandatory redeemable preferred stock

Start-up business corporations generally have no real means with which to repay debt, so the initial start-up capital will be some form of equity, probably common stock or a sort of preferred stock, depending on who the early investors are.

The real measure and ingredient for success in capital raising revolves around the company's story and prospects for business success. The story and prospects for success obviously play into an investor's mindset, consisting of fear and greed. The fear element is *not* the fear of losing one's investment. It is the fear of missing out on the next grand slam home run like Google! Greed is the element of investing $1 and receiving back $4 or $8. These are the real motivators behind an investment decision.

What can make investors reach for their checkbook and (in some respects) throw caution and reason to the wind?

- Fear
- Greed
- Great, exciting story
- Change-the-world technology
- Great cocktail party conversation
- *Your personal and business credibility*

Large amounts of money can be raised based on the founder's credibility. That credibility comes from past successes (i.e., people will throw money at you if you have made money for them in the past) and evidence that you can and do accomplish what you say you can. (Achieving company milestones is how you demonstrate this kind of credibility; missing those milestones is how you destroy it.)

Do not ever be misled into believing that start-up enterprises cannot raise capital through debt. As we have indicated, people will invest based on what you are able to tell them and take the risk. Straight debt that is coming due for repayment can always be converted into equity or perhaps purchased by another investor who is willing to convert the debt—kind of like a chain letter. Here the funds go directly to the original investor, and the second investor gets equity.

Convertible debt can be raised in a start-up enterprise with investors who believe that the story is so attractive that the investors will make substantially more money from converting the debt into shares of stock of the company and watching that stock value rise to a point at which the greed factor outstrips the inherent risk of debt financing for a start-up.

Another factor that is critical in the money-raising process is persistence. It has been said that "time kills all deals." That is very true. The passage of time can cause a deal to stall, wither, and die. That philosophy speaks to moving as quickly as possible to get a deal done.

The flip side of that philosophy is "perseverance gets deals done." It is all too easy to give up and abandon a difficult situation—people who are winners never give up and persevere to victory.

TIPS AND TECHNIQUES

Perseverance cannot be overemphasized. I have been involved in the formation of businesses and raising capital for more than 40 years and sometimes have been accused of being too dumb to quit. However, perseverance is always recognized and demonstrates to outsiders your level of commitment and confidence in the business enterprise. This attitude often instills sufficient confidence for investors to overcome fear (the other kind), throw caution to the wind, and get out that checkbook to fund your corporation.

Capital Sources

We have identified a variety of sources of capital, including:

- Angel investors
- Venture capital
- Private placements

Each of these sources really represents a form of private placement, since securities are being offered privately to a select group of investors. The difference is the sophistication of the ultimate investor. The more sophisticated the investor, the more sophisticated and involved the process and paperwork. Unfortunately, this fact is potentially one of the major areas where pitfalls occur.

Because even an offering to a few family and friends (angel investors) still constitutes a private placement, its informality does not negate the necessity for following rules and regulations governing such offerings. Subscription documents, accredited investor questionnaires, and other documents still are required but often are overlooked, thus creating potential securities law issues for the company and its officers.

TIPS AND TECHNIQUES

Overdocumenting securities transactions is not a bad thing. The preparation of such documentation often goes a long way toward *avoiding* future problems at times when the existence of such problems may, in and of itself, be a deal breaker.

As we have discussed, the source of the capital is an exhaustive challenge that will inevitably lead you through heaven to angels and on to venture capitalists (VCs), who may represent the other end of the spectrum (where it is constantly hot), and into structured private placements as a compromise alternative.

Angels are the best source of early and friendly capital because they probably are already in your address book. Friends and family are the best places to start to find early capital in the hope that they can turn you on to other angels. By concentrating on this area, you may be able to capitalize your company sufficiently to reach a first milestone; doing so makes it somewhat easier to attract the next level of funding. Despite the friendly nature of the relationships, it is best to utilize documents that clearly state that these angel investors are:

- Accredited investors
- Purchasing the securities with an intent to not resell the securities
- Aware of the illiquidity of their investment
- Aware of the business and financial plan for the company
- Cognizant of the risks inherent in such an investment

 TIPS AND TECHNIQUES

The devil is always in the details. Even if you do not use an attorney, you can develop basic documents (with the exhibits provided on www.wiley.com/go/capitalformation) to communicate the required information and document it to protect you and the company.

Moving on to venture capital funding requires an introduction. As we have mentioned, VCs receive hundreds of business plans daily. Unless you have a way of being introduced, the likelihood of your business plan being read by a VC is somewhere between slim and none. However, do not be dismayed. Each person or VC whom you contact regarding your company may be in a position to introduce you to the next person who may be a funding source. Again, perseverance is critical and necessary.

With a VC funding, there will be terms and governance issues as well as the issue of control. VCs typically expect at least one seat on the board of directors and terms that could conceivably punish the failure to achieve certain milestones. They also rarely look at a deal that is below $3 million in size.

Despite the relative ease of obtaining a significant amount of capital with one or two VC checks, you will have to yield a certain amount of control, and that is before you start the negotiation process involving the issues of valuation and dilution.

Rarely will the VC's perception of valuation coincide with yours. You may believe that the streets are paved with gold; the VC will have the opposite view. At issue here is the portion of the company that will be represented by the VC's investment—hence, dilution. A large amount of dilution will further compound and confound the issue of control and governance, since now the VC has a more than insignificant ownership percentage of the company as well as a seat or two on the board of directors.

IN THE REAL WORLD

In today's challenging and unfavorable financial markets, the opportunity to strongly capitalize a company with a few investors should not be rejected on the sole basis of valuation. Use it as a beginning point in the negotiations, but remember: The most expensive money you ever raised is that which you did not raise.

In the absence of venture capital funding, the best and sole alternative is some sort of structured private placement. Remember that a wide variety of corporate finance transactions come under the broad category of private placement. These might include senior and subordinated debt, asset-backed securities, and equity issues. The attractiveness of a private placement lies in the potential to place the securities through a placement agent to a group of high-net-worth investors (often referred to as retail investors). Retail investors invest more on the basis of prospects and tend to pay far less attention to pricing (or valuation), hence the term "retail."

Although using a placement agent does involve some fees, it moves the selling effort away from the company and to a third party, thus relieving the company of some effort. The trade-off for that is the necessity to prepare a formal and involved private placement memorandum (PPM) that provides a lot of information about the company, financial statements, and risk factors.

From a risk perspective, the most important thing to keep in mind regarding private placements is that they are not exempt from the antifraud provisions of the securities laws. Consequently, although the placement is technically a private placement, you still must be continually mindful of certain requirements under the securities laws.

IN THE REAL WORLD

In today's financial markets, the private placement form of financing should be viewed as a legitimate and desirable alternative that could be a real source of capital, despite troubled and distrustful market conditions. Care should be taken with the placement agents, if any, to ensure that you do not pay up-front fees and that they can keep their promises.

Going Public

In Chapters 5, 6, and 7 we discussed the merits and methods of going public, from a traditional initial public offering to a reverse merger. The real and perceived benefits of going public are numerous and include:

- Improved financial condition
- Greater marketability
- Improved value
- Portfolio diversification
- Capital to sustain growth
- Greater access for future financing
- Pathways to mergers and acquisitions
- Improved corporate image
- Listing on a stock exchange

Like a coin, going public has two sides, and the drawbacks can be equally disconcerting. These include items like:

- Loss of control
- Sharing success with others
- Loss of privacy
- Loss of some freedom to act

- Continuous and periodic reporting
- Increased expenses
- Unrealistic shareholder expectations
- Restrictions on selling
- Fiduciary responsibilities

You have to decide whether the advantages outweigh the drawbacks as well as whether the time is right for such a significant change in status. Will such a move doom the company to Bulletin Board hell? That could be a worse fate than remaining a private company.

With the change in status comes a different mode of operations. Operating a public company is in many ways different from operating a private company. The two biggest differences probably remain living in a fishbowl and making decisions that have a short-term benefit versus decisions that have a negative short-term benefit but a much more significant long-term benefit to overall earnings.

At the same time these decisions are being made, you have to keep your exit strategies in mind. An exit strategy, as described in Chapter 8, depends on a flawless strategic plan as well as flawless execution. This is true whether the company is public or private. The execution of a strategic exit, resulting in the sale of the company to either a financial or a strategic buyer, also requires flawless planning and execution. This execution is on a transaction level (only focused on the exit) versus an operational execution (worrying about tomorrow and the day after and the day after).

The key is in knowing all the right steps, as pictured in the cartoon.

Summary

I have tried to summarize 40 years of experience with four public companies and three going-public transactions in a way that provides you, the reader, with practical insight into all the essential opportunities and challenges of:

- Forming a business
- Capitalizing a business
- Operating a business
- Exiting that business

The business life cycle, from giving birth through an exit, is not for the faint of heart. This book will not answer all your questions or provide you with a road map through all the obstacles, known or unknown. I hope it does provide you with good practical insight into the steps along the way, as well as those life lessons sometimes only learned through the painful act of falling on your butt. And I hope that, by reading this book, you can avoid some of life's painful lessons. In addition, the book should provide you with the knowledge that there are a few choice points always to bear in mind:

- **Don't ever give up!** Success comes to those who persevere, and perseverance wins in the end. Sometimes the race is not won by the fastest entrant but by the one who lasts the longest.

- **Don't ever take no for an answer!** Just because you run into some roadblocks and even your professional advisors are advising you that there is no alternative, there still may be one. Keep looking and talking to people. By so doing, you will find the unconventional solution that has never been tried before, yet works.

 IN THE REAL WORLD

Many times people thought I was crazy to persevere as I did with all my endeavors. Maybe so, but in the last company in which I worked, a development-stage medical diagnostics company, over a period of seven years, I was able to raise capital when no one else could, outlasted all my investment bankers, transitioned it to a public company, and received Food and Drug Administration marketing clearance for its first product—all while being told it was pointless to continue.

Remember, the goal is always to maximize shareholder value!

Nothing worthwhile in life is easy. If it was, everyone would be doing it. Use the guidance in this book and the last two points and you can accomplish almost anything. Good luck and, above all, have some fun doing it!

About the Author

David H. Fater (Delray Beach, Florida) is an experienced financial executive with more than 40 years experience in the corporate world and capital markets. He is the founder and CEO of ALDA & Associates International, Inc., a business and financial consulting firm providing capital formation, capital allocation, and profit optimization services primarily to the healthcare and life sciences industries. He is also the Chairman, President, and Chief Executive Officer of Vicor Technologies, Inc., (OTCBB:VCRT) a biotechnology company focused on the development of innovative, noninvasive medical diagnostics, where he is responsible for overseeing the planning, direction, finance, and management of the company including Research & Development, the clinical trial activities, and business and product development. Prior to his founding ALDA, Mr. Fater served as a senior executive and Chief Financial Officer with three public healthcare companies, including two in which he led the initial public offering process and one which he led to a NYSE listing and a $1 billion market capitalization. Fater is also a former managing partner with Ernst & Young. He is on the board of directors of Financial Executives International and the National Executive

Service Corps. He holds a B.S. in Accounting from the University of North Carolina. He is a Certified Public Accountant in Georgia, Illinois, North Carolina, and New York.

Index

Index